Harry Collingwood

**A Pirate of the Caribbees**

Harry Collingwood

**A Pirate of the Caribbees**

ISBN/EAN: 9783743306127

Manufactured in Europe, USA, Canada, Australia, Japa

Cover: Foto ©ninafisch / pixelio.de

Manufactured and distributed by brebook publishing software (www.brebook.com)

Harry Collingwood

**A Pirate of the Caribbees**

# A PIRATE OF THE CARIBBEES

OF

# THE CARIBBEES

BY

## HARRY COLLINGWOOD

AUTHOR OF "AN OCEAN CHASE" "FOR TREASURE BOUND"
"JACK BERESFORD'S YARN" ETC. ETC.

*ILLUSTRATED BY C. J. DE LACY*

GRIFFITH FARRAN BROWNE & CO. LIMITED
35 BOW STREET, COVENT GARDEN
LONDON

*The Rights of Translation and of Reproduction are Reserved.*

# CONTENTS

| CHAP. | | PAGE |
|---|---|---|
| I. | A FRIGATE FIGHT IN MID-ATLANTIC | 7 |
| II. | THE *ALTHEA* FOUNDERS | 28 |
| III. | THE GIG IS CAUGHT IN A HURRICANE | 43 |
| IV. | WE FALL IN WITH AND CAPTURE A SCHOONER | 65 |
| V. | WE PROCEED IN SEARCH OF THE *ALTHEA'S* BOATS | 86 |
| VI. | WE FIND THE LAUNCH | 105 |
| VII. | A DARING ACT OF PIRACY | 122 |
| VIII. | WE CAPTURE A SPANISH INDIAMAN | 142 |
| IX. | WE ENCOUNTER AND FIGHT THE *GUERRILLA* | 157 |
| X. | SEÑOR JOSÉ GARCIA | 173 |
| XI. | CARIACOU—AND AFTERWARD | 189 |
| XII. | I BECOME THE VICTIM OF A VILLAINOUS OUTRAGE | 209 |
| XIII. | IN THE POWER OF THE ENEMY | 228 |
| XIV. | I SEIZE THE FELUCCA | 247 |
| XV. | HEAVY WEATHER | 263 |
| XVI. | THE LAST OF THE FELUCCA | 279 |
| XVII. | CAPTAIN LEMAITRE | 294 |
| XVIII. | A DOUBLE TRAGEDY | 310 |
| XIX. | THE END OF THE *GUERRILLA* | 326 |

# LIST OF ILLUSTRATIONS

| | |
|---|---|
| THE RAFT PROVED TO BE SURPRISINGLY BUOYANT | *Frontispiece* |
| IN LESS THAN A MINUTE TWO GUNS SPOKE OUT | *Facing page* 21 |
| "BACK WATER FOR YOUR LIVES!" | ,, 51 |
| THE BOAT SEEMED TO BE FULL OF DEAD | ,, 115 |
| "HEAVE A SHOT ACROSS THE RASCAL'S FORE-FOOT" | ,, 160 |
| TEN MINUTES SUFFICED US TO SPIKE THE GUNS | ,, 196 |
| I SEIZED THE TILLER AND KEPT HER AWAY ANOTHER POINT | ,, 258 |
| STILL, BY A MIRACLE, MORILLO HIMSELF SURVIVED | ,, 340 |

IN LESS THAN A MINUTE TWO GUNS SPOKE OUT.

*To face page 21.*

"BACK WATER FOR YOUR LIVES!"

*To face page* 51.

THE BOAT SEEMED TO BE FULL OF DEAD.

*To face page* 115.

"HEAVE A SHOT ACROSS THE RASCAL'S FORE-FOOT."

*To face page 160.*

TEN MINUTES SUFFICED US TO SPIKE THE GUNS.

*To face page 196.*

I SEIZED THE TILLER AND KEPT HER AWAY ANOTHER POINT.

*To face page* 258.

STILL, BY A MIRACLE, MORILLO HIMSELF SURVIVED.

# A PIRATE OF THE CARIBBEES

---

## CHAPTER I

### A FRIGATE FIGHT IN MID-ATLANTIC

"EIGHT bells, there, sleepers; d'ye hear the news? Rouse and bitt, my hearties! Show a leg! Eight bells, Courtenay! and Keene says he will be much obliged if you will relieve him as soon as possible!"

These words, delivered in a tone of voice that was a curious alternation of a high treble with a preternaturally deep bass—due to the fact that the speaker's voice was "breaking"—and accompanied by the reckless banging of a tin pannikin upon the deal table that adorned the midshipmen's berth of H.M. frigate *Althea*, instantly awoke me to the disagreeable consciousness that my watch below had come to an end, especially as the concluding portion of the harangue was addressed to me personally, and accompanied by a most uncompromising thump upon the side of my hammock. So I surlily growled an answer—

"All right, young 'un; there's no occasion to make all that hideous row! Just see if you can make yourself useful by finding Black Peter, will you, and telling him to brew some coffee."

The lad was turning away to do my bidding when a pattering of naked feet became audible as their owner approached, while a husky voice ejaculated—

"Who's dat axin' for Brack Petah? Was it you, Mistah Courtenay?" And at the same instant the shining, good-natured, grinning visage of a gigantic negro appeared in the narrow doorway, through which the fellow instantly passed into the berth, bearing a big pot of steaming hot coffee.

"Ay, you black demon, I it was," answered I. "Is that coffee you have there? Then find my cup and fill it, there's a good fellow, and I'll owe you a glass of grog."

"Hi, yi!" answered the black, his eyes sparkling and his teeth gleaming hilariously, "who you call 'brack demon,' eh, sah? Who eber hear of brack demon turnin' out at four o'clock in de mornin' to make coffee for young gentermen, eh? And about de grog, Mistah Courtenay; how many glasses do dis one make dat you now owe me, eh, sah? Ansah me dat, sah. You don' keep no account, I expec's, sah, but *I* do. Dis one makes seben, Mistah Courtenay, and I'd be much obleege, sah, if you'd pay some of dem off. It am all bery well to say you'll *owe*

# A FRIGATE FIGHT IN MID-ATLANTIC

'em to me, sah, but what's de use ob dat if you don' nebber *pay* me, eh?"

"*Pay* you, you rascal?" shouted I, as I sprang to the deck and began hastily to scramble into my clothes, "do you mean to say that you have the impudence to actually expect to be *paid*? Is it not honour and reward enough that a gentleman condescends to become *indebted* to you? Pay, indeed! why, what is the world coming to, I wonder?"

"Bravo, Courtenay, well spoken!" shouted young Lindsay, the lad who had so ruthlessly interrupted my slumbers, "how well you express yourself; you ought to be in Parliament, man! Give it him again; bring him to his bearings. The impudence of the fellow is getting to be past endurance! Now then, you black swab, where's the sugar? Do you suppose we can drink that stuff without sugar?"

After a search of some duration the sugar was eventually found in a locker, in loving contiguity to an open box of blacking, some boot brushes, a box of candles, a few fragments of brown windsor,—one of which had somehow found its way into the bowl,—and a few other fragrant trifles. In my haste to get on deck, and betrayed by the feeble light of the purser's dip, which just sufficed to render the darkness visible, I managed to convey this stray morsel of soap into my coffee along with the sugar wherewith I intended to sweeten it, and only discovered what I had done barely in time to avoid gulping down the soap along with the scalding liquid into which I had plunged it. A midshipman, however, soon loses all sense of squeamishness, so I contented myself with muttering a sea blessing upon the head of the unknown individual who had deposited this "matter in the wrong place," and dashed up the hatchway to relieve the impatient Keene.

I shivered and instinctively buttoned my jacket closely about me as I stepped out on deck, for, mild and bland as the temperature actually was, it felt raw and chill after the close, stifling atmosphere of the midshipman's berth. It was very dark, for it was only just past the date of the new moon, and the thin silver sickle—which was all that the coy orb then showed of herself—had set some hours before; moreover, there was a thin veil of mist or sea fog hanging upon the surface of the water, through which only a few of the brighter stars could be faintly distinguished near the zenith. There was no wind—it had fallen calm the night before about sunset, and we were in the Horse latitudes—and the frigate was rolling uneasily upon a short, steep swell that had come creeping up out from the north-east during the middle watch, the precursor, as we hoped, of the north-east trades—for we were in the very heart of the North Atlantic, and bound to the West Indies. I duly received the anathemas of my shipmate Keene at my tardy appearance on deck, hurled a properly spirited retort after him down the hatchway, and then made my way up the poop ladder to tramp out my watch on the lee side of the deck—if there can be such a thing as a lee side when there is no wind.

It was dreary work, this tramping fore and aft, fore and aft, with nothing whatever to engage the attention, and nothing to do. I therefore eagerly watched for, and hailed with delight, the first faint pallid brightening of the eastern sky that heralded the dawn; for with daylight there would at least be the ship's toilet to make—the decks to holystone and scrub, brasswork and guns to clean and polish, the paintwork to wash, sheets and braces to flemish-coil, and mayhap something to see, as well as the possibility that with the rising of the sun we might get a small slant of wind to push us a few miles nearer to the region where the trade wind was merrily blowing.

The dawn came slowly—or perhaps it merely *seemed* to my impatience to do so—and with daylight the mist that had hung about the ship all night thickened into a genuine, unmistakable fog, so thick that when standing by the break of the poop it was impossible to see as far as the jib-boom end.

The fog made Mr. Hennesey, our second lieutenant and the officer of the watch, uneasy,—as well it might, for we were in the early spring of the year 1805, and Great Britain was at war with France, Spain, and Holland, at that time the three most formidable naval powers in the world, next to ourselves, and the chances were that every second ship we might meet would be an enemy,—and at length, just as seven bells were being struck, he turned to me and said—

"Mr. Courtenay, you have good eyes; just jump up on to the main royal yard, will you, and take a look round. This fog packs close, but I do not believe it reaches as high as our mastheads, and I feel curious to know whether anything has drifted within sight of us during the night."

I touched my hat, and forthwith made my way into the main rigging, glad of even a journey aloft to break the dismal monotony of the blind, grey, stirless morning, and in due time swung myself up on to the slender yard, the sail of which had been clewed up but not furled. But, alas! the worthy second luff was mistaken for once in his life; it was every whit as thick up there as it was down on deck, and not a thing could I see but the fore and mizzen-masts, with their intricacies of standing and running rigging, their tapering yards, and their broad spaces of wet and drooping canvas, hanging limp and looming spectrally through the ghostly mist-wreaths. I was about to hail the deck and report the failure of my experimental journey, but was checked in the very act by feeling something like a faint stir in the damp, heavy air about me; another moment and a dim yellow smudge became visible on the port beam, which I presently recognised as the newly risen sun struggling to pierce with his beams the ponderous masses of white vapour that were now slowly working as though stirred by some subtle agency. By imperceptible degrees the pallid vision of the sun brightened and strengthened, and presently I became conscious of a faint but distinct movement of the air from off the port quarter, to which the cloths of the sail against which my feet dangled responded with a gentle rustling movement.

"On deck, there!" I shouted, "it is still as thick as a hedge up here, sir, but it seems inclined to clear, and I believe we are going to have a breeze out from the north-east presently."

"So much the better," answered the second luff, ignoring the first half of my communication; "stay where you are a little longer, if you please, Mr. Courtenay."

"Ay, ay, sir!" answered I, settling myself more comfortably upon the yard. And while the words were still upon my lips the stagnant air about me once more stirred, the great spaces of canvas beneath me swelled sluggishly out with a small pattering of reef-points from the three topsails, and a gentle creak of truss and parrel, as the strain of the filling canvas came upon the yards; and I saw the brightening disc of the sun begin to sweep round until it bore broad upon our larboard quarter. Then some sharp words of command from the poop, in Mr. Hennesey's well-known tones,—dulcet as those of a bull-frog with a bad cold,—came floating up to me, followed by the shrill notes of the boatswain's pipe and his hoarse bellow of, "Hands make sail!" A few minutes of orderly confusion down on deck and on the yards below me now ensued, and when it ceased the *Althea* was running square away before the languid but slowly strengthening breeze, with studding-sails set on both sides.

Meanwhile the fog was gradually clearing, for it was now possible to see to a distance of fully three lengths of the ship on either hand, before the curling and sweeping wreaths of vapour shut out the tiny dancing ripples that seemed to be merrily racing the ship to port and starboard. Occasionally a break or clear space in the fog-bank swept down upon and overtook us, when it would be possible to see for a distance of a quarter of a mile for a few seconds; then it would thicken again and be as blinding as ever. But every break that came was wider than the one that preceded it, showing that the windward edge of the bank was rapidly drawing down after us; and as these breaks occurred indifferently on either side of, or sometimes on both sides at once, with now and then a clear space right astern to give a spice of variety to the proceedings, my eyes, as may be guessed, were kept pretty busy.

At length an opening, very considerably wider than any that had thus far reached us, came sweeping down upon our starboard quarter, and as I peered into it, endeavouring to pierce the veil of fog that formed its farther extremity, I suddenly became aware of a vague shape indistinctly perceptible through the intervening wreaths of mist that were now sweeping rapidly along before the steadily freshening breeze. I saw it but during the wink of an eyelid, when it was shut in again, but I knew at once what it was; it could be but one thing—a ship, and I forthwith hailed—

"On deck, there! there's a strange sail about a mile distant, sir, broad on our starboard quarter!"

"Thank you, Mr. Courtenay," promptly responded the "second." "What do you make her out to be?"

"It is impossible at present to say anything definite about her, sir," I answered. "I saw her but for a second, and then only very indistinctly, but she loomed up through the fog like a craft of about our own size."

"Very well, sir," answered Hennesey; "stay where you are, and keep a sharp lookout for her next appearance."

Once more I returned the stereotyped, "Ay, ay, sir!" as I sent my glances searching round the ship for further openings. The next that overtook us swept down upon our port quarter; it was fully a mile and a half wide, and when it bore about four points abaft the beam another shape slid into it, not vague and shadowy this time, as the other shape had been, but clearly distinct—a frigate, unmistakably, under a similar spread of canvas to our own, and as nearly as possible our own size. So close indeed was the resemblance that for a second or two I was disposed to fancy that by some strange trick of light and reflection the fog was treating me to a picture of the old *Althea* herself, but a more steadfast scrutiny soon dispelled the illusion. There were certain unmistakable points of difference between this second apparition and ourselves, some of which were so strongly characteristic that I at once set her down as a French frigate.

The plot was thickening, and it was not wholly without a certain feeling of exhilaration that I again hailed the deck—

"A frigate broad on our port quarter, sir, with a very Frenchified look about her!"

"Thank you again, Mr. Courtenay," answered Hennesey, with an unmistakable ring of delight in his jovial Irish accent, which, by the way, had a trick of growing more pronounced under the influence of excitement. "Ah, true for you, there she is," he continued, "I have her! Mr. Hudson, have the kindness to jump below and fetch me my glass, will ye, and look alive, you shmall anatomy!"

A gentle ripple of subdued laughter from the forecastle at this sally of our genial "second" floated up to me from the forecastle, a glimpse of which I could just catch under the foot of the foretopsail, and I could see that the men were all alive down there with pleasurable excitement at the prospect of a possible fight. Young Hudson—a smart little fellow, barely fourteen years old, and the most juvenile member of our mess—was soon on deck again with the second lieutenant's telescope; but by this time the fog had shut the stranger in again, so, for the moment, friend Hennesey's curiosity had to remain unsatisfied. Not for long, however; the presumably French frigate had not been lost sight of more than two or three minutes when I caught a second glimpse of the other craft—the one first sighted—on our starboard quarter.

"There is the other fellow, sir!" I shouted. "You can see her distinctly now. And she too is a frigate, and French, unless I am greatly mistaken."

"By the powers, Mr. Courtenay, I hope you may be right," answered Hennesey. "Ay, there she is," he continued, "as plain as mud in a wineglass! And if she isn't French her looks belie her. Mr. Hudson, you spalpeen, slip down below and tell the captain that there are a brace of suspicious-looking craft within a mile of us. And ye may call upon Misther Dawson and impart the same pleasant information to him." Then, turning his beaming phiz up to me, he continued—

"Mr. Courtenay, it's on the stroke of eight bells, but all the same you'd better stay where you are for the present, until the fog clears, since you know exactly the bearings of those two craft. And I'll thank ye to keep your weather eye liftin', young gentleman; there may be a whole fleet of Frenchmen within gun-shot of us, for all that we can tell."

"Ay, ay, sir!" I cheerfully answered, my curiosity having by this time got the better of my keen appetite for breakfast; moreover, having been the discoverer of the two sail already sighted, I was anxious to add to the prestige thus gained by being the first to sight any other craft that might happen to be in our neighbourhood.

My stay aloft, however, was not destined to be a long one, for the fog was now clearing fast, and within ten minutes it had all driven away to leeward of us, revealing the fact that there were but the two sail already discovered in sight—unless there might happen to be others so far ahead as to be still hidden in the fog-bank to leeward. But before I left the royal yard I had succeeded in satisfying myself, by means of my glass—which had been sent up to me bent on to the signal halliards—that the two strangers were frigates, and almost certainly French. They were exchanging signals at a great rate, but we could make nothing of their flags, which at least proved that they were not British. To make assurance doubly sure, however, we had hoisted our private signal, to which neither ship had been able to reply. There was no doubt that they were enemies; and this fact having been satisfactorily established, I was permitted to descend and snatch a hasty breakfast.

And a hasty one it was, for I had scarcely been below five minutes when we were piped to clear for action, and I was obliged to hurry on deck again. But a hungry midshipman can achieve a good deal in the eating line in five minutes, and in that brief interval I contrived to stow away enough food to take the keen edge off my appetite, promising myself that I would make up my leeway at dinner-time—provided that I was still alive when the hour for that meal came round. This last thought sobered me down somewhat, and to a certain extent subdued my hilarious spirits; but they rose again as, upon gaining the deck, I looked round and saw the cheerful yet resolute faces of the captain and officers, and noted the gaiety with which the men went about their duty.

The strangers had by this time shown their bunting,—the tricolour,—so there was no further question of their nationality or of the fact that we were booked for a sharp fight, for they had the heels of us and were overhauling us in grand style; we could not therefore have escaped, had we been ever so anxious to do so. And, had we made the attempt, we should certainly have been quite justified, for it had now been ascertained that they were both forty-gun ships, while we mounted only thirty-six pieces on our gun deck. Escape, however, was apparently the very last thought likely to occur to Captain Harrison; for although he kept the studding-sails abroad while the ship was being prepared for action, no sooner had the first lieutenant reported everything ready than the order was given to shorten sail; and a pretty sight it was to see how smartly and with what beautifully perfect precision everything was done at once, the studding-sails all collapsing and coming in together at exactly the same moment that the three royals were clewed up and the flight of staysails on the main and mizzen masts hauled down.

"Very prettily done, Mr. Dawson," said the skipper approvingly. "Our friends yonder will see that they have seamen to deal with, at all events, even though we cannot sport such a clean pair of heels as their own."

The two Frenchmen were by this time within less than half a mile of us, converging upon us in such a manner as to range up alongside the *Althea* within the toss of a biscuit on either hand, but neither of them manifested the slightest disposition to follow our example by shortening sail. Perhaps they believed that, were they to do so, we should at once make sail again and endeavour to escape, whereas by holding on to everything until they drew up alongside us, we should fall an easy prey to their superior strength, if indeed we did not surrender at discretion.

And, truly, the two ships formed a noble and a graceful picture as they came sweeping rapidly down upon us with every stitch of canvas set that they could possibly spread, their white sails towering spire-like into the deep, tender blue of the cloudless heavens, with the delicate purple shadows chasing each other athwart the rounded bosoms of them as the hulls that upbore them swung pendulum-like, with a little curl of snow under their bows, over the low hillocks of swell that chased them, sparkling in the brilliant sunlight like a heaving floor of sapphire strewed broadcast with diamonds.

They stood on, silent as the grave, until the craft on our larboard quarter—which was leading by about a couple of lengths—had reached to within a short quarter of a mile of us, when, as we all stood watching them intently, a jet of flame, followed by a heavy burst of white smoke, leapt out from her starboard bow port, and the next instant the shot went humming close past us, to dash up the water in a fountain-like jet a quarter of a mile ahead of us.

"That, I take it, is a polite request to us to heave-to and haul down our colours," remarked Captain Harrison to the first lieutenant, with a smile. "Well, we may as well return the compliment, Mr. Dawson. Try a shot at each of them with the stern-chasers. If we could only manage to knock away an important spar on board either of them it might so cripple her as to cause her to drop astern, leaving us to deal with the other one and settle her business out of hand. Yes, aim at their spars, Mr. Dawson. It would perhaps have been better had we opened fire directly they were within range, but I was anxious not to make a mistake. Now that they have fired upon us, however, we need hesitate no longer."

The order was accordingly given to open fire with our stern-chasers, and in less than a minute the two guns spoke out simultaneously, jarring the old hooker to her keel. We were unable for a moment to see the effect of the shots, for the smoke blew in over our taffrail, completely hiding our two pursuers for a few seconds; but when it cleared away a cheer broke from the men who were manning the after guns, for it was seen that the flying-jib stay of our antagonist on the port quarter was cut and the sail towing from the jib-boom end, a neat hole in her port foretopmast studding-sail showing where the shot had passed. The other gun had been less successful, the shot having passed through the head of the second frigate's foresail about four feet below the yard and half-way between the slings and the starboard yardarm, without inflicting any further perceptible damage.

"Very well meant! Let them try again," exclaimed the skipper approvingly. And as the words issued from his lips we saw the two pursuing frigates yaw broadly outward, as if by common consent, and the next instant they both let drive a whole broadside at us. I waited breathlessly while one might have counted "one—two," and then the sound of an ominous crashing aloft told me that we were wounded somewhere among our spars. A block, followed by a shower of splinters, came hurtling down on deck, breaking the arm of a man at the aftermost quarter-deck gun on the port side, and then a louder crash aloft caused me to look up just in time to see our mizzen-topmast go sweeping forward into the hollow of the maintopsail, which it split from head to foot, the mizzen-topgallant mast snapping short off at the cap as it swooped down upon the maintopsail yard. Two topmen were swept out of the maintop by the wreckage in its descent, and terribly—one of them fatally—injured, and there were a few minor damages, which, however, were quickly repaired. Then, as some hands sprang aloft to clear away the wreck, our stern-chasers spoke out again, the one close after the other, and two new holes in the enemy's canvas testified to the excellent aim of our gunners; but, unfortunately, that was the extent of the damage, both shots having passed very close to, but *just missed*, important spars.

The French displayed very creditable smartness in getting inboard the flying-jib that we had cut away for them, and by the time that this was accomplished they had drawn up so close to us that by bearing away a point or two to port and starboard respectively, both craft were enabled to bring their whole broadsides to bear upon us, which they immediately did, taking in their studding-sails, and otherwise reducing their canvas at the same time, until we were all three under exactly the same amount of sail—excepting, of course, that we had lost our mizzen-topsail with all above it, while theirs still stood intact. As for us, our guns were all trained as far aft as the port-holes would permit, and as our antagonists ranged up on either quarter, within pistol-shot, each gun was fired point-blank as it was brought to bear. And now the fight began in real, grim downright earnest, the crew of each gun loading and firing as rapidly as possible, while the French poured in their broadsides with a coolness and precision that extorted our warmest admiration, despite the disagreeable fact that they were playing havoc with us fore and aft, one of our guns having been dismounted within three minutes of the arrival of the enemy alongside us, while the tale of killed and wounded was growing heavier with every broadside that we received. But if we were suffering severely we were paying our punishment back with interest, as we could see by glancing at the hulls of our antagonists, the sides of which were torn and splintered and pierced all along the broad white streak that marked the line of ports,—some of which were knocked two into one,—while their yellow sides were here and there broadly streaked with crimson as the blood drained away through their scuppers. It is true they were fighting us two to one, but, after all, their advantage was more apparent than real, for, running level with us as they were, they could only fight one of their batteries, while we were fighting both ours, and our guns—every one of them double-shotted—were being better and more rapidly served than theirs.

I will not attempt to describe the fight in detail, for indeed any such attempt could only result in failure. And as a matter of fact there was very little to describe. We simply ran dead away to leeward, the three of us, fighting almost yardarm to yardarm, and exchanging broadsides as rapidly as the guns could be loaded and run out. After the first ten minutes of the fight there was little or nothing to be seen, for the wind was fast dropping again, and the three ships were wrapped in a dense white pall of smoke that effectually concealed everything that was going on at a greater distance than some fifty feet from the observer. The most impressive characteristic of the struggle was *noise*—the incessant crash of the guns, the discharge of which set up a continuous tremor of the ship throughout the entire fabric of her; the rending and splintering of timber as the enemy's shot tore its way through the frigate's sides; the shrieks and groans of the wounded and dying, cut into at frequent intervals by some sharp order from the captain or the first lieutenant; the curt commands of the captains of the guns: "Stop the vent! run in! sponge! load! run out!" and so on; the creak of the tackle blocks, the rumble of the gun carriages, the clatter of handspikes, the dull thud of the rammers driving home the shot, the rattling volleys of musketry from the marines on the poop, the occasional rending crash of a falling spar, and the terrific babble of the Frenchmen on either side of us, sounding high and clear in the occasional brief intervals when all the guns happened to be silent together for a moment,—I can only compare it all to the horrible confusion raging through the disordered imagination of one in the clutches of a fiercely burning fever. Our people fought grimly and in silence, save for an occasional cheer at some unusually successful shot; but the Frenchmen jabbered away incessantly, sometimes reviling us and shaking their fists at us through their open ports, and more often squabbling among themselves.

At length, when the fight had lasted about half an hour, the wind dropped to a dead calm, and the Frenchman on our starboard side, who had forged somewhat ahead of us, made an effort to lay himself athwart our bows before he lost way altogether.  But we were too quick for him, for his mainmast was towing alongside and stopped his way; so we did with him what he tried to do to us, driving square athwart his bows as his bowsprit came thrusting in between our fore and main masts, when we lost not a moment in lashing the spar to our main rigging.  But, after all, it resolved itself into tit for tat, for the other fellow put his helm hard aport and just managed to drive square athwart our stern, where he raked us most unmercifully for fully five minutes, until he drove clear, bringing down all three of our masts before he left us.  Of course we could only retaliate upon him with our stern-chasers, which we played upon him with considerable effect; but what we lacked in the way of adequate retort to him we amply made up for to his consort, raking her time after time with such good-will that in a few minutes her bows were battered into a mere mass of torn and splintered timber.  Somebody on board her cried out that they had struck, but as her marines kept up their fire upon us from the poop, while her main-deck guns continued to blaze away whenever she swung sufficiently for any of them to bear, no notice was taken of this intimation; and presently our skipper gave the order to cut her adrift, so that her people might have no chance to board—a proceeding that would have proved exceedingly awkward for us in our then weakened condition.

But it presently became evident that they had no

thought of boarding us; on the contrary, their chief anxiety was clearly to escape from the warm berth that they had thrust themselves into; for a few minutes later, the fire on both sides having slackened somewhat, we observed that both craft had their boats in the water and were doing their best to tow off from us, and almost immediately afterwards the French ceased firing altogether. I believe our skipper—fire-eater though he was—felt unfeignedly thankful at this cessation of hostilities, for he immediately followed suit, giving the order for the men to leave the guns and proceed to repair damages. This was no light task, for not only were we completely dismasted, but the hull of the ship was terribly knocked about, the carpenter reporting five feet of water in the hold and twenty-seven shot-holes between wind and water, apart from our other damages, which were sufficiently serious. Moreover, our "butcher's bill" was appallingly heavy, the list totalling up to no less than thirty-eight killed and one hundred and six wounded, out of a total of two hundred and eighty!

## CHAPTER II

### THE *ALTHEA* FOUNDERS

THE French having ceased firing, and manifesting an unmistakable anxiety to withdraw from our proximity, we bestowed but little further attention on them, for it quickly became clear to us that our own condition was quite sufficiently serious to tax our energies to the utmost. The first task demanding the attention of the carpenter and his mates was of course the stoppage of our leaks, and a very difficult task indeed it proved to be, owing to the rapidity with which the water was rising in the hold; by manning the pumps, however, and employing the entire available remainder of the crew in baling, we succeeded in plugging all the shot-holes and clearing the hold of water by noon, when the men were knocked off to go to their well-earned dinner. Then, indeed, we found time to look around us and to ask ourselves and each other where the French were and what they were doing. There was no difficulty in furnishing a reply to either question, for our antagonists were only a bare four miles off, and close together. But bad as our own plight was, theirs was very much worse; for we now saw that the frigate which we had raked so unmercifully was in a sinking condition, having settled so low in the water indeed that the sills of her maindeck ports were awash and dipping with every sluggish heave of her upon the low and almost imperceptible swell, while her own boats and those of her consort were busily engaged in taking off her crew. With the aid of my telescope I could distinctly see all that was going on, and I saw also that the end of the gallant craft was so near as to render her disappearance a matter of but a few minutes. Hungry, therefore, as I was, I determined to remain on deck and see the last of her. Nor had I long to wait; I had scarcely arrived at the decision that I would do so, when, as I watched her through my glass, I saw the boats that hung around her shoving off hurriedly one after the other, until one only remained. Presently that one also shoved off, and, loaded down to her gunwale, pulled, as hastily as her overloaded condition would permit, toward the other frigate. She had scarcely placed half a dozen fathoms between herself and the sinking ship before the latter rolled heavily to port, slowly recovered herself, and then rolled still more heavily to starboard, completely burying the whole tier of her starboard ports as she did so. She hung thus for perhaps half a minute, settling visibly all the time; finally she *staggered*, as it were, once more to an even keel, but with her stern dipping deeper and deeper every second until her taffrail was buried, while her battered bows lifted slowly into the air, when, the inclination of her decks rapidly growing steeper, she suddenly took a sternward plunge and vanished from sight in the midst of a sudden swirl of water that was distinctly visible through the lenses of the telescope. The occupants of the boat that had so recently left her saw their danger and put forth herculean efforts to avoid it; they were too near, however, to escape, and despite all their exertions the boat was caught and dragged back into the vortex created by the sinking ship, into which she too disappeared. But a few seconds afterwards I saw heads popping up above the water again, here and there, while a couple of boats that had just discharged their cargo of passengers dashed away to the rescue and were soon paddling hither and thither among the little black spots that kept popping into view all round them. I waited until all had seemingly been picked up, and then went below to secure what dinner might be remaining for me.

When, after a hurried meal, I again went on deck, the horizon away to the northward and eastward was darkening to a light air from that quarter, that came gently stealing along the glassy surface of the ocean, first in cat's-paws, then as a gentle breathing that caused the polished undulations to break into a tremor of laughing ripples, and finally into a light breeze, before which the surviving French frigate bore up with squared yards, leaving us unmolested.

Meanwhile the crew, having dined, turned to again for a busy afternoon's work, which consisted chiefly in clearing away the wreck of our fallen spars, and saving as many of them and as much of our canvas and running gear as would be likely to be of use to us in fitting the ship with a jury-rig. And so well did the men work, that by sunset we were enabled to cut adrift from the wreck of our lower masts, and to bear up in the wake of the Frenchman, who by this time had run us out of sight in the south-western quarter.

But, tired as the men were, there was no rest for them that night, for it was felt to be imperatively necessary to get the ship under canvas again without a moment's delay; moreover, despite the fact that the shot-holes had all been plugged, it was found that the battered hull was still leaking so seriously as to necessitate a quarter of an hour's spell at the pumps every two hours. The hands were therefore kept at work, watch and watch,' all through the night, with the result that when day broke next morning we had a pair of sheers rigged and on end, ready to rear into position the spars that had been prepared and fitted as lower masts. The end of that day found us once more under sail, after a fashion, and heading on our course to the southward and westward.

For the following two days all went well with us, save that the ship continued to make water so freely as to necessitate the use of the pumps at the middle and end of every watch, a fair breeze driving us along under our jury-canvas at the rate of five to six knots per hour. Toward evening, however, on the second day, signs of a change of weather began to manifest themselves, the sky to windward losing its rich tint of blue and becoming pallid and hard, streaked with mares' tails and flecked with small, smoky-looking, swift-flying clouds, while the setting sun, as he neared the horizon, lost his radiance and became a mere shapeless blotch of angry red that finally seemed to dissolve and disappear in a broad bank of slate-hued vapour. The sea too changed its colour, from the clear steel-blue that it had hitherto worn to the hue of indigo smirched with black. Moreover, I heard the captain remark to Mr. Dawson that the mercury was falling and that he feared we were in for a dirty night.

And, indeed, so it seemed; for about the middle of the second dog-watch the wind lulled perceptibly and we had a sharp rain-squall, soon after which it breezed up again, the wind coming first of all in gusts and then in a strong breeze that, as the night wore on, steadily increased until it was blowing half a gale, with every indication of worse to come. The sea, too, rose rapidly, and came rushing down upon our starboard quarter, high, steep, and foam-crested, causing the frigate to roll and tumble about most unpleasantly under her jury-rig and short canvas. Altogether, the prospects for the night were so exceedingly unpromising that I must plead guilty to having experienced a selfish joy at the reflection that it was my eight hours in.

When I went on deck at midnight that night, I found that the wind had increased to a whole gale, with a very high and confused sea running, over which the poor maimed *Althea* was wallowing along at a speed of about eight and a half knots, with a dismal groaning of timbers that harmonised lugubriously with the clank of the chain pumps and the swash of water washing nearly knee-deep about the decks—for the hooker laboured so heavily that she was leaking like a basket, necessitating the unremitting use of the pumps throughout the watch. And—worst of all—Keene whispered to me that, even with the pumps going constantly, the water was slowly but distinctly gaining. And thus it continued all through the middle watch.

It was hoped that the gale would not be of long duration, but at eight bells next morning the news was that the mercury was still falling, while the wind, instead of evincing a disposition to moderate, blew harder than ever. And oh, what a dreary outlook it was when, swathed in oilskins, I passed through the hatchway and stepped out on deck! The sky was entirely veiled by an unbroken mass of dark, purplish, slate-coloured cloud that was almost black in its deeper shadows, with long, tattered streamers of dirty whitish vapour scurrying wildly athwart it; a heavy, leaden-hued, white-crested, foam-flecked sea was running, and in the midst of the picture was the poor crippled frigate, rolling and labouring and staggering onward like a wounded sea-bird under her jury-spars and spray-darkened canvas, with a miniature ocean washing hither and thither athwart her heaving deck, and a crowd of panting, straining, half-naked men clustering about her pumps, while others were as busily employed in passing buckets up and down through the hatchways; the whole set to the dismal harmony of howling wind, hissing spray, the wearisome and incessant wash of water, and the groaning and complaining sounds of the labouring hull. The skipper and the first luff were pacing the weather side of the poop together in earnest converse, and at each turn in their walk they both paused for an instant, as by mutual consent, to cast a look of anxious inquiry to windward.

Presently I saw the carpenter coming along the deck with the sounding-rod in his hand. I intercepted him just by the foot of the poop ladder and remarked—

"Well, Chips, what is the best news you have to tell us?"

"The best news?" echoed Chips, with a solemn shake of the head; "there ain't *no* best, Mr. Courtenay, it's all worst, sir; there's over four foot of water in the hold now, and it's gainin' on us at the rate of five inches an hour; and if this here gale don't break pretty quick I won't answer for the consequences!"

And up he went to make his report to the skipper.

This was bad news indeed, especially for the unfortunate men who were compelled by dire necessity to toil unceasingly at the back-breaking labour of working the pumps; but I felt no apprehension as to our ultimate safety. Five inches of water per hour was a formidable gain for a leak to make in spite of all the pumping and baling that could be accomplished, yet it would take so many hours at that rate to reduce the frigate to a waterlogged condition that ere the arrival of that moment the gale would certainly blow itself out, the labouring and straining of the ship would cease, the leak would be got under control again, and all would be well.

But when, at noon that day,—the gale showing no symptoms whatever of abatement,—the captain gave orders for the upper-deck guns to be launched overboard, I began to realise that our condition was such as might easily become critical. And when, about half an hour before sunset, orders were given to throw the *main*-deck guns overboard, it became borne in upon me that matters were becoming mighty serious with us.

With the approach of night the gale seemed rather to increase in strength than otherwise, while the sea was certainly considerably heavier; and the worst of it was that there was no indication of an approaching change for the better. As for the poor *Althea*, she certainly did not labour quite so heavily now that she was relieved of the weight of her guns, but the water in the hold still gained steadily upon the pumps, and the more experienced hands among us were beginning to hint at the possibility of our being compelled to leave her and take to the boats. And these hints received something of confirmation when, shortly after the commencement of the first watch, the carpenter and his mates were seen going the rounds of the boats and examining into their condition with the aid of lanterns. Nevertheless, and despite these omens, the men stuck resolutely to the pumps and the baling all through the night, the captain and the first lieutenant animating and encouraging them by their presence throughout the long, dismal, dreary hours of darkness.

About three bells in the morning watch the welcome news spread throughout the ship that the mercury had at length begun to rise again; and with the approach of dawn it became apparent that the gale was breaking, the sky to windward gave signs of clearing, and hope once more sprang up within our breasts. But the men, although still willing and even eager to continue the heart-breaking work of pumping and baling, were by this time utterly worn out; the water in the hold steadily and relentlessly gained upon them, despite their most desperate efforts, and by the arrival of breakfast-time it had become perfectly apparent to everybody that the poor old *Althea* was a doomed ship!

If, however, there was any doubt as to this in the minds of any of us, it was quickly dispelled, for after breakfast the order was passed to knock off baling; and the men thus relieved were at once set to work under the first and second lieutenants, the one party to prepare a sea anchor, and the other to attend to the provisioning of the boats and get them ready for launching. I was attached to the first lieutenant's party, or that which undertook the preparation of the sea anchor; and as the idea impressed me as being rather ingenious, I will describe it for the benefit of those who may feel interested in such matters, prefacing my description with the explanation that, in consequence of the springing up of the gale so soon after our action with the Frenchmen, our jury-rig was of a very primitive and incomplete character, such as would enable us to run fairly well before the wind, but not such as would permit of our lying-to; hence the need for a sea anchor, now that the necessity had arisen for us to launch our boats in heavy weather.

The sea anchor was the offspring of the first lieutenant's inventiveness, and it consisted of an old foretopsail bent to a couple of booms of suitable length and stoutness. The head of the sail was bent to one of the booms with seizings, in much the same manner as it would have been bent to a topsail yard, while the clews were securely lashed to the extremities of the other boom. Then to the boom which represented the topsail yard was attached a crow-foot made of two spans of stout hawser, having an eye in the centre of them to which to bend the cable. The lower boom was well weighted by the attachment to it of a number of pigs of iron ballast, as well as our stream anchor; after which the starboard cable was paid out and passed along aft, outside the fore rigging, the end being then brought inboard and bent on to the crow-foot. The whole was then made up as compactly as possible with lashings, after which, by means of tackles aloft, it was hoisted clear of the bulwarks and lowered down over the side; the lashings were then cut and the sail dropped into the water, opening out as it did so, when, the lower boom sinking with the weight attached to it, a broad surface was exposed, acting as a very efficient sea anchor. At the moment when everything was ready to let go, the ship's helm was put hard over, bringing her broadside-on to the sea, when, as she drove away to leeward, she brought a strain upon her cable that at once fetched her up head to wind. This part of the process having been successfully accomplished, it was an easy matter to bend a spring on to the cable and heave the ship round broadside-on to the sea once more, in which position she afforded an excellent lee under the shelter of which to launch our boats, which, but for this contrivance, must have inevitably been swamped.

By the time that all this was done the boats were ready for launching, and the captain gave orders for this to be at once proceeded with, beginning with the launch; this being the heaviest boat in the ship, and the most difficult to get into the water. I felt exceedingly doubtful as to the ability of our jury-spars to support the weight of so heavy a craft, but, by staying them well, the delicate task was at length successfully accomplished, when the worst cases among the wounded were brought on deck and carefully lowered over the side into the boat beneath, the doctor, with his instruments and medicine-chest, being already there to receive them. And as soon as she had received her complement, the launch was veered away to leeward at the end of a long line—but still under the shelter of the ship's hull—to make room for the first cutter. The rest of the boats followed in succession—the men preserving to the very last moment the most admirable order and discipline—until only the captain's gig, of which I was placed in command, remained. The proper complement of this boat was six men, in addition to the coxswain; but in order that the wounded—who were placed in the launch and the first and second cutters—might be as little crowded as possible, the remainder of the boats received rather more than their full complement, in consequence of which my crew numbered ten, all told, instead of seven. We were the last boat to leave the ship, the skipper having gone below to his cabin for some purpose at the last minute; and I assure you that, the bustle and excitement of getting the men out of the ship being now all over, I found it rather nervous and trying work to stand there in the gangway, waiting for the reappearance of the captain on deck. For the ship was by this time in a sinking condition and liable to go down under our feet at any moment, having settled so low in the water that she rolled her closed maindeck ports completely under with every sickly lurch of her upon the still heavy sea that was now continuously breaking over her, while the water could be distinctly heard washing about down below.

At length the skipper came out of his cabin, bearing in his hand a large japanned tin box.

"Jump down, Mr. Courtenay, and stand by to take this box from me," he cried; and down the side I went, needing no second bidding. The box was carefully passed down to me, and I stowed it away in the stern-sheets. When I had done so, and looked up at the ship, Captain Harrison was standing in the gangway with his hat in his hand, looking wistfully and sorrowfully along the deserted decks and aloft at the jury-spars that, with their rigging, so pathetically expressed the idea of a mortally wounded creature gallantly but hopelessly struggling against the death that was inexorably drawing near. Some such fancy perhaps suggested itself to him, for I distinctly saw him dash his hand across his eyes more than once. At length he turned, descended the side-ladder, and, watching his opportunity, sprang lightly into the boat.

"Shove off, Mr. Courtenay!" he ordered, as he wrapped himself in his boat cloak.

"Shove off!" I reiterated in turn, and forthwith away

we went, the men nothing loath, as I could clearly see, for the ship was now liable to founder at any moment; indeed the wonder to me was that she remained afloat so long, for she had by this time sunk so deep that her channels were completely buried, only showing when she rolled heavily away from us. Poor old barkie! what a desolate and forlorn object she looked as we pulled away from her, with little more than her bulwarks showing above water, with the seas making a clean breach over her bows continually, as she rolled and plunged with sickening sluggishness to the great ridges of steel-grey water that incessantly swooped down upon her and into which her bows, pinned down by the weight of water within her hull, occasionally bored, as though, tired of the hopeless struggle for existence, she had at length summoned resolution to take the final plunge and so end it all. Again and again I thought she was gone, but again and yet again she emerged wearily and heavily out of the deluges of water that sought to overwhelm her; but at length an unusually heavy sea caught her with her bows pinned down after a plunge into the trough; clear, green, and unbroken it brimmed to her figure-head and poured in a foaming cataract over her bows, sweeping the whole length of her from stem to stern until her hull was completely buried. As the wave left her it was seen that her bows were still submerged, and a moment later it became apparent that the end had come and she was taking her final plunge.

"There she goes!" shouted one of the men; and as the fellow uttered the words the captain rose to his feet in the stern-sheets and doffed his hat, as though he had been standing beside the grave of a dear friend, watching the dear old barkie as, with her stern gradually rising high, she slid slowly and solemnly out of sight, the occupants of the boats giving her a parting cheer as she vanished. The captain stood motionless until the swirl that marked her grave had disappeared, then he replaced his hat, resumed his seat, and remarked—

"Give way, men! Mr. Courtenay, be good enough to put me aboard the launch, if you please."

## CHAPTER III

### THE GIG IS CAUGHT IN A HURRICANE

UPON reaching the launch, the captain's first care was to satisfy himself as to the well-being and comfort of the poor wounded fellows aboard her; but the doctor had already attended to this matter, with the result that they were as comfortable as the utmost care and forethought could render them. The master, meanwhile, had been ascertaining the exact latitude and longitude of the spot where the frigate had gone down, and he now communicated the result of his calculations to the captain, who thereupon gave orders for the boats to steer southwest on a speed trial for the day, the leading boat to heave-to at sunset and wait for the rest to close. I had not the remotest notion as to the meaning of this somewhat singular order, but my obvious duty was to execute it; so I forthwith made sail upon the gig, and a very few minutes sufficed to demonstrate that we were the fastest boat of the whole squadron. Nor was this at all surprising, for the gig was not an ordinary service boat; she was the captain's own private property, having been built to order from his own design, with a special view to the development of exceptional sailing powers, boat-sailing being quite a hobby with him. She was a splendid craft of her kind, measuring thirty feet in length, with a beam of six feet, and she pulled six oars. She was a most beautiful model of the whale-boat type, double-ended, with quite an unusual amount of sheer fore and aft, which gave her a fine, bold, buoyant bow and stern; moreover, these were covered in with light turtle-back decks, that forward measuring six feet in length, while the after turtle-back measured five feet from the stern-post. She was fitted with a keel nine inches deep amidships, tapering off to four inches deep at each end; was rigged as a schooner, with standing fore and main lug and a small jib, and, with her ordinary crew on board and sitting to windward, required no ballast even in a fresh breeze. Small wonder, therefore, was it that, having such a boat under us, we had run the rest of the fleet out of sight by midday, the wind still blowing strong, although it was moderating rapidly.

The first lieutenant was, like the captain, fond of inventing and designing things, but his speciality took the form of logs for determining the speed of craft through the water; and in the course of his experiments he had provided each of the frigate's boats with an ingenious spring arrangement which, attached to an ordinary fishing-line with a lead weight secured to its outer end,

## THE GIG IS CAUGHT IN A HURRICANE 45

which was continuously towed astern, registered the speed of the boat with a very near approach to perfect accuracy.

The day passed uneventfully away, the wind moderating steadily all the time, and the sun breaking through considerably before noon, enabling me to secure a meridian altitude wherefrom to compute my latitude. The sea, too, was going down, and when the sun set that night the sky wore a very promising fine-weather aspect. As the great golden orb vanished below the horizon we rounded the boat to, lowered our sails, and moored her to a sea anchor made of the oars lashed together in a bundle with the painter bent on to them. And later on, when it fell dark, we lighted a lantern and hoisted it to our foremasthead, as a beacon for which the other boats might steer. The gig had behaved splendidly all through the day, never shipping so much as a single drop of water, and now that she was riding to her oars she took the sea so easily and buoyantly that I felt as safe as I had ever done aboard the poor old *Althea* herself, and unhesitatingly allowed all hands to turn in as best they could in the bottom of the boat, undertaking to keep a lookout myself until the other boats had joined company.

The first boat to make her appearance was the service gig in charge of Mr. Flowers, the third lieutenant; she ranged up alongside and hove-to about two hours after sunset, soon afterwards following our example by throwing out a sea anchor. Then came the first and second cutters, in command of the first and second lieutenants; the first cutter arriving about an hour after Mr. Flowers, while the second cutter appeared about a quarter of an hour later. The launch followed about half an hour astern of the second cutter; but this was not to be wondered at, the former being rather deep, owing to the very generous supply of water that the doctor had insisted on carrying for the comfort of the wounded. Then, some three-quarters of an hour later, came the jolly-boat in charge of the boatswain; and finally the dinghy, carrying four hands and in charge of my friend and fellow-mid, Jack Keene, turned up close upon midnight.

Long ere this, however, we had each in succession spoken the launch, reporting the distance that we had traversed up to sunset. And, with the data thus supplied, the master had gone to work upon a calculation which formed the basis of a sort of table showing the ratio of the speeds of the several boats, with the aid of which the officer in charge of each boat could estimate with a moderate degree of accuracy the position of each of the other boats at any given moment—so long, that is to say, as the wind held fair enough to allow the boats to steer a given course. A copy of this table was then furnished to the officer in command of each boat, after which the captain ordered Mr. Flowers to make the best of his way to Barbadoes, with instructions to report the loss of the frigate immediately upon his arrival, with a request to the senior naval officer that a craft of some sort might be forthwith despatched in search of the other boats. Similar instructions were next given to me, except that my port of destination was Bermuda. Of course we each carried a written as well as a verbal message to the senior naval officer of the port to which we were bound; and equally, of course, it was impressed upon us both that if we happened to encounter a friendly craft *en route*, and could induce her to undertake the search, it would be so much the better. Having received these instructions, and taken young Lindsay out of the launch, which was a trifle over-crowded, I at once made sail and parted company, the occupants of the other boats giving us the encouragement of a farewell cheer as we did so; they also making sail at the same time on a west-south-westerly course, which would afford them about an even chance of being picked up by a craft either from Bermuda or Barbadoes; while, in the event of their being found by neither, they stood a very good chance of hitting off one or another of the Leeward Islands.

For the remainder of that night we sped gaily onward, with the wind about two points free, making splendid progress; although I am bound to admit that, with the height of sea and the strength of wind that still prevailed, there were moments when the task of sailing the boat became exciting enough to satisfy the cravings of even the most exacting individual. Lindsay and I relieved each other at the tiller, watch and watch, with one hand forward to keep a lookout ahead and to leeward, the rest of the poor fellows being so thoroughly worn out by their long spell at the pumps that rest and sleep was an even more imperative necessity for them than it was for us.

By the time of sunrise the wind had dwindled away to a topgallant breeze, with a corresponding reduction in the amount of sea; we were therefore enabled to shake out the double reef that we had thus far been compelled to carry in our canvas, while the aspect of the sky was more promising than it had been for several days past. The weather was now as favourable as we could possibly wish, the wind being just fresh enough to send us along at top speed, gunwale-to, under whole canvas, while the sea was going down rapidly. But, as the day wore on, the improvement in the weather progressed just a little too far; it became even finer than we wished it, the wind continuing to drop steadily, until by noon we were sliding over the long, mountainous swell at a speed of barely four knots, with the hot sun beating down upon us far too ardently to be pleasant. Needless to say, we kept a sharp lookout for a sail all through the day, but saw nothing; the flying-fish that sparkled out from the ridges of the swell and went skimming away to port and starboard, gleaming as brilliantly in the strong sunlight as a handful of new silver dollars, being the only objects to break the solitude that environed us. By sunset that day the wind had died completely out, leaving the ocean a vast surface of slow-moving, glassy undulations, and I was reluctantly compelled to order the canvas to be taken in, the masts to be struck, and the oars to be thrown out. Then, indeed, as the night closed down upon us and the stars came winking, one by one, out of the immeasurable expanse of darkening blue above us, the silence of the vast ocean solitude that hemmed us in became a thing that might be felt. So oppressive was it that, as by instinct, our conversation gradually dwindled to the desultory exchange of a few whispered remarks, uttered at lengthening intervals, until it died out altogether; while the profound stillness of air and ocean seemed to become accentuated rather than broken by the measured roll of the oars in the rowlocks, and the tinkling lap of the water under the bows and along the bends of the boat. We pulled four oars only instead of six, in order that we might have two relays, or watches, who relieved each other every four hours. The men pulled a long, steady, easy stroke, of a sort that enabled them to keep on throughout the watch without undue fatigue, by taking a five minutes' spell of rest about once an hour; but it was weary work for the poor fellows, after all, and our progress soon became provokingly slow.

About three bells in the middle watch that night, as I half sat, half reclined in the stern-sheets, drowsily steering by a star, and occasionally glancing over my shoulder at the ruddy, glowing sickle of the rising moon, then in her last quarter, we were all suddenly startled by the sound of a loud, deep-drawn sigh that came to us from somewhere off the larboard bow, apparently at no great distance from the boat; and while we sat wondering and listening, with poised oars, the sound was repeated close aboard of us, but this time on our starboard quarter, accompanied by a soft washing of water; and turning sharply, I beheld, right in the shimmering, golden wake of the moon, a huge, black, shapeless, gleaming bulk noiselessly upheave itself out of the black water and slowly glide up abreast of us until it was alongside and all but within reach of our oars.

"A whale!" whispered one of the men, in tones that were a trifle unsteady from the startling surprise of the creature's sudden appearance.

"Ay," replied the man next him, "and that was another that we heard just now; bull and cow, most likely. I only hopes they haven't got a calf with 'em, because if they have, the bull may take it into his head to attack us; they're mighty short-tempered sometimes when they have young uns cruisin' in company! I minds one time when I was aboard the old *Walrus*—a whaler sailin' out of Dundee—that was afore I was pressed"—

Another long sigh-like expiration abruptly interrupted the yarn, and close under our bows there rose another leviathan, so closely indeed that, unless it was a trick of the imagination, I felt a slight tremor thrill through the boat, as though he had touched us! Involuntarily I glanced over the side; and it was perhaps well that I did so, for there, right underneath the boat, far down in the black depths, I perceived a small, faint, glimmering patch of phosphorescence, that, as I looked, grew larger and more distinct, until, in the course of a very few seconds, it assumed the shape of another monster rising plumb underneath us.

"Back water, men! back water, for your lives! There is one of them coming up right under our keel!" I cried; and, at the words, the men dashed their oars into the water and we backed out of the way, just in time to avoid being hove out of the water and capsized, this fellow happening to come up with something very like a rush. Meanwhile, others were rising here and there all around us, until we found ourselves surrounded by a school of between twenty and thirty whales. It was a rather alarming situation for us; for although the creatures appeared perfectly quiet and well-disposed, there was no knowing at what moment one of them might gather way and run us down, either intentionally or inadvertently; while there was also the chance that another might rise beneath us so rapidly as to render it impossible for us to avoid him. One of the men suggested that we should endeavour to frighten them away by making a noise of some sort; but the former whaler strongly vetoed this proposition, asserting—whether rightly or wrongly I know not—that if we startled them the chances were that those nearest at hand would turn upon us and destroy the boat.

We therefore deemed it best to maintain a discreet silence; and in this condition of unpleasant suspense we remained, floating motionless for a full half-hour, the whales meanwhile lying as motionless as ourselves, when suddenly a stir seemed to thrill through the whole herd, and all in a moment they got under way and went leisurely off in a northerly direction, to our great relief. We gave them a full quarter of an hour to get well out of our way, and then the oars dipped into the water once more, and we resumed our voyage.

At daybreak the atmosphere was still as stagnant as it had been all through the night, the surface of the ocean being unbroken by the faintest ripple, save where, about a mile away, broad on our starboard bow, the fin of a solitary shark lazily swimming athwart our course turned up a thin, blue, wedge-shaped ripple as he swam. There was, however, a faint, scarcely perceptible mistiness in the atmosphere that led me to hope we might get a small breeze from somewhere—I little cared where—before the day grew many hours older. At nine o'clock I secured an excellent set of sights for my longitude,—having taken the precaution to set my watch by the ship's chronometer before parting company with the launch,—and it was depressing to find, after I had worked out my calculations, how little progress we had made during the twenty-one hours since the previous noon. As the morning wore on the mistiness that I had observed in the atmosphere at daybreak passed away, but the sky lost its rich depth of blue, while the sun hung aloft, a dazzling but rayless globe of palpitating fire. A change of some sort was brewing, I felt certain, and I was somewhat surprised that, with such a sky above us, the atmosphere should remain so absolutely stagnant.

As the day wore on, the thin, scarcely perceptible veil of vapour that had dimmed the richness of the sky tints in the early morning gradually thickened and seemed to be assuming somewhat of a distinctness of shape. I just succeeded in securing the meridian altitude of the sun, for the determination of our latitude, but that was all. Half an hour after noon the haze had grown so dense that the great luminary showed through it merely as a shapeless blur of pale, watery radiance, and within another hour he had disappeared altogether from the overcast sky. Still the wind failed to come to our help; the atmosphere seemed to be dead, so absolutely motionless was it; and although the sun had vanished behind the murky vapours that were stealthily and imperceptibly veiling the firmament, the heat was so distressing that the perspiration streamed from every pore, the manipulation of the oars grew more and more languid, and at length, as though actuated by a common impulse, the men gave in, declaring that they were utterly exhausted and could do no more. And I could well believe their assertion, for even I, whose exertions were limited to the steering of the boat, felt that even such slight labour was almost too arduous to be much longer endured. The oars were accordingly laid in, we went to dinner, and then the men flung themselves down in the bottom of the boat, and, with their pipes clenched between their teeth, fell fast asleep, an example which was quickly followed by Lindsay and myself, despite all our efforts to the contrary.

When I awoke it was still breathlessly calm, and I thought for a moment that night had fallen, so dark was it; but upon consulting my watch I found that it still wanted nearly an hour to sunset. But, heavens! what a change had taken place in the aspect of the weather during the four hours or so that I had lain asleep in the stern-sheets of the boat! It is quite possible that, had I remained awake, I should scarcely have been aware of more than the mere fact that the sky was steadily assuming an increasingly sombre and threatening aspect; but, awaking as I did to the abrupt perception of the change that had been steadily working itself out during the previous four hours, it is not putting it too strongly to say that I was startled. For whereas my last conscious memory of the weather, before succumbing to the blandishments of the drowsy god, had been merely that of a lowering, overcast sky, that might portend anything, but probably meant no more than a sharp thunder-squall, I now awakened to the consciousness that the firmament above consisted of a vast curtain of frowning, murky, black-grey cloud, streaked or furrowed in a very remarkable manner from about east-south-east to west-nor'-west, the lower edges of the clouds presenting a curious frayed appearance, while the clouds themselves glowed here and there with patches of lurid, fiery red, as though each bore within its bosom a fiercely burning furnace, the ruddy light of which shone through in places. I had never before beheld a sky like it, but its aspect was sufficiently alarming to convince the veriest tyro in weather-lore that something quite out of the common was brewing; so I at once awoke the slumbering crew to inquire whether any of them could read the signs and tell me what we might expect.

The newly-awakened men yawned, stretched their arms above their heads, and dragged themselves stiffly up on the thwarts, gazing with looks of wonder and alarm at the portentous sky that hung above them.

" Well, if we was in the Chinese seas, I should say that a typhoon was goin' to bust out shortly," observed one of them—a grizzled, mahogany-visaged old salt, who had seen service all over the world. "But," he continued, "they don't have typhoons in the Atlantic, not as ever I've heard say."

" No, they don't have typhoons here, but they has hurricanes, which I take to mean pretty much the same thing," remarked another.

" You are right, Tom," said I, thus put upon the scent, as it were, "a Chinese typhoon and a West Indian hurricane are the same thing under different names. A third name for them is ' cyclone '; and as this threatening sky seems to remind Dunn so powerfully of a Chinese typhoon, depend upon it we are going to have a taste of a West Indian hurricane, or cyclone. I have read somewhere that they frequently originate out here in the heart of the Atlantic."

"If we're agoin' to have a typhoon, or a hurricane, or a cyclone—whichever you likes to call it—all I say is, 'The Lord ha' mercy upon us,'" remarked Dunn. "Big ships has all their work cut out to weather one o' them gales; so what are *we* agoin' to do in this here open boat, I'd like to know?"

"Have you ever been through a typhoon, Dunn?" I asked.

"Yes, sir, I have, and more than one of 'em," was the reply. "I was caught in one off the Paracels, in the old *Audacious* frigate,—as fine a sea-boat as ever was launched, —and, in less time than it takes to tell of it, we was dismasted and hove down on our beam-ends; and it took us all our time to keep the hooker afloat and get her into Hong-Kong harbour. And the very next year I was catched again—in the Bashee Channel, this time—in the *Lively* schooner, of six guns. We knowed it was comin'; it gived us good warnin' and left us plenty of time to get ready for it; so Mr. Barker—the lieutenant in command— gived orders to send the yards and both topmasts down on deck, and rig in the jib-boom; and then he stripped her down to a close-reefed boom foresail. But we capsized—reg'larly 'turned turtle'—when the gale struck

## THE GIG IS CAUGHT IN A HURRICANE 57

us, and only five of us lived to tell the tale. As to this here boat, if a hurricane anything at all like them Chinee typhoons gets hold of her, why, we shall just be blowed clean away out o' water and up among the clouds! And that's just what's goin' to happen, if signs counts for anything."

Wherewith the speaker thrust both hands into his trouser pockets, disgustedly spat a small ocean of tobacco-juice overboard, and subsided into gloomy silence.

It was a sufficiently alarming retrospect, in all conscience, to which we had just listened, and the prophetic utterance wherewith it had been wound up, while powerfully suggestive of a highly novel and picturesque experience in store for us, was certainly not attractive enough to cause us to look forward to its fulfilment with undisturbed serenity; nevertheless, I did not feel like tamely giving in without making some effort to save the boat and the lives with which I had been entrusted, so I set myself seriously to consider how we could best utilise such time as might be allowed us, in making some sort of preparation to meet the now confidently-expected outburst. I looked over our resources, and found that they consisted, in the main, of eight oars, two boat-hooks, two masts, two yards, three sails, half a coil of two-inch rope that some thoughtful individual had pitched into the boat when getting her ready for launching, half a coil of ratline and two large balls of spun-yarn, due to the forethought of the same or some other individual, a painter some ten fathoms long, and the boat's anchor, together with the gratings, stretchers, and other fittings belonging to the boat, and a few oddments that might or might not prove useful.

Was it possible to do anything with these? After considering the matter carefully I thought it was. The greatest danger to which we were likely to be exposed seemed to me to consist in our being swamped by the flying spindrift and scudwater or by the breaking seas, and if we could by any means contrive to keep the water out there was perhaps a bare chance that we might be able to weather the gale. And, after a little further consideration, I thought that what I desired to do might possibly be accomplished by means of the boat's sails, which were practically new, and made of very light, but closely woven canvas, that ought to prove watertight. So, having unfolded my ideas to the men, we all went to work with alacrity to put them to the test of actual practice.

Of course it was utterly useless to think of scudding before the gale; our only hope of living through what was impending depended upon our ability to keep the boat riding bows-on to the sea, and to do this it became necessary for us to improvise a sea anchor again. This was easily done by lashing together six of our eight oars in a bundle, three of the blades at one end and three at the other, with the boat anchor lashed amidships to sink the oars somewhat in the water and give them a grip of it. A span, made by doubling a suitable length of our two-inch rope, was bent on to the whole affair, and the boat's painter was then bent on to the span, when the apparatus was launched overboard, and our sea anchor was ready for service.

Our next task was to cut the two lug-sails adrift from their yards. The mainsail was then doubled in half, and one end spread over the fore turtle-back and drawn taut. Over this, outside the boat and under her keel, we then passed a length of our two-inch rope, girding the boat with it and confining the fore end of the sail to the turtle-back, when, with the aid of one of the stretchers, we were able to heave this girth-rope so taut as to render it impossible for the sail to blow away. But before heaving it taut, we passed a second girth-rope round the boat over the after turtle-back, next connecting both girth-ropes together by lengths of rope running fore and aft along the outside of the boat underneath the edge of the top strake. The doubled mainsail was then strained taut across the boat, and its edges tucked underneath the fore-and-aft lines outside the boat; the foresail was treated in the same way, but with its fore edge overlapped by about a foot of the after edge of the mainsail. Our girth-ropes were then hove taut, with the finished result that we had a canvas deck covering the boat from the fore turtle-back to within about six feet of the after one. The edges of the sails were next turned up and secured by seizings on either side, and our deck was complete. But, as it then stood, I was not satisfied with it, for at the after extremity of it there was an opening some six feet long, and as wide as the boat, through which a very considerable quantity of water might enter—quite enough, indeed, to swamp the boat. And with our canvas deck lying flat, as it then was, there was no doubt that very large quantities of water would wash over it, and pour down through the opening, should the sea run heavily. Our deck needed to be sloped upward from the forward to the after end of the boat, so that any water which might break over it would flow off on either side before reaching the opening to which I have referred. We accordingly laid the boat's mainmast along the thwarts fore and aft, amidships, and lashed the heel firmly to the middle of the foremost thwart. Then, by lashing our two longest stretchers together, we made a crutch for the head or after end of the mast to rest in; when, by placing this crutch upright in the stern-sheets against the backboard, we were able to raise the mast underneath the sails until it not only formed a sort of ridge-pole, converting the sails into a sloping roof, but it also strained the canvas as tight as a drum-head, rendering it so much the less liable to blow away, while it at the same time afforded a smooth surface for the water to pour off, and it also possessed the further advantage that it gave us a little more head-room underneath the canvas deck or roof. This completed our preparations—none too soon, for it was now rapidly growing dark, and the light of our lantern was needed while putting the finishing touches to our work.

Our task accomplished, we of course at once extinguished our lantern,—for candles were scarce with us,— and we then for the first time became aware of the startling rapidity with which the night seemed to have fallen; for with the extinguishment of the lantern we found ourselves enwrapped in darkness so thick that it could almost be felt. This, however, proved to be only transitory, for with the lapse of a few minutes our eyes became accustomed to the gloom, and we were then able not only to discern the shapes of the vast pile of clouds that threateningly overhung us, but also their reflections in the oil-smooth water, the latter made visible by the dull, ruddy glow emanating from the clouds themselves, which was even more noticeable now than it had been before nightfall, and which was so unnatural and appalling a sight that I believe there was not one of us who was not more or less affected by it. It was the first time that I had ever beheld such a sight, and I am not ashamed to confess that the sensation it produced in me was, for a short time, something very nearly akin to terror, so dreadful a portent did it seem to be, and so profoundly impressed was I with our utter helplessness away out there in mid-ocean, in that small, frail boat, with no friendly shelter at hand, and nothing to protect us from the gathering fury of the elements—nothing, that is to say, but the hand of God; and—I say it with shame—I thought far too little of Him in those days.

Not the least trying part of it all was the painful tension of the nerves produced by the suspense—the enforced *waiting* for the awful ordeal that lay before us. There was nothing for us to do, nothing to distract our attention from that awful, threatening sky, that looked as though it might momentarily be expected to burst into a devastating flame that would destroy the world! Some of the men, indeed, frankly avowed that the sight was too terrible for them, and crept away under the canvas, where they disposed themselves in the bottom of the boat, and strove to while away the time in sleep.

At length—it would be about the close of the second dog-watch—we became conscious that the swell, which had almost entirely subsided, was gathering weight again, coming this time out from the north-west. At first the heave was only barely perceptible, but within half an hour it had grown into a succession of long, steep undulations, running at right angles athwart the old swell, causing the boat to heave and sway with a singularly uneasy movement, and frequent vicious, jerky tugs at her painter. Then we noticed that the clouds—which had hitherto been motionless, or so nearly so that their movement was not to be detected—were working with a writhing motion, as though they were chained giants enduring the agonies of some dreadful torture, while the awful ruddy light which they emitted glowed with a still fiercer and more lurid radiance, lighting up the restlessly heaving ocean until it burned like the flood of Phlegethon. Anon there appeared a few scattered shreds of smoky scud speeding swiftly athwart the fiery canopy, and almost immediately afterwards, with a low, weird, wailing sound, there swept over us a scurrying blast that came and was gone again in a second. It came out from the north-west, and judging that this was probably the direction from which the gale itself would come, we at once rigged out over the stern one of the two oars remaining in the boat, and swept the bows of the gig round until they pointed due north-west. Scarcely had we accomplished this when a second scuffle came whistling down upon us from the same direction, and before it had swept out of hearing astern there arose a low moaning to windward, that increased in strength and volume with appalling rapidity. The sky suddenly grew black as ink ahead, a lengthening line of ghostly white appeared stretching along the horizon ahead and bearing down upon us with frightful speed; the moan grew into a deep, thunderous, howling roar, and from that to a yell which might have issued from the throats of a million fiends in torment; the white wall of foam and the yelling fury of wind struck us at the same instant; and the next thing I knew was that I was lying flat in the stern-sheets, hatless, and with my face stinging as though it had been cut with a whip; while the boat trembled and quivered from stem to stern with the scourging of wind and water, and the spray blew in a continuous sheet over the opening above me and into the sea astern, not a drop falling into the boat. The long-expected hurricane was upon us; and now all that remained was to see how long our frail craft could withstand the onslaught of the terrific forces arrayed against her.

## CHAPTER IV

### WE FALL IN WITH AND CAPTURE A SCHOONER

THE air was thick with scud-water, so thick, indeed, that it was like fog, it being impossible to see farther than some twenty fathoms from the boat. This scud-water swept horizontally along in a perfect deluge, and stung like shot when, by way of experiment, I exposed one of my hands to it. As for the wind, it was like an invisible wall driving along; it was simply impossible to stand up against it; it scourged the surface of the ocean into a level plain of white froth, which was torn away and hurled along like a shower of bullets. Our sea anchor fortunately maintained a sufficient hold upon the water to keep the gig riding head to wind, but that was as much as it could do; with the painter strained taut for its whole length, the boat was driving away to leeward, stern-first, at a speed of — according to my estimate — fully seven miles an hour! And it was, perhaps, a fortunate thing for us that such was the case; for had we been riding to a sea anchor powerful enough, and sunk deep enough in the water to have held us nearly stationary, I believe we should have been swamped within five minutes of the outburst of the hurricane. Even as it was, and despite all the precautions that we had taken to make our canvas covering perfectly secure, the wind tugged at it and beat upon it with such vehement fury that I momentarily expected to see it torn bodily off the boat and go driving away to leeward in tatters. Probably the thorough soaking that it almost instantly received—and which caused the fabric to shrink up and strain still tighter than it was before—may have had something to do with the stubborn resistance that it offered to the gale. Be that as it may, it held intact; and to that circumstance I attribute the fact that the gig was not instantly swamped. But no woven fabric, however stout,—scarcely wood itself,—could long withstand such a furious pelting of scud-water as our sails were now enduring, and in about ten minutes the water began to drip through, first in single drops, here and there, then in a few small streams, that rapidly increased in number until there seemed in the thick darkness to be hundreds of them; for in endeavouring to avoid one stream we only succeeded in encountering two or three more. To add to the unpleasantness of the situation, it was impossible for us to light the lantern; for although we were sheltered from the direct violence of the gale by the canvas, the wind somehow managed to penetrate beneath, creating quite a formidable little scuffle there, and easily frustrating all our efforts to obtain a light. And very soon we had another annoyance to contend with, in the shape of a gradual accumulation of water in the boat, whether caused by a leak in the hull, or by the drainage of the water through the canvas we knew not; but it obliged us to have recourse to baling, which proved to be a singularly awkward operation in such cramped quarters and such pitchy darkness.

The first mad fury of the outburst lasted for about three-quarters of an hour,—it *seemed* a perfect eternity to us, in our condition of overpowering suspense, but I do not believe it was longer than three-quarters of an hour at the utmost,—and then it subsided into a heavy gale of wind, and the sea began to get up so rapidly that within another hour we were being flung hither and thither with such terrific violence that in a very short time our bodies were covered with bruises, while some of the men actually became sea-sick! And now, too, a new danger threatened us; for as the sea rose it commenced to break, and it was not long ere we had the seas washing, in rapidly increasing volume, over the boat, and pouring down through the opening over the stern-sheets. This kept us baling in good earnest, not only with our solitary bucket but with hats and boots as well, to save the boat from being swamped. And the bitterest hardship of it all was that there was no relief, not a moment's intermission throughout the whole of that dreadful, interminable night. We were in continuous peril of death with every breath that we drew; every second saw us trembling upon the verge of eternity, and escaping destruction as by a constantly recurring succession of miracles. It was a frightful experience, so frightful that language is utterly powerless to describe it; the most eloquent pen could do no more than convey a poor, feeble, and miserably inadequate idea of the terror and suffering of it. No one who has not undergone such an experience can form the remotest conception of its horrors.

All things mundane have an end, however, sooner or later; and at length the welcome light of day once more made its appearance, piercing slowly and with seeming reluctance through the dense canopy of black, storm-torn cloud and flying scud that overhung us. And then we almost wished that it had remained night, so dreary and awe-inspiring was the scene that met our aching gaze. The heavens gave no sign of relenting, the sky looked wild as ever,—although the awful ruddy glow had long since faded out from the clouds,—while the ocean seemed to be lashed and goaded by the furious wind into an endless succession of rushing mountain waves, every one of which, as it swept with hissing, foam-white crest down upon us, seemed mercilessly bent upon our destruction. As I stood up and gazed about me, —for I could do so now, by leaning well forward against the wind,—it seemed a marvellous thing to me that the gig continued to live through it; for, light and buoyant though she was, every sea she met swept her from stem to stern; and it was plain enough to us all now that it was nothing but the canvas covering that saved her. As it was, we shipped so much water that it was as much as three of us could do—that being all who could work in the opening at one time—to keep her from filling. To add still further to our misery, we were one and all by this time dead tired, worn out, in fact, with the terror and anxiety of the past night; yet we dared not yet attempt to seek the comfort and refreshment of sleep, for our critical situation continued to demand our utmost watchfulness and our unremitting exertions; and when at length we sought to renew our strength by means of a meal, the grievous discovery was made that the whole of our small stock of ship's bread was spoiled and rendered uneatable by the salt water. And, as though this misfortune was not in itself sufficiently serious, when we sought to quench our thirst we discovered that the bung of the water-breaker had somehow got out of the bung-hole, allowing so much salt water to mingle with our small stock of fresh that the latter had been rendered almost undrinkable.

Our first gleam of hope and encouragement came to us about half an hour before noon that day, when our anxious watching was rewarded by the appearance of a small, momentary break in the sky, low down toward the horizon to windward; it showed but for a moment, and then was lost again. But presently a wider and more pronounced break appeared which did *not* vanish; on the contrary, it widened, until presently a fitful gleam of wan and watery sunshine pierced through it and lighted up the bleak, desolate expanse of raging ocean for a few seconds. And almost simultaneously with the welcome appearance of this transient but welcome gleam of pallid sunshine, we became aware of a slight but unmistakable diminution in the fury of the gale; a change productive of such profound relief to us, worn out as we all were by long-protracted toil and anxiety, that we actually greeted it with a feeble cheer! Nor was the hope thus aroused fallacious; for from this moment the sky began to clear, until within a couple of hours the storm-clouds had all swept away to leeward, leaving the sky a clear, pure blue, streaked here and there, it is true, with a tattered, trailing streamer of pinky grey, that, however, soon vanished; and once more we revelled in the glorious warmth and radiance of the unclouded sunlight, while the wind dropped so rapidly that, but for the sea, which still ran with dangerous weight, we might have made sail again by sunset. As it was, we were all so completely worn out that I think we were really thankful for an excuse to leave the boat riding to her sea anchor a few hours longer, while we sought and obtained what was even more necessary to us than food and drink —sleep.

All actual danger was by this time past, so we arranged

that each of us should keep a look out for an hour while the rest slept, there being sufficient of us to carry us through the night at this rate; and I undertook to keep the first look out. That hour was, I think, the longest sixty minutes I had ever up to then experienced; for, now that constant watchfulness was no longer necessary to insure our safety, the incentive to watchfulness was gone, and overtaxed nature craved so vehemently for repose that the effort to remain awake was absolutely painful. I continued, however, to perform the task that I had undertaken, and, when my hour had expired, flung myself down in the stern-sheets, where I instantly sank into a profound and dreamless sleep, having first, of course, aroused young Lindsay, and cautioned him to maintain a bright lookout for passing ships—a caution which I gave orders should be passed on from man to man throughout the night.

When I awoke I found that I had maintained all through the night the precise attitude in which I had flung myself down to sleep some hours before; it appeared to me that I had not stirred by so much as a hair's-breadth all through those hours of unconsciousness. I awoke spontaneously, with the light of the sun shining strongly through my still closed eyelids. The first thing after that of which I became conscious was that the boat was rising and falling easily with a long, steady, swinging motion; then I opened my eyes, and immediately noticed that the sun was some two hours high. A very soft, warm, gentle breeze fanned my cheek, and the only audible sounds were the snores and snorts of many sleepers near me, mingling with the gentle lap of water along the boat's planking. All hands save myself were sound asleep! I was not greatly surprised at this, though naturally a trifle vexed that my orders as to the maintenance of a lookout had not been more strictly observed. But it was not until I had risen to my feet and flung an inquiring glance round the horizon that I realised how miserably unfortunate this negligence had been. For there, away in the western board, distant some fourteen miles, gleamed the sails of a large ship; and a more intent scrutiny revealed the tantalising circumstance that she was steering such a course as had undoubtedly carried her past us about an hour before daybreak at a distance of little more than three miles; and, had a proper watch been maintained, we could have intercepted and boarded her without difficulty. Whether she happened to be a friend or an enemy was a matter of very secondary import just then, in our miserable plight as regarded our stock of provisions and water; our situation was such that even to have fallen into the hands of the enemy would have been better than to be left as we were.

I at once roused all hands, and we forthwith went to work to cut adrift the sails that had served us so well, and to bend them afresh to the yards; while the others hauled aboard our sea anchor, cut its lashings adrift, and took to the oars with the object of going in pursuit of the distant sail. For there was yet a chance for us. If we could keep her in sight long enough there was just a possibility that some one or another of her crew, working aloft, might cast a glance astern and catch sight of our tiny sail, when he would at once recognise it as that of a boat, and report it; when, if the skipper happened to be a humane man, he would assuredly heave-to and wait for us to close. So we all went to work with a will, and soon had the boat all ataunto once more, and in pursuit of the stranger as fast as oars and sails together could put her through the water. But the experience of the first hour sufficed to demonstrate beyond all question the hopelessness of our attempt to overtake the ship; she was leaving us rapidly, and unless someone aloft happened to sight us, our prospects of rescue, so far as she was concerned, were not worth a moment's consideration. The men, partially restored by their night's sound sleep, toiled like tigers at the oars, in their anxiety to prolong the chance of our being sighted to the latest possible moment, frequently relieving each other. But it was all of no avail; strive as they would, the stranger steadily increased her distance from us until, after we had been in pursuit of her for fully three hours, the heads of her royals sank below the western horizon, and we lost her for good and all. Then the men sullenly laid in their oars, declaring that they were worn out and could do no more. Then they began to savagely inquire among themselves who was the individual to whose culpable carelessness we were all indebted for our present disappointment. The culprit was soon discovered in the person of a little Welshman— the man whose watch followed Lindsay's. This man declared that he had remained awake throughout his watch, and had duly called his successor before resuming his slumbers. But there was some reason to doubt this statement; and even if it happened to be true, he was still culpable, according to his own showing, for he was obliged to confess that he had not waited to assure himself that his successor was properly awakened, but had satisfied himself with a single shake of the sleeper's shoulder, accompanied by the curt announcement that it was time to turn out, and had then flung himself down and gone to sleep. As for the man whom the Welshman was supposed to have awakened, he disclaimed all responsibility upon the ground that, if called at all—which he did not believe—he had been called so ineffectively as to be quite unconscious of the circumstance. At the conclusion of the inquiry, his comrades were so furiously incensed with the Welshman for his culpable—almost criminal—neglect, that they seemed strongly disposed to take summary vengeance upon him; and it needed the exertion of all my authority to protect the fellow from their violence, which broke out anew when at noon we went to dinner, and were compelled to make out the best meal we could upon raw salt beef washed down with water so brackish that we could scarcely swallow it.

## WE CAPTURE A SCHOONER

Reduced to such a condition as this, it will scarcely be wondered at that I should be brought to something very nearly approaching despair when my observations that day revealed the disconcerting fact that, thanks to our excessive drift during the gale, we were still fully six hundred miles from our port of destination—a distance which we scarce dared to hope might be covered, even under the most favourable circumstances, in less than five days.

But it soon appeared as though even this protracted period of privation and exposure was to be increased, for, as the afternoon wore on, the wind, still continuing to drop, grew so light that our speed dwindled down to a bare three knots by the hour of sunset; and by midnight it had still further fallen to such an extent that our sails became useless to us, and the oars had once more to be resorted to.

The return of daylight found us in the midst of a stark calm, under a cloudless sky, out of which the sun soon began to dart his scorching beams so pitilessly that the task of pulling shortly became a labour little less than torture to people in our exhausted condition; indeed, so severe did the men find it, that, after persevering until about four bells in the afternoon watch, they gave it up, declaring themselves to be quite incapable of further exertion. And thus, for the remainder of the day, we lay motionless upon that oil-smooth sea, under the blistering rays of the burning sun, with our tongues cleaving to our palates as we began to experience the first fierce torments of unquenchable thirst. For our supply of water—all but undrinkable as it was—was growing so short that it became imperatively necessary to husband it with the most jealous care, and to reduce our allowance to the very smallest quantity upon which life could possibly be sustained. The men sought to forget their sufferings in sleep, disposing themselves in the bottom of the boat, under the shelter of the now useless sails; but I was far too anxious to be able to sleep, for I began to realise that our boat voyage threatened to develop into an adventure that might easily terminate in a ghastly tragedy.

Half an hour before sunset I called the men, and we went to supper; and with the going down of the sun the oars were once more thrown out, and we resumed our weary voyage, all hands of us being equally anxious to avail ourselves to the utmost of the comparatively cool hours of darkness, to shorten, as much as possible, the distance that still intervened between us and deliverance. All through the hot and breathless night we toiled, in an unspeakable agony of thirst, and when morning once more dawned out of a brilliant and cloudless sky, my companions presented so wild and haggard an appearance, with their cheeks sunken with famine and their eyes ablaze with the fever of thirst and starvation, that they were scarcely recognisable. Half an hour after sunrise we partook of our loathsome breakfast of putrid meat

## WE CAPTURE A SCHOONER

and nauseous water, and then composed ourselves to sleep—if we could—through the long hours of the blazing day, maintaining, however, a one-man hourly watch, in order that we might be duly warned of any change in the weather.

And, late that afternoon, a change came—a change of so welcome a character that I believe I may, without exaggeration, say it saved our lives. For, about noon, when I was aroused by the man on watch to get the meridian altitude of the sun for the determination of the latitude, I observed a bank of purple-grey clouds gathering in the south-western quarter, their rounded edges as sharply defined as though they had been cut out of paper. There was no mistaking their character; they portended a thunderstorm. And a thunderstorm we had about four o'clock that afternoon, of truly tropical violence. There was not a breath of wind with it, but it brought us a perfect deluge of rain,—thrice-welcome and blessed rain,—pouring from the overcharged clouds in sheets of warm water, soft and sweet as nectar. We let not a drop escape us that it was possible to save; we saw that it was coming, and prepared for it by spreading the sails across the boat, and caught the welcome stream in the depressions that we had arranged for its reception, drinking out of the hollowed canvas until we could drink no more. Then, as the rain still continued to fall, we did a desperate deed; we threw away every drop of our drinking water, in the hope of being able to refill our breakers with the sweet, fresh rain-water. And we were successful. God in His infinite mercy allowed the floodgates of heaven to remain open until we had filled every available receptacle at our disposal; and then the rain ceased, the storm drifted away to the north-eastward, and the sun disappeared below the horizon in a blaze of cloudless splendour.

But our sufferings were not yet over; for now that the hellish torments of thirst were assuaged, the pangs of hunger assailed us with redoubled fury, hourly growing in intensity, until some time during the night—while Lindsay and I were asleep, and the boat was in charge of one of the men—they became so utterly unendurable that, in a fit of madness, the famished crew fell upon the slender remainder of our stock of eatables, devouring the whole at one fell swoop, except Lindsay's and my own portion, which, despite their famished condition, they loyally set aside for us!

Another day of breathless calm; another twelve hours of scorching heat under the rays of the pitiless sun; and then, with nightfall, the men once more threw out their oars and resumed the heart-breaking task of shortening by a few miles the still formidable stretch of ocean that lay between us and safety. But nothing that we could say would induce a single one of them to accept ever so small a share of the provisions that they had apportioned as the share belonging to Lindsay and myself; they declared that their last meal had so far satisfied and reinvigorated them, that they were no longer hungry, while one or two of them spoke hopefully of the possibility that they might catch a fish or two on the morrow.

It was somewhere about ten o'clock that night that we detected the first symptoms of another change in the weather, the first subtle indication that the long period of calm which had so nearly destroyed us was about to end. And, best of all, the indication was of such a character as permitted us to indulge the hope that, although the calm was about to give way to a breeze, we were likely to be favoured with weather fine enough to permit of our pursuing our voyage under the most favourable conditions. This symptom of approaching change merely consisted in the gathering in the heavens of a thin veil of mottled, fine-weather cloud, just dense enough to obscure most of the lesser stars and render the night rather dark, while a few of the brighter stars peeped through the openings between the clouds at tolerably frequent intervals, permitting us to steer our course without having recourse to the lantern or compass. The prospect of a coming breeze seemed to cheer the men and endow them with renewed vigour, for they gave way with something like a will, while they occasionally went so far as to exchange a muttered ejaculation of encouragement one with another.

It happened to be my trick at the yolk-lines until midnight, I having relieved young Lindsay at four bells. I was sitting in the stern-sheets, with my eyes intently fixed upon a particularly bright star that gleamed out through the clouds at frequent intervals right over the boat's nose, at an altitude of about thirty degrees above the horizon, and which I had consequently selected as a suitable guide to steer by.

It is a curious fact, well known to sailors, that an object can be better seen on a dark night at sea by looking at the sky slightly *above* or to one side of it, rather than directly *at* it; hence it was that, as I kept my eye intently fixed upon the star immediately ahead, I suddenly became aware of the presence of a small, dark object some three points on our starboard bow. I immediately looked straight at it, but could then see nothing; whereupon I looked into the sky rather above the point where I knew it to be, when I again caught sight of it. To make quite sure, I sheered the boat some four points off her course, when it became quite distinct, although only as a small, black, shapeless shadow against the dark sky immediately ahead.

I held up my hand warningly to the men, and at the same moment gave the order, "Oars!"

The men, somewhat wonderingly, instantly obeyed, staring hard at me inquiringly, while two or three who were lying down in the bottom of the boat, trying unavailingly to sleep, raised themselves upon their elbows, as though to ascertain what was the matter.

"Lads," said I, in low, cautious tones, "not a sound, for your lives! There is a small craft of some sort out there becalmed, and it is my intention to run her alongside. But we cannot of course tell whether she is a friend or an enemy, so I think it will be well for us to get alongside without attracting the attention of her crew, if we can manage it. If she proves to be a friend, well and good; but if she is an enemy, we must take her at all costs; for we are in a starving condition, as you are all aware, while we are still five days distant from Bermuda, and I do not believe we could possibly live to reach the island without provisions. So muffle your oars as well as you can; have your cutlasses ready; and I will put you alongside. H-u-s-h! not a sound! That craft is a good three miles away, but sounds travel far on such a night as this, and we must not allow the crew of her to discover that we are in their neighbourhood. Now muffle your oars, and we will soon find out who and what she is."

Without a moment's hesitation, the men forthwith proceeded to muffle their oars with portions of their clothing; and in another five minutes we were heading for the small, dark blot. When we had been pulling silently for about a quarter of an hour, a small, thin sound came creeping across the water to us, that within another five minutes had resolved itself into the strains of the

Marseillaise played upon an accordion and sung by a fairly good tenor voice, to which several others were almost instantly added. That was sufficient; the craft, whatever else she might be, was assuredly French, and we were relieved of the anxiety of approaching a vessel uncertain as to whether she was friend or foe. The song was sung through to the end with great enthusiasm, and then, after a slight pause, another song was started, also French, so far as could be made out. It was cut short, however, before a dozen bars had been reached, by a hoarse, gruff voice loudly demanding, in clear, unmistakable French, " what, in the name of all the saints, the singer meant by arousing all hands at that hour of the night with his miserable braying?" This rendered assurance doubly sure, and we proceeded with increased caution—if that were possible—laying in all but a single pair of oars, with the double object of resting the men as much as possible prior to the attack, and at the same time approaching our quarry slowly enough to allow her crew to coil away about the decks, and go to sleep again if they would.

Paddling slowly and with the utmost circumspection, taking care that the oars entered and left the water without the slightest splash, we were a full hour and more traversing the distance that separated us from the stranger; but long ere we reached her we had made her out to be a schooner of somewhere about one hundred and forty tons, and by her taunt spars, as well as by the fact of her being where she was,—nicely in the track of our homeward-bound West Indiamen,—I judged her to be a privateer. When first discovered she must have been lying nearly broadside-on to us, but the swing of the swell gradually slewed her, as we stealthily approached, until she presented her stern fairly at us, affording us an admirable opportunity to get alongside her undetected. And this we did, gliding up under her starboard quarter and alongside, and actually climbing in on deck over her low bulwarks before the alarm was raised. Then, from the neighbourhood of the wheel, there suddenly arose a muttered execration in French, followed by a sharp inquiry in the same language of, "Who goes there?"

"British," I answered, in the inquirer's own lingo. "Surrender, or we will drive every man of you overboard!"

"The British! ah, sac-r-r-r-e! Yes, monsieur, oh yes, we surrender," gurgled the man, as I seized him by the throat and threatened him with my cutlass, while Lindsay led the hands forward to the forecastle. There were a few drowsily muttered ejaculations in that direction, quickly succeeded by a volley of execrations, a scuffling of feet, the slamming of the hatch over the fore-scuttle, and Lindsay sang out that the schooner was ours. Even as he did so, two figures in rather scanty clothing rushed up on deck through the companion; and before I could fully realise what was happening, one of them snapped his pistol at me, while the other aimed a blow at my head with a sword. Fortunately the bullet missed me, finding its billet in the body of the man whose throat I still grasped, while I managed to catch the blow of the other fellow on my own blade; and in a moment we were at it "hammer and tongs"—that is to say, the swordsman and myself, the other fellow making a dash at me now and then, aiming fierce blows at me with the butt-end of his pistol, until, in self-defence, I seized my opportunity and cleft his skull with my cutlass at the same instant that I launched out with my left hand and sent his companion reeling to the deck with a blow planted fairly between the eyes.

At this moment young Lindsay came rushing aft, with half a dozen of our fellows at his heels, to know what was the matter; so, bidding a couple of the men to securely bind the prisoners, I descended the companion ladder, with Lindsay at my heels, to see whether there were any more Frenchmen to be fought. There were not, however; the close, stuffy little cabin was empty; so we went on deck again, and, leaving two men to keep watch and ward at the after end of the ship, went forward, where I personally superintended the operation of effectually securing the crew, who we afterwards passed down into the hold. The cook, however, we left free, and, being ravenously hungry, gave him orders to at once light the galley fire and cook us the best meal the ship could afford, all hands taking the keen edge off our appetites, meanwhile, by munching some excellent biscuits that Lindsay discovered snugly stored away in the pantry. Our next care was to hoist in the gig that had served us so well ; and, this done, we settled down to wait for our dinner and the breeze that promised to come ere long.

## CHAPTER V

### WE PROCEED IN SEARCH OF THE *ALTHEA*'S BOATS

THE wind came away about an hour and a half before sunrise, a gentle breeze out from the north-east, coming down to us first of all in the form of a few wandering cats'-paws, that just wrinkled the oil-smooth surface of the ocean and were gone again, and finally settling into a true breeze that fanned us along at a speed of some four knots, the schooner proving to be a fairly speedy little vessel.

Long ere this, however, I had carefully thought out a line of action for myself, in order that when the wind came I might be prepared for it. It will be remembered that before parting company with the launch I had been furnished by the master with a table showing the relative speeds of the various boats, and from that moment I had, with the assistance of the table, carefully calculated the supposed position of each boat at noon; so that I now knew, to within a few miles, where any particular boat ought to be looked for, upon the assumption that all had gone well with them. And somehow I thought it had; I was very strongly impressed with the belief that the gale which we had encountered had not extended far enough to the south-east to reach the launch and the rest of the squadron. Flowers it *might* have overtaken, but my observations upon the bearings of the centre of the storm and its direction led me to entertain a very strong hope that the rest of the boats had escaped. This being so, I determined to act upon the assumption that they had done so, and to proceed in search of them in the direction where they ought, upon that assumption, to be found. Of course, with their different rates of sailing, they would now be strung out in a fairly long line; and the question that exercised me most strongly was whether I should first seek the leading boat, and, having found her, dodge about in waiting for the others, or whether I should first seek the dinghy, and, having found her, run down the wind in the track of the others. The direction from which the wind might happen to spring up would necessarily influence my decision to a great extent; but when it came away out from the north-east, and I discovered that the schooner could fetch, upon an easy bowline, the spot where the sternmost boat might be expected to be found, I hesitated no longer, but at once made up my mind to first look for the dinghy.

As the morning wore on the breeze freshened somewhat, and the schooner's speed increased to fully seven knots. I employed the early part of the forenoon in satisfying myself that the prisoners were properly secured, —taking the precaution to have them all put in irons, as, in the exhausted condition of my own crew, I could not afford to run any unnecessary risks,—and as soon as I had eased my mind of that anxiety, I personally investigated the condition of the schooner's storeroom. To my great joy I discovered that we possessed an ample supply of provisions and water, together with a liberal quantity of wines, spirits, and other luxuries—enough of everything, in fact, to maintain the whole of the survivors of the *Althea* upon full allowance for at least a month. The schooner, moreover,—she proved to be the *Susanne*, privateer, of St. Malo, —was nearly new, a stout, substantially built little craft of one hundred and thirty-four tons register, as tight as a bottle, well found, and armed with six long six-pounders in her batteries, with a long nine-pounder mounted on a pivot on her forecastle, and her magazine nearly full.

Nothing of any importance happened, either on that day or the next, except that the sky gradually became overspread with those peculiar patches of fleece-like clouds called "trade-clouds"—showing that at length we had hit off the north-east trade winds that seemed to have been evading us for so long. According to my reckoning, and upon the assumption that the wind would now hold fairly steady, we ought to hit off the track of the boats about six bells in the morning watch, on the third morning after the capture of the schooner, which would allow us some eleven hours of daylight in which to prosecute our search; and, to give ourselves the best possible chance of finding the objects of our quest, I took care, on the preceding midnight, to haul the schooner as close to the wind as she would lie, so that there should be no possibility of hitting upon their track to leeward instead of to windward of them, and so running *away* from instead of *after* them. And at six bells on that morning I was called, in accordance with previous instructions, in order that I might work up the reckoning to the very last moment, and so make certain of getting as accurately as possible upon the track. My calculations now showed that it would be nearly eight bells instead of six before we should reach the imaginary line for which we were making; and at a quarter to eight — having previously sent a hand aloft to take a careful look round—I gave the order to up-helm and bear away upon a west-south-west course, and to pack the studding-sails upon the little hooker. The men—thanks to good feeding and all the rest I could give them consistent with the maintenance of proper discipline — had by this time completely recovered from the effects of our boat voyage, and were one and all as keen as needles on the lookout for the boats from the moment that we squared away, the watch, all but the helmsman, taking to the rigging — without any orders from me — immediately that they had finished breakfast, and disposing themselves upon the royal and topgallant yards in their eagerness to catch the earliest possible glimpse of their shipmates. I calculated that at about five bells in the forenoon watch we ought to overtake the dinghy,—the slowest boat in the fleet,—and as that moment drew near our anxiety reached a most painful pitch, the men on the yards straining their eyes to the utmost as they peered intently into the distance from right ahead to broad on either beam, carefully and slowly scanning the horizon for the little blot of gleaming canvas that should proclaim the success of our quest. But the fateful moment came and went, leaving the horizon a blank. Noon arrived, and I secured an excellent observation for my latitude, by means of which I was enabled to check my previous dead reckoning, which tallied to within less than a mile of what it ought to be; and still there was no sign of the missing boat, although my calculations showed that we had overrun by some fifteen miles the spot where we expected to find her. I hailed the yards, inquiring whether there was any possibility of our having run past the dinghy without observing her; but the men assured me that they had maintained so bright a lookout that had she been anywhere within the boundaries of our horizon they would assuredly have seen her.

This was rather disconcerting, yet I felt that I had no real cause for disappointment; the boats might have met with rather fresher winds than I had estimated for, in which case the likelihood was that they were still many miles ahead of us. My calculations had been based upon the supposition that they had been evenly maintaining the same rate of speed from the moment when we parted with them, and I knew that this was in the last degree improbable. Yet it was the only basis I had upon which to make my calculations; for it was impossible for me to judge by the weather which we had ourselves experienced. Of one thing I felt tolerably well convinced, which was that, keeping so much farther to the southward than we had done in the gig, the other boats would not have met with the calms that had so seriously delayed us; and that consequently — unless they too had been caught in the hurricane that had so nearly proved our destruction—they must be somewhere directly ahead of us as we were then steering. There was nothing for it, therefore, but to keep all on as we were until we found them.

In this condition of anxiety and suspense we continued to run away to the west-south-west until sunset, without sighting anything; and then, fearful of running past one or more of the objects of our quest during the night-time without seeing them, I hove the schooner to under foresail and jib, with the topsail aback, so that we might remain as nearly as possible where we were—excepting for our lee drift — all through the night. I also caused three lanterns to be hoisted, one over the other, from our maintopmast stay, as a fairly conspicuous signal, pretty certain to attract attention in the event of either of the boats coming within sight of us during the hours of darkness, and of course gave the strictest injunctions for the maintenance of a bright lookout all through the night.

The night passed uneventfully, and at daybreak, after

having first gone aloft and personally but unavailingly examined the horizon and the entire visible expanse of the ocean through the ship's telescope,— an excellent instrument, by the way,— we made sail again upon the schooner, and resumed our search.

Shortly after breakfast I secured an observation for my longitude, and, having worked out my calculations, found that, if the boats were still afloat, and had continued to steer the course which I had been told they would, we must certainly find them that day. As on the preceding day, the men spent their watch upon the yards, maintaining so keen a lookout that even I, anxious as I was, felt satisfied they would allow nothing to escape them. Yet the day passed, and evening arrived without the discovery of any sign of the missing boats; while my anxiety grew more painfully intense with the lapse of every hour of daylight. And when at length the night closed down upon us, and the stars came winking mistily out from between the driving clouds, the conviction came to me that something had gone lamentably wrong, and that to continue the search any further in the direction that we had been pursuing would be useless.

The question was: What had happened? I could think of but two possible explanations of our failure to find the boats; one of which was that they had been fallen in with and been picked up by a passing ship, while the other was that they had experienced bad weather, which had driven them out of their course. If the first explanation happened to be the correct one, well and good—our missing comrades were safe; but if the second explanation was to account for our non-success, in what direction ought we to continue our search? The question was a very difficult one to answer with any approach to accuracy, but an approximation to the truth might be arrived at. I reasoned thus: The boats were undoubtedly within the limits of the trade wind when we parted with them, and the only disturbing influence that they would be likely to meet with in that region would be that of the hurricane that we had encountered. Reasoning thus, I went below and produced a chart of the North Atlantic, —it was a French one, reckoning its longitude from the meridian of Paris; but that difficulty was to be easily overcome,—and upon it I forthwith proceeded to prick off, as accurately as the data in my possession would permit, first, the spot where we had parted company with the other boats; secondly, our own course and distance up to the moment when the hurricane struck us; and thirdly, the supposititious course and distance of each of the boats up to the moment when the hurricane would probably strike them. The observations I had personally made as to the bearing and course of the centre of the storm had originally led me to the conclusion that the other boats had probably escaped it altogether; and now, as I went over the matter afresh, I could not persuade myself that they had encountered anything worse than a mere fringe of it, a breeze strong enough perhaps to compel them to run before it for a few hours, but nothing more.  Assuming, then, this to be the case, I calculated as nearly as I could the probable direction of the wind when the gale struck them, and the number of hours during which they would be likely to be compelled to run before it, pricking off upon the chart their probable whereabouts at the moment when they would be likely to find themselves once more able to head for, say, St. Thomas or St. Kitts.  From this point I laid off a course for the former island, and then calculated their probable position on that line at the moment, compared this with the position then occupied by the schooner, and thus arrived at the new direction in which I ought to seek for them. Having reached thus far, I went on deck, set the new course, and then, with Lindsay's assistance, went over all my calculations again, verifying every figure of them.

Luckily for our anxiety, the trade wind was now blowing so fresh that, on an easy bowline as we were, a whole mainsail, foresail, and topsail, with royal and topgallant sails stowed, was as much as we could stagger under, the little witch dancing along at a good, clean eleven knots under this canvas; the consequence being that in thirty-eight hours from the moment of bearing up we had reached the spot where I intended that my new search for the missing boats should begin.

This time, however, I intended to adopt a course of procedure exactly opposite to that which I had followed while prosecuting my former search.  Then, I had gone

# WE SEARCH FOR THE *ALTHEA'S* BOATS

to windward of the spot when I expected to find the boats, and had run down to leeward along the course which I thought it probable they had taken; but now my uncertainty as to their precise position necessitated a search over a belt of ocean several miles in width. I therefore determined to get well to leeward of the spot where my calculations indicated that I ought to find them, and from there work to windward on an easy bowline, making stretches of some twenty-six miles in length. I had already ascertained the height of our royal yard above the sea-level, and from that had calculated that a look-out stationed at that elevation would command a circular area having a radius of thirteen miles. If, therefore, I made stretches across a circle of twenty-six miles' diameter, I should practically command a belt of ocean of fifty-two miles in width; and this I deemed sufficient for my purpose.

Accordingly, having reached our cruising ground at two bells in the forenoon watch, and having one hand on the royal yard as a lookout, with two more on the top-sail yard by way of additional precaution, we made our first reach of thirteen miles in a south-easterly direction. Then, nothing being in sight, we tacked and stood to the northward for twenty-six miles. Still nothing in sight; so we hove about again, and this time reached to the southward and eastward for a distance of twenty-six miles, continuing our search thus throughout the entire day, without success. At sunset we hove about again, and, reaching to the northward, until we had arrived at the track which the boats, if still afloat, would probably pass over, we hove-to for the night, hoisting three lanterns, as before, to attract their attention should they happen to arrive within sight of us during the hours of darkness. It was some relief to us that the night was tolerably clear, with a fair sprinkling of stars and a moon well advanced in her first quarter; so that, during the first half of the night, we had a very fair amount of light.

I did not keep the lookout men aloft at night, deeming it useless, as the light, although—as I have said—fairly good, was not bright enough to reveal a small object like a boat at a greater distance than some two or three miles, and up to that distance it was possible to see really better from the level of the deck than from the more lofty elevation of the yards; but I had three men continuously on the lookout at the same time, namely, one on the jib-boom end, and one each to port and starboard in the waist. We were hove-to on the starboard tack. Needless to say, that although we had these three men thus stationed for the express purpose of keeping a lookout and doing nothing else, Lindsay and I also kept our eyes well skinned, going even to the length of blinding the skylight with an old sail in order that our eyes might not be dazzled by even the dim light of the cabin lamp.

It happened to be my eight hours in that night, and I had taken advantage of the circumstance to turn in early, for the anxiety attending upon this dishearteningly fruitless search was beginning to tell upon me, and I had suffered for the last night or two from an inability to sleep. On this particular occasion, however, I felt somewhat drowsy, and therefore went to my bunk in the hope of getting two or three hours' rest; and, as a matter of fact, I did sleep, but my rest was so disturbed by frightful dreams of men enduring unheard-of suffering in open boats, that at length, awaking in a paroxysm of horror, I turned out and went on deck, to find that it was seven bells, and that under any circumstances I should have been called in another half-hour.

The moon was within a very short time of setting when I reached the deck, and I stood watching her half-disc creeping insensibly nearer and nearer to the horizon, lighting up the sky that way with a soft, mysterious, brownish-green light, and casting a long, tremulous wake of ruddy gold athwart the tops of the running surges. Lindsay was standing beside me, yawning the top of his head nearly off, poor lad; for although he too was anxious as to the fate of those who we were seeking, his anxiety had not, thus far, interfered with his rest, and his watch was now so nearly up that he was quite ready for the four hours' sleep that awaited him.

I was in the very act of telling him that, as I should not go below again, he might turn in if he chose,—my eyes being all the while fixed upon the setting moon,— when suddenly, almost immediately under the luminary,

I caught a momentary glimpse of a small black object—small as a pin-head—as it were hove-up on the back of a sea against the luminous sky. Stopping short in what I was saying, I sprang to the rail, and from thence into the main rigging, half a dozen ratlines of which I ascended in order to gain a horizon clear of the run of the nearer seas. From this elevation I again looked out, instinctively shading my eyes under my hand, and in another moment I had again caught sight of the object, and not only so, but had also detected an intermittent flashing, as of the moonlight off the wet blades of oars.

"A boat! a boat!" I shouted, in the fulness of my delight. "Hurrah, lads! we have one of them at last! Let draw the jib-sheet! Fill the topsail! Up helm there, my man, and let her go broad off!"

As I rapidly issued these orders I swung myself out of the rigging, and, running to the binnacle, took the bearing of the moon, allowing half a point to the northward of her as the course to steer for the boat.

"Where is the gunner?" I shouted; "pass the word for Mr. Robbins!"

"Here I am, sir," answered Robbins—for my words had thrilled through the little craft like an electric shock, and already the watch below were scrambling up through the hatchway, carrying their clothing in their hands, in their eagerness to get a glimpse of the newly discovered boat.

"Mr. Robbins," said I, "have the goodness to clap a blank cartridge into one of the guns, and fire it as an encouragement to those poor fellows out there; they will guess, by our firing, that we have seen them."

"Ay, ay, sir," answered Robbins, shambling away with alacrity upon his errand; and a few minutes later one of our guns rang out what I hoped would prove a thrice-welcome message to our shipmates. Somehow I never for a moment doubted that it was one of the frigate's boats that I had seen; I felt as sure of it as though we had her already alongside, although of course I could form no sort of surmise as to which of them it would prove to be.

It took us but a very few minutes to run down to the boat, when, judging our distance, we rounded-to and laid the topsail aback, so close to windward of the little craft that one of our people was able to heave a rope's-end into her, and we hauled her alongside. Then, to our supreme disappointment, we discovered that it was *not* either of the boats that we were looking for, but the long-boat of a merchantman, with eleven people in her, all of whom were in a very wasted and exhausted condition, partly from famine and partly from wounds, most of them being swathed about the head or limbs with bloodstained bandages.

Concealing our disappointment as well as we could, we helped the poor creatures up over the side,—discovering, during the process, that the rescued party were our fellow-countrymen,—and then, having removed everything from the boat that promised to prove of the slightest value, we cast her adrift, having no room on our decks for her. Meanwhile, the unhappy strangers, being too weak to stand, had sunk down upon the deck, pointing to their parched throats and feebly gasping the word "water"; in response to which appeal some of our own people had gone to work, under my supervision, to supply them cautiously with small quantities of water slightly dashed with brandy. This treatment had a wonderfully stimulative and revivifying effect upon them, so much so, indeed, that they managed to stagger to their feet and earnestly beg for food. This, of course, we supplied them with forthwith, in the form of ship's bread broken small and softened by steeping in weak brandy and water. I gave them this pending the preparation of a more substantial and appetising meal by the cook; and it was perhaps well that circumstances obliged me to do so, for I afterwards learned that the administration of a solid, substantial meal to people in their famished condition would probably have had fatal results. Having satisfied to some small extent their first ravenous craving for food and drink, we got them below and provided them with such makeshift sleeping accommodation as the resources of the schooner would permit, that they might seek in sleep such further recuperation as was to be obtained, pending the production of the meal in preparation for them. Having thus disposed of the rescued men, nothing remained for us but to await, with such patience as we could muster, the return of daylight, to enable us to resume the search for the lost frigate's boats.

It was nearly noon next day ere any of the rescued

party appeared on deck, the first to do so being a fine, sailorly-looking man of some forty or forty-five years of age, who introduced himself to me as "Captain" Tucker of the late British barque *Wyvern*, of Bristol, outward-bound to the West Indies with a general cargo of considerable value. He informed me that all had gone well with him until eight days previously, when, about noon, a strange sail was sighted in the south-western board, standing to the northward, close-hauled on the starboard tack.

"You may be sure," said Tucker, "that I kept a sharp eye upon her, for I knew that, for every honest merchant-man that I happened to meet down here, I was likely to meet with a dozen rogues, in the shape of picaroons, privateers, or other craft of the enemy, or even our own men-o'-war—no offence meant to *you* in saying so, Mr. Courtenay ; but *you* know, sir, as well as I do, that some of our men-o'-war treat British merchantmen pretty nearly as bad as if they were enemies, boarding them and impressing all their best men, and leaving them with so few hands that if they happen to meet with bad weather it's ten chances to one of their being able to take their ship to her destination. Well, knowing this, I kept both eyes on the stranger, which I soon made out to be an uncommonly smart and heavy brigantine, that, close-hauled as she was, seemed to be travelling three feet to our one. She had a particularly wicked look about her that I didn't half like ; and I liked it still less when, having drawn well up on our larboard beam, at a distance of some five miles,

I suddenly discovered that she was edging away for us. We were already under stunsails, so I could do no more in the way of making sail; but we mounted eight brass nine-pounders,—very pretty pieces they were, too,—so I had them cleared away and loaded, in readiness for the worst; for I took her to be a French or Spanish privateer, and I had no notion of yielding my ship to any such vermin without making a fight for it; and my own lads were quite of the same mind as myself, not liking the idea of being locked up for years in a French or a Spanish prison.

"Well, sir, that brigantine came bowling along at such a pace that within half an hour of the time when I noticed her to be edging down for us she was within gun-shot; and no sooner was this the case than, yawing broad off for a moment, she pitched a shot—an eighteen-pounder I took it to be—across our fore-foot, as a polite hint to us to heave-to. But I wasn't in the humour for heaving-to just then, so I hoisted my ensign and kept all on as I was going.

"I expected that, seeing this, the brigantine would give us a sight of her bunting, and open fire upon us in good earnest; but she didn't do either. She just kept edging away, until in another five minutes she was broad on our larboard quarter, running the same way that we were, and creeping up with the evident intention of running us alongside. Seeing this, I ordered Mr. Thomson, my mate, to ram an extra shot down upon the top of those we had already loaded our guns with, and to depress the muzzles, so that we could fire down upon the brigantine's low deck as she ranged up alongside. But I tell you, sir, that I didn't half like the look of things; for by this time the craft was so close to us that we saw down upon her decks quite distinctly, and she seemed to be full of men—swarthy, greasy, black-bearded cut-throats, every one of them, if looks went for anything. In another minute or so she was within biscuit-toss of us,—so close that we could hear the hissing shear of her sharp stem through the water, and the moan of the wind in the hollows of her canvas,—when up jumps a fellow upon her rail and hailed us in what I took to be Spanish,—it wasn't French, I know, because I can speak a little of that lingo,—at the same time pointing to his gaff-end, up to which another ruffian at once began to hoist a *black flag*.

"'So ho!' thinks I; 'so it's *pirates* we have to deal with, eh? Well, that means neck or nothing, so here goes:' And with that I sings out to the mate to throw open the ports—we'd kept them closed until now—and let the rascals have it hot. No sooner said than done. Thomson gave the word, the ports were thrown open, the nine-pounders run out, and the next second four of our shot went smashing through the brigantine's bulwarks, bowling over like ninepins every man that happened to be standing in their way. The man on the rail jumped down off his perch as nimbly as if he was scalded, and I heard him shout 'Car-r-r-r-amba!' or something like it, as he waved his hand to the man at the wheel. At the same moment the brigantine delivered her broadside, and before the smoke had time to clear away I heard and felt the crash of her as she dropped alongside us fair in the waist. The next second—so it seemed to me—our rail was alive with the dirty, garlic-smelling blackguards, who came swarming over upon our decks until it seemed that there was no room for more. Well, I had a pair of pistols and a sword, and each of our lads had his cutlass, and for three or four minutes there was as pretty a fight as you'd wish to see going on aboard the old *Wyvern*. Then, while I was doing my best to hold my own against four of the rascals who came crowding round me, I got a knock on the head from behind that made me see about a million stars before I dropped senseless to the deck."

## CHAPTER VI

### WE FIND THE LAUNCH

"HOW long I remained unconscious I don't know, but it must have been at least half an hour, I should say; for when at length I came round I found myself lying, bound hand and foot, on the deck, along with such of my crew as had not been killed in the defence of the ship, while the *Wyvern* was hove-to under topsails, with her hatches off, and a regular mob of the dirty, greasy Spaniards swarming round the main hatchway and hoisting out the cargo that another gang was breaking out down below. They had hoisted out all our boats, too, I soon found, and were using them to transfer such goods as they required to the brigantine— all, that is to say, except the long-boat, which, for some reason that I did not then understand, was lying unused in the starboard gangway. They took their time over the job of picking and choosing from among the stuff that we carried, but I noticed that all the while they had a hand aloft on the main-royal yard keeping a lookout.

They kept at it until it was too dark to see what they were about, and then they left us, one boat remaining alongside for fully twenty minutes after the rest had gone, while some of her people were busy down below. At length, however, they shoved off as well, leaving me and my people lying on the deck trussed up like so many chickens. Two or three minutes later I heard some orders given, immediately followed by the cheeping of blocks and the creaking of yard parralls, by which I knew that they were filling upon the brigantine and leaving us.

"I could not understand why they had left us all there, alive, but bound hand and foot as we were. I suspected some villainy, however, and my first idea was that they had set the barque on fire. But I could not detect any smell of burning, and then the thought came to me that perhaps they had scuttled her, intending us to go down with the ship. The idea of either fairly made my blood run cold, I can tell you; but it stirred me up too, and I went to work to see if I could work my hands free. I might just as well have tried to fly; the scoundrels had made sure work of me, and no mistake. Then I sang out to the others to try if they could work themselves adrift; and after a bit first one and then another answered that it was no use, they were lashed altogether too securely.

"'Well, lads,' says I, 'if none of us can work ourselves free, I'm afraid it's all up with us; for my notion is that those Spanish devils have scuttled the ship, and if so it won't be so very long before she'll founder, taking us with her.'

"That set the men muttering among themselves, and presently the man that was lying nearest me said—

"'If you can manage to work your way near enough to me, sir, for me to get a feel of your lashings with my fingers, I'll see what I can do towards loosenin' of 'em for yer.'

"'All right, my lad,' says I, 'I will!' No sooner said than done. I worked and wriggled myself up alongside of him somehow, and presently I felt his fingers fumbling about with my lashings. This particular chap, I ought to tell you, was uncommonly clever with his fingers, especially in the matter of handling rope; and sure enough, in about twenty minutes, I'm blessed if he hadn't worked those lashings so loose that I presently managed to slip my hands clear of 'em altogether. The moment that I was free I set to work to chafe my fingers and get the life back into them,—for they had lashed me so tight that I had lost all feeling in my hands,—and as soon as I was able to tell once more that I'd got a complete set of fingers, I whipped a knife out of my pocket and cut the lashings off my feet, after which I went the round of the party, cutting them adrift as quick as I could. Then, while they were getting the benumbed feeling out of their limbs, I swung myself down through the open hatchway to investigate. It was as I had feared;

they had scuttled the ship, for already there was something like three feet of water in the hold. You may be sure I didn't waste much time down below after making that discovery; I just scrambled up on deck again as quick as ever I could, and told the men what had happened. The barque was bound to go, of course,—we could do nothing to keep her afloat,—so I jumped to the side to see after the boats. They were gone, all but the longboat, which, as I told you just now, was lying in the starboard gangway. I crossed the deck to take a look at her, and then saw why the pirates had left her there unused; she was stove in on the starboard side, her planks being crushed and her timbers broken over a space measuring some six feet by two. As she was then she would not float two minutes; she would have filled the moment we dropped her into the water. But when Chips came to overhaul her he had a notion that he could patch her up enough to make her carry us. As a matter of fact, it rested between that and the whole lot of us drowning; for the barque was filling so fast that there was no time for us to put a raft together. So the carpenter fetched his tools and went to work there and then, the rest of us lending a hand and fetching things as Chips sung out for them. First of all, he gently coaxed the broken timbers and planking back into their places, as nearly as he could get them; then he got a couple of strips of canvas big enough to cover the hole, one of which he dressed with tallow on both sides, working the grease

## WE FIND THE LAUNCH

well into the fabric. Then, with small, flat-headed tacks, spaced close together, he nailed this first piece of canvas over the hole, allowing it plenty of overlap. Then he took the other piece of canvas,—which was cut an inch larger each way than the first piece,—tarred it well, and strained it tightly over the first piece. Then he cut a third piece of canvas, which he fixed over the hole on the *inside* of the boat, nailing the bottom and two ends of the canvas so that it formed a sort of pocket. Then he got a lot of oakum, which he first soaked in tar and then stuffed into this pocket arrangement until it was packed as tightly as it was possible to pack it. This was to keep the broken planks and timbers in place. And finally he nailed up the top of the pocket, declaring, as he flung down his tools, that the boat was now ready for hoisting out. And it was high time, too, for by the time that the job was finished the barque had settled to her chainplates, and was liable to go down under our feet at any moment. Accordingly, we hooked on the tackles, and, watching the roll of the ship, managed to hoist out the boat and get her into the water without accident. Then we hurriedly pitched into her a couple of breakers of water and such provisions as we could lay our hands upon,—and that wasn't much, for by this time the cabin was all afloat and the lazarette under water,—and tumbled over the side into her, I only waiting long enough behind the others to secure the ship's papers and the chronometer. We shoved off in a hurry, I can tell you, for while I was securing those few matters that I've just mentioned the poor old hooker gave an ugly lurch or two that told me her time was up; and, sure enough, we hadn't pulled above fifty fathoms away from her when down she went, stern first.

"Our first anxiety was, of course, as to the carpenter's repairing job; but we soon found that we needn't greatly trouble ourselves about that. There was just a draining of water that somehow worked its way through, but a few minutes' spell with the baler about once an hour was sufficient to keep the boat fairly dry and comfortable. All the same, I wasn't very keenly anxious for a long boat voyage in such a craft as that, so we shaped a course to the west'ard, hoping to fall in with and be picked up by an outward-bounder of some sort. But not a blessed sail did we see for seven mortal days, until we sighted your upper canvas last night, and pulled so as to cut you off. And if you hadn't picked us up, I believe we should all have been dead by this time, for our provisions soon ran out; and when it was too late, we discovered that both our breakers were full of *salt* instead of fresh water!"

Such was the tragic story related by the skipper of the ill-fated *Wyvern*, a story that was replete with every element necessary for the weaving of a thrilling romance; yet it was told baldly and concisely, without the slightest attempt at embellishment; told precisely as though to be attacked by pirates, to have one's ship rifled and scuttled, one's boats stolen, and then to be left, bound hand and foot on deck, to helplessly perish, were one of the most ordinary and commonplace incidents imaginable. Truly, they who go down to the sea in ships, and do business on the great waters, meet with so many extraordinary experiences, and see so many strange and unaccountable sights, that the capacity for wonder is soon lost, and the most astonishing and—to shore-abiding folk—incredible occurrences are accepted as a matter of course.

During the whole of that day we continued to make short tacks to windward as before, with half the watch aloft on the look out; but nothing was sighted, and at nightfall we again hove-to, maintaining our position as nearly as possible in the same spot until the next morning.

With the first sign of daylight I sent aloft the keenest-sighted man we had on board, that he might take a good look round ere we filled upon the schooner to resume our disheartening search. So eager was I, that when the man reached the royal yard, the stars were still blinking overhead and down in the western sky, and it was too dark to see to any great distance. But the dawn was paling the sky to windward, and as the cold, weird, mysterious pallor of the coming day spread upward, and warmed into pinkish grey, and from that into orange, and from orange to clearest primrose, dyeing the weltering undulations of the low-running sea with all the delicate, shifting tints of the opal, I saw the fellow aloft suddenly rise to his feet and stand upon the yard, with one arm round the masthead to steady himself against the quick, jerky plunges of the schooner, while he shielded his eyes with the other hand, as he steadfastly gazed into the distance to windward.

"Royal yard, there, do you see anything?" I hailed eagerly; and the sudden ecstasy of renewed hope which sprang up within my breast now fully revealed to me how nearly I had been driven to the confines of despair by the long-protracted non-success of the search upon which I had so confidently entered.

"I ain't quite sure, sir," was the unsatisfactory reply that came down to me; "it's still a trifle dusky away out there, but I thought just now that—ay, there it is again! There's *something* out there, sir, about six or seven mile away, but I can't yet tell for certain whether it's a boat or no; it's somewheres about the size of a boat, sir."

"Keep your eye on it," I answered. "I will get the glass and have a look for myself."

So saying, I went hastily to the companion, removed the ship's telescope from the beckets in which it hung there, and quickly made my way aloft.

"Now," said I, as I settled myself upon the yard, "where is the object?"

"D'ye see that long streak of light shootin' up into the sky from behind that bank of cloud, sir?" responded the man. "Well, it's about half a p'int, or maybe nearer a p'int, to the south'ard of that."

"Ah, I see it!" ejaculated I, as I caught sight for a moment of a small, scarcely distinguishable speck that appeared for an instant and then vanished again, apparently in the hollow between two waves. A few seconds later I caught it again, and presently I had it dancing unsteadily athwart the field of the instrument. But even then I was unable to definitely settle whether it was or was not a boat; as the man at my side had remarked, it looked like a boat, it was about the size of a boat, as seen nearly end-on, but there was no indication of life or movement about it; it seemed to be floating idly to the run of the seas. Just at this moment the sun's upper limb flashed into view over the edge of the cloud-bank, darting a long gleam of golden radiance athwart the heaving welter to the schooner, and I looked again, half expecting to catch the answering flash of wet oar-blades; but there was nothing of the kind to be seen. Undoubtedly, however, there was *something* out there,—something that might prove to be a boat,—and I determined to give it an overhaul without loss of time. So, carefully noting its bearing and distance, and cautioning the lookout not to lose sight of it for an instant, I descended to the deck and straightway gave the necessary orders for making sail and beating up to it.

The object being nearly dead to windward, it was a full hour before we reached it, but little more than half that time sufficed to satisfy us that it really was a boat, and a further quarter of an hour established the fact that it was none other than the *Althea's* launch; but my heart was full of foreboding as I observed that, although we fired gun after gun to attract attention, there was no answering sign of life to be discovered on board her, although from the moment when she became visible from the deck, either Lindsay or I kept the telescope constantly bearing upon her. Yet the depth at which she floated in the water showed that she was not empty. Lindsay suggested that her crew might have been taken out of her by some craft that had fallen in with her, and that the reason why she floated so deep was that she was half-full of water. But I could not agree with this view; there was a buoyancy of movement about her as she rose and fell upon the surges, which was convincing proof to my mind that she was loaded down with something much more stable than water.

At length, when we had drawn up to within a cable's length of her, the man on the royal yard sang out that there were people in her, but that they were all lying down in the bottom of the boat, and appeared to be dead.

"We shall have to pick her up ourselves," said I to Lindsay. "Let one hand stand by to drop into her from the fore chains with a rope's end as we bring her alongside. Lay your topsail aback, Mr. Lindsay, and let your jib-sheet flow, if you please."

And as I sprang up on the rail to con the schooner alongside, Lindsay gave the necessary orders.

With the topsail aback, and the mainsheet eased well off, the schooner went drifting slowly down toward the launch, that, as we now approached her, looked old, battered, and weather-stained almost out of recognition. We steered so as to shave past her close to windward, and as she came drifting in under our fore chains, the man who was waiting there with a rope's-end dropped neatly into her, and, springing lightly along the thwarts into the eyes of her, deftly made fast the rope to the iron ring bolt in her stem. Then he turned himself, and looked at the ghastly cargo that the boat carried, and as he gazed he whitened to the lips, and a look of unspeakable horror crept into his eyes as he involuntarily thrust out his hands as though to ward off the sight of some dreadful object. And well he might, for as I gazed down into that floating charnel-house I turned deadly sick and faint, as much at what met my sight as at the horrible odour that rose up out of her and filled my nostrils. The boat seemed to be full of dead, lying piled upon one another, as though they had been flung there; yet the first glance assured me that some of those who were on board her, on the night when I parted company in the gig, were now missing. The captain and the doctor were lying side by side in the stern-sheets; the rest of the ill-fated party were lying heaped one upon the other, or doubled up over the thwarts in the other part of the boat. The two masts were standing, but the sails were lowered and lay, unfurled, along the thwarts, on top of the oars and boathook.

There was no trace of food of any kind to be seen, and the water-breakers were without bungs, and to all appearance empty.

So ghastly and repulsive was the sight which the boat presented, that our people hung in the wind for a moment or two when I ordered them to jump down into her and pass the bodies up over the side; but they rallied at once and followed me when I led the way. The skipper and the doctor were both lying upon their faces, and as I raised the former and turned him over, it is difficult to say which shocked me most, whether the startling ease with which I lifted his wasted body, or the sight of his withered, drawn, and shrunken features—which were so dreadfully altered that for a moment I was doubtful whether it really was or was not the body of Captain Harrison that I held in my arms. I passed him up out of the boat without difficulty, and then did the same with the doctor. It struck me that the latter was not quite dead, and I sang out to Lindsay to get some very weak brandy and water and moisten the lips of each man as he was passed up on deck; for if life still lingered in any of them, it might be possible to save them even now by judicious and careful treatment. Ten of our inanimate shipmates we singled out as possibly alive, but with the rest the indications of dissolution were so unmistakable that I deemed it best not to interfere with them, but to cover the bodies with a sail, weight

## WE FIND THE LAUNCH

it well down with ballast pigs, and then pull the plug out of the boat and cast her adrift, after reading the burial service over the poor relics of humanity that she contained.

That, however, was a duty that might be deferred until we had attended to those who had been passed up out of her as possibly alive; we therefore dropped her under the stern, and allowed her to tow at the full scope of a complete coil of line, while we devoted ourselves to the task of attempting to resuscitate the other ten. As I had suspected, the doctor proved to be alive, · for after diligently painting his blue and shrivelled lips for about a quarter of an hour with a feather dipped in weak brandy and water, his eyelids quivered, a fluttering sigh passed his lips, followed by a feeble groan, and his eyes opened, fixing themselves upon Lindsay and myself in a glassy, unrecognising stare.

"Water! water, for the love of God!" he murmured in a thick, dry, husky whisper.

I raised his head gently and rested it against my shoulder, while Lindsay held the pannikin of weak grog to his lips. For a few seconds he seemed to be incapable of swallowing, then, like a corpse galvanised into the semblance of life, he suddenly seized the edge of the pannikin between his clenched teeth as in a vice, and held it until he had drained it to the dregs. Luckily, there were but two or three spoonfuls left in it, or—as he afterwards assured me—that draught would probably have been his last.

"Ah!" he ejaculated, with a sigh of unspeakable relief, "nectar! nectar! Give me more." Adding quickly, "No, no; not yet, not yet! A single teaspoonful every five minutes! Oh, my God, what anguish! Why did I not die? Is that Courtenay, or am I dreaming? Where is the captain?"

I whipped off my jacket and placed it under his head, as I allowed him to sink gently back on the deck, for at this moment Lindsay whispered to me that the captain was coming round, and I turned to render what assistance I could. Captain Harrison's eyes were now open, but it was perfectly plain to us both that his wandering glances were as yet devoid of recognition; and it was not until some ten minutes later that he began to evince some understanding of who we were and what had happened. His first inquiry was after the well-being of those who had been with him in the boat, and to this I felt constrained to give an evasive but encouraging reply, as he was so terribly weak that I feared the effect upon him of a straightforward answer giving the actual state of the matter. We got him and the doctor down below and put them to bed as quickly as possible, and by the time that this was done the other eight poor souls had also been successfully brought round, when they too were conveyed below and made as comfortable as circumstances would permit. This done, we disposed of the dead with all due reverence, and then resumed our search to windward with renewed hope arising out of the happy discovery of the launch.

It was drawing well on toward eight bells in the afternoon watch that day when the man whom I had stationed in the cabin to keep an eye upon the captain and the doctor came up on deck with the news that both were now awake, and that the captain wished to see me. I at once obeyed the summons, and was greatly rejoiced to find that both of my patients were much stronger, and wonderfully the better in every way for their long sleep. They lost no time in explaining that they were ravenously hungry; whereupon I sent word forward to the galley, and in less than five minutes both were busily engaged in disposing of a bowl of strong broth, prepared from two of the small remaining stock of chickens that we had found on board the schooner when we took her.

The moment that the soup had disappeared the captain began to ask me questions, in reply to which I gave him a succinct account of our adventures from the moment when we parted company from the rest of the boats; and when I had finished he paid me a high compliment upon what he was pleased to term the skill and judgment that I had displayed throughout. He then recounted what had befallen the launch, from which I learned that the entire flotilla of boats had remained together — the faster boats accommodating their pace to the slower craft — until caught in the tail-end of the hurricane, — which with them only reached the strength of a moderate gale, — when they were perforce compelled to separate, from which time the launch had seen none of the others again. It appeared that the launch, deeply loaded as she was, suffered very nearly as much as we in the gig did; the few in her who were capable of doing any work having their hands full in keeping her above water. The sea had broken over them heavily, all but swamping them upon several occasions, and destroying the greater part of their provisions, so that within three days after the cessation of the gale they found themselves without food and face to face with starvation. Then followed a terrible story of protracted suffering, ending in many cases in madness and death, of fruitless effort to work the heavy boat, and finally of utter helplessness, despair, and—oblivion. The captain informed me that he had little hope that any of the other boats had outlived the gale, but believed that if they were still afloat they would be found some forty miles or so to the northward and eastward of where we had fallen in with the launch.

In that direction therefore we continued our search, scouring the whole ocean thereabout over an area of fully one hundred miles square, but we found none of the other boats; and at length, when we had been cruising for a full week, the captain, who by this time was rapidly regaining strength, reluctantly gave the order for us to desist and bear up for Jamaica. And I may as well here mention that none of the other boats were ever again heard of, there being little doubt that they all foundered during the gale.

# CHAPTER VII

### A DARING ACT OF PIRACY

THE captain, having thus sorrowfully and reluctantly abandoned all hope of finding the missing boats, at once became keenly anxious to reach Port Royal with all possible expedition, in order that the painful business of our trial by court-martial for the loss of the frigate might be got over without delay. We therefore carried on night and day; and so smartly did the little schooner step out, that on the seventh day after bearing up we found ourselves at daybreak within sight of Turk's Island, running in for the Windward Passage before the rather languid trade wind. Most of the people were by this time getting about once more, so that, with our own men and the *Wyvern* party, our decks looked rather crowded; and as we went below to breakfast the captain remarked upon it, expressing his satisfaction that the time was so near at hand when we could exchange our cramped quarters aboard the schooner for the more roomy ones to be found in the

Kingston hotels or the houses of the hospitable Jamaica planters.

We were still dawdling over breakfast in the close, stuffy little cabin of the schooner, when Lindsay, who was looking out for me, poked his head through the open skylight to report that there were two sail ahead—a ship and a brigantine—hove-to in somewhat suspicious proximity; and that Captain Tucker—who had been aloft to get a better view of the strangers—declared his belief that the brigantine was none other than the piratical craft the crew of which had pillaged and destroyed the *Wyvern*.

"How do they bear, Mr. Lindsay?" demanded the captain.

"Straight ahead, sir," answered Lindsay.

"And how far distant?" was the next question.

"About ten miles, sir," replied Lindsay.

"And what are we going at the present moment?" asked the captain.

Lindsay withdrew his head from the skylight to glance over the rail, and then replaced it again to answer, "A bare five, sir, I should say; the wind seems to be growing more scant. Shall I heave the log, sir?"

"No, thank you," answered the captain; "I have no doubt your judgment is nearly enough correct for all practical purposes, Mr. Lindsay. Let a hand be sent aloft to keep an eye on the strangers, and tell him to report anything unusual that he may see. I shall be on deck myself in a few minutes."

Excusing myself, I slipped up on deck to have a look at the two craft, the upper canvas of which was visible above the horizon directly ahead of us. As Lindsay had said, the one was a full-rigged ship, while the other was a fine big brigantine; both were hove-to, and in such close proximity that the merest tyro might shrewdly guess at what was going on there just beyond the horizon. But, to make assurance doubly sure, I took the ship's glass, and went up on the topgallant yard, from whence I was able to obtain a full view of them. It was as I had expected; boats were passing rapidly to and fro between the two craft, those which left the ship being heavily laden, while those which left the brigantine were light.

I was still aloft, working away with the telescope, when the captain emerged from the companion-way, and at once catching sight of me, hailed—

"Well, Mr. Courtenay, what do you make of them?"

"It is undoubtedly a case of piracy, sir," I replied. "The brigantine is rifling the ship, and the latter has all the appearance of a British West Indiaman."

"Whew!" I heard the skipper whistle, as he walked to the rail and looked thoughtfully down at the foam bubbles that were gliding past our bends. "If she is an Indiaman she will have passengers aboard her," he remarked to the doctor, who at that moment joined him.

The doctor seemed to acquiesce, although he spoke in

so low a tone that I could not catch his words. The two stood talking together for a few minutes, and then the captain hailed me again.

"What do you judge our distance from those two craft to be, Mr. Courtenay?" he asked.

"A good eight miles, sir, I should say," answered I.

"Thank you, Mr. Courtenay; you may come down, sir," returned the skipper, which I took to be a hint that he wanted me. I accordingly slung the glass over my shoulder, swung myself off the yard on to the backstay, and so descended to the deck.

"Did you notice whether they seemed to have more wind than we have?" inquired the captain, as I joined him.

"Pretty much the same, sir, I should think," answered I. "It looks as though it would fall calm before long."

"I am afraid not; no such luck," remarked the skipper, cocking his weather eye skyward and carefully studying the aspect of the heavens. "I fervently wish it would; then we could nab that fellow beautifully with the boats."

"Might we not try, sir, as it is?" inquired I eagerly. "We have enough people—that is, counting the *Wyvern's* men, who, I have no doubt, would all volunteer," I hastened to add, as my eye fell upon three or four of those whom we had taken out of the launch, and who, what with starvation and their still unhealed wounds, looked more fit for a hospital than for boat duty.

"Thank you, Mr. Courtenay," answered the skipper, with a smile, evidently reading my unspoken thoughts. "No, I am afraid it would not do. In the first place, I question whether we really *have* sufficient men to justify such an attempt; and, in the next place, if we had, it would still be desirable, in my opinion, to defer the attempt until we are much nearer. At present nobody can tell what we are. The schooner is such a small affair that I am in hopes the brigantine will take no notice of us until we are within striking distance of her; while, if I were to send the boats away, she would probably make off at once. No; it is rather trying to the patience to remain idly aboard here, drifting along at this snail's pace, but I am convinced that it is the correct thing to do. Perhaps, if we show only a few men about the decks, the brigantine may be tempted to tackle us."

"Ah! if only she would, sir!" I ejaculated, with such intensity of feeling that the captain laughed.

"Why, I declare you are developing into a regular fire-eater!" he exclaimed.

"Think of the passengers, sir, some of them women, most likely!" I said.

"I *am* thinking of them, sir!" answered the captain through his clenched teeth, and with a sudden glitter in his eye that foreboded evil to the brigantine's people, should we be fortunate enough to get within striking distance of them.

I turned away and walked forward to where I saw

Black Peter, the whilom servant of the midshipmen's mess aboard the *Althea*. He was one of those whom we had found still alive in the launch, and he had picked up wonderfully since then, having become almost his old self again. He was lounging on the forecastle near the port cat-head, with his bare, brawny arms crossed on the rail as he gazed ahead at the two craft, with which we were slowly closing.

"Peter," said I, "get the grindstone ready. And Green, get the cutlasses up on deck and give them a thorough good sharpening. We may want them by and by."

"Ay, ay, sir," answered Green, with a grin, as he shambled away to get the weapon, while Peter bestirred himself with alacrity to prepare the grindstone for its work by drawing a bucket of water and pouring it into the trough. A few minutes later Peter, his eyes gleaming with excitement and every one of his ivories bared in a broad grin of delight, was whirling the handle round at a furious speed, as Green and another hand stood on either side of the stone, each pressing a bare blade to its fiercely buzzing disc.

We continued to drift along at an exasperatingly slow pace before the languid breeze until we had arrived within about four miles of the two craft, when the skipper gave orders to clear the decks and cast loose the guns; but he instructed me that the galley fire was not to be extinguished and the magazine opened until the last moment.

Apparently he had his doubts as to the probability of the brigantine attacking us. And, if so, his doubts were soon confirmed; for when we had reduced the distance by another mile the lookout aloft reported that the brigantine was filling away; and in another minute or two she turned her stern to us, rigged out her studding-sail booms, and went off before the wind, setting her studding-sails as she went.

"Ah!" ejaculated the captain, "it is as I feared! She smells a rat, and does not mean to wait for us! Hoist out the gig at once, Mr. Courtenay, and pull for your life to that ship; too probably it is a case of the *Wyvern* over again, and if there are any people left aboard her they must be saved. Let the men go fully armed, but do not take more than the boat's proper complement, as you are not likely to have any fighting to do, while you may want all the room in the boat that you can spare."

We were by this time moving so slowly that it was unnecessary to heave-to in order to hoist out the gig. No time, therefore, was lost in getting her into the water, and within five minutes of the issuing of the order by the captain we were afloat and away from the schooner, with the men—a picked crew, consisting of the strongest and smartest men in the ship—bending their backs as they drove the beautifully modelled boat at racing speed through the water.

We had barely got away, however, before I detected

light wreaths of smoke curling up between the masts of the distant ship; and at the same moment I observed that although her mainyards were still braced aback she seemed to be no longer hove-to, for, as I watched, her bows fell off until she was nearly before the wind, and she went drifting slowly away to leeward, sometimes heading in one direction and sometimes in another, yawing about all over the place, with a difference of fully four points on either side of the general direction in which she was driving. This was most exasperating, as although she was drifting slowly she was still drifting, and that, too, in the same general direction that we were steering, thus prolonging the time that must necessarily elapse ere we could overtake her, while it would greatly increase the expenditure of energy on the part of the oarsmen to enable us to get alongside.

"Give way with a will, men," I cried. "The rascals have not only set fire to the ship, but they have also cast loose her wheel, so that she is now running away from us to leeward. The harder you pull the sooner shall we catch her, and the better chance will there be for us to put out the fire. And remember, for aught that we know, her crew may be lying there upon her deck, bound hand and foot, utterly helpless, to roast alive, unless we can get alongside in time to save them!"

This appeal was not without effect upon the men; hard as they had been pulling, they now put out every available ounce of strength they possessed, their brawny muscles standing out like ropes upon their bare arms, while the perspiration literally poured off them, and the stout ash blades bent like wands, as they all but lifted the gig clean out of the water at every stroke. We tore along over the low, oil-like ridges of the swell at the speed of the dolphin, leaving the schooner as though she were at anchor; yet to my eager impatience our headlong pace seemed to be little better than a crawl, for the light wreaths of smoke that I had seen winding lazily upward from the ship's hull and twining about her spars increased in volume with startling rapidity, while it momentarily grew darker in colour, until, within ten minutes of its first appearance, it had become a dense cloud of dun-coloured smoke, completely enveloping the ship, in the heart of which long, forking tongues of flickering flame presently appeared. They had apparently set fire to the poor old barkie in at least half a dozen places, and she was burning like match-wood.

"Pull, men, pull!" I cried, "or we shall be too late; she is well alight even now, and in another quarter of an hour she will be a blazing furnace if she goes on at her present rate. Heaven above! if there are people aboard her what must their feelings be now?"

A groan of sympathy burst from the men in response to this ejaculation of mine, and they tugged at the oars with a strength and energy that filled me with amazement. We were coming up with the ship hand over hand; but, fast as the boat flew, the fire grew still faster, and presently

I saw the flames climbing aloft by way of the well-tarred shrouds until they reached the sails, when there arose a sudden blaze of flame among the spars, and in two or three minutes every shred of canvas had been consumed, and the crawling tongues of fire were circling about the masts and yards, feebly at first, but steadily increasing until they were all ablaze. Meanwhile the ship, deprived of her canvas, gradually fell broadside-on to the wind, and from that position as gradually drifted round until she lay bows-on to us. By this time we were within three-quarters of a mile of her, and now that she was no longer driven to leeward by her sails, we neared her rapidly. But my heart sank within me as I watched her, for the destruction of her sails, which I had at first thought a fortunate circumstance,—inasmuch as she no longer blew away from us,— I now recognised as a dreadful happening; for, stationary as she now lay on the water, the light draught of wind had full power to fan the fire that raged aboard her, and by the time that we drew up under her bows and hooked on to her bobstay, she was a roaring mass of flames from stem to stern.

I shinned up the bobstay and so got on to her bowsprit, and from there made my way into her head; but I could go no farther, for the fore part of her deck was a sheet of fire, upon which no living thing could exist for more than a few seconds of unspeakable torment, and even where I stood the heat was all but unendurable. I could not see very far aft for the flames and smoke,

Her fore scuttle was open, and a pillar of flame roared out of it as from a chimney on fire; and some ten feet abaft it was her foremast, ablaze from the deck to the truck; and immediately abaft it again was the blazing framework of what had shortly before been a deck-house. Beyond that I could see nothing. One thing was quite certain, and that was that if there were living people still aboard her —which I could not believe possible—they must be aft, and it was there that we must seek them. So I scrambled down into the gig again, and ordered the men to back off and pull round under the ship's stern.

They lost no time in obeying my order; and it was well for us all that they exhibited so much alacrity, for as we swept round and gave way an ominous cracking and rending sound was heard aboard the ship, and a moment later her blazing foremast toppled over and fell with a crash into the sea, missing the gig by a bare boathook's length.

"Look out for the other masts; they'll be comin' down too in a jiffy!" sang out one of the men; and they all pulled for their lives. But the alarm was a false one, the main and mizzen masts standing for full ten minutes longer.

But when we got under the ship's stern it became perfectly clear that no living thing could be aboard her, for she was even more fiercely ablaze aft than she was for'ard, the whole of her, from the mainmast to the taffrail, being a veritable furnace of roaring flame, with tongues and jets of fire leaping from her cabin windows and from every port and scuttle. It was impossible to board her in this direction; it would have simply been an act of suicide to have attempted it; even her outside planking, right down to the water's edge, was so hot that it was unbearable to the touch; and it was beyond all doubt that if those fiends in the brigantine had left the crew, or any portion of them, on board, the unhappy creatures must have perished long ere we had reached the ill-fated craft. I therefore took a note of her name,—the *Kingston Trader* of Bristol,—and reluctantly gave the word to haul off to a safe distance to wait until the schooner should run down and pick us up.

This occurred about a quarter of an hour later, and the moment that the gig was fairly clear of the water we crowded sail after the brigantine; but, fast as the schooner was, the pirate craft easily ran away from us, and by sunset had vanished below the horizon.

Nothing further of importance happened to us until our arrival at Port Royal, which occurred on the evening of the following day, when we just saved the last of the sea breeze into the harbour. The captain went ashore and reported himself that same night, dining with the admiral afterwards; but I did not go ashore until late the next day, as there was a great deal of business that I had to attend to. Captain Harrison was of course most anxious that our trial by court-martial for the loss of the frigate should take place as speedily as possible, because he could not hope for another command until that was over; and it happened by a quite exceptional piece of luck that there were enough ships in the harbour to allow of its being held at once. It was consequently arranged to take place on board the flag-ship, on the fourth day following our arrival. It was, of course, only a formal affair, the loss of the frigate being due to causes quite beyond our control,—unless, indeed, we had chosen to run from the two French ships instead of fighting them, —so it was soon over, and before noon we were all honourably acquitted, and our side-arms returned to us with much congratulatory handshaking on the part of the officers present. Captain Harrison, the doctor, Lindsay, and I were invited to dine with the admiral at his Pen that evening, and we accordingly drove out with the last of the daylight, arriving at the house just as the sun was setting over Hunt Bay. The admiral was the very soul of hospitality, and we were therefore a large party, several officers from Up Park Camp and a sprinkling of civilians being present "to take off the salt flavour" likely to prevail from a too exclusive gathering of the naval element, as our host laughingly put it.

Somewhat to my surprise, I found myself the lion of the evening, Captain Harrison having most generously made the utmost of my exploit in capturing the French schooner and my subsequent search for the frigate's boats; and so many compliments were paid me that, being still young and comparatively modest, I had much difficulty in maintaining my self-possession and making suitable replies.

After dinner, and while the rest of us were chatting and smoking over our wine, the admiral, apologising for being obliged to temporarily absent himself, withdrew, taking Captain Harrison with him. They were absent for nearly an hour, and when they returned there was noticeable in the skipper's manner a subdued but joyous exultation that told of good news. I did not, however, learn what it was until we had left the Pen and were driving back to our hotel in Kingston by the dazzling silver radiance of a tropical full moon. And, prior to that, the admiral had said to me as I bade him good-night—

"Come and see me in my office to-morrow about noon, Mr. Courtenay; I want to have a talk to you."

As soon as we were clear of the Pen grounds and fairly on our road to Kingston, the skipper said to me—

"Mr. Courtenay, do you happen to have noticed that fine frigate, the *Minerva*, lying just inshore of the flagship?"

"Yes, sir, I have," said I. "She is a beauty, and is said to be a wonderful sailer, especially on a taut bowline. I heard yesterday that her captain is ashore, down with yellow fever."

"Very true," answered the skipper. "The poor fellow died this morning, and the admiral has been pleased to give the command of her to me."

"I congratulate you with all my heart, sir," said I.

"I thought I could read good news in your face this evening when you returned to the dining-room. She is a magnificent vessel, and I sincerely hope that you will have abundant opportunity to distinguish yourself in her. And I hope, sir, that you will take me with you."

"Thank you, Courtenay, thank you!" exclaimed the skipper, evidently touched by the sincerity of my congratulations; "if we can only manage to fall in with the enemy frequently enough, never fear but I will distinguish myself—if I live. As to taking you with me, I would do so with the greatest pleasure, and as a matter of course, were I permitted to have my own way; but I believe, from what the admiral let drop to me to-night, that he has his own plans for you, and, if so, you may rest assured that they will be far more to your advantage than would be your accompanying me to the *Minerva*. Let me see—how much longer have you to serve before you are eligible for examination?"

"Only four days more, sir," I answered, with a laugh; "then I shall go up as early as possible."

"Only four days more?" exclaimed the skipper in surprise; "I thought it was more like two months!"

"Only four days, I assure you, sir," repeated I.

"Um! well, I suppose you know best," was the answer, given in a musing tone, to which was presently added, "So much the better! So much the better!"

"May I ask, sir, whether that remark has any reference to me?" I inquired.

"Certainly, Courtenay, certainly; there cannot be any possible objection to your asking, but I am not bound to answer, am I?" replied the skipper, with a laugh. "No," he continued, "I must not tell you anything, except that I have reason to believe that the admiral is very much pleased with your behaviour, and that he contemplates marking his approval in a manner which, I am sure, will be very pleasing to yourself."

And that was all I could get out of the gallant captain; but it was sufficient to cause me to pass a sleepless night of pleasurable speculation.

Prompt to the second I presented myself at the admiral's office next morning, and was at once shown into the great man's presence.

"Morning, Mr. Courtenay!" exclaimed he, as I entered. "Bring yourself to an anchor for a minute or two, will ye, until I have signed these papers; then I shall be free to have a talk to you. Jenkins, clear away a chair for Mr. Courtenay."

The orderly sergeant reverently removed a pile of books and papers from a chair, dusted it, and placed it near an open window, and I amused myself by looking out upon the busy scene in the harbour, while the admiral proceeded to scrawl his signature upon document after document.

"There!" he exclaimed, with a sigh of relief, as he signed the last one and pushed it away from him, "thank goodness that job is finished! Now, Mr. Courtenay—by the way, Captain Harrison told me last night that he believed you would soon be eligible for your examination. Is that so?"

"Yes, sir," answered I; "I shall have served my full time in three days more."

"Three days!" exclaimed the admiral. "Is that all?"

I replied that it was.

"And I understand that you are a good seaman and navigator," resumed the admiral. "I suppose you have no fear of failing when you go up for your examination?"

I modestly replied that I had not, provided that I was treated fairly, and had not a lot of catch-questions put to me.

"Just so," responded the admiral musingly. "Your navigation, I have no doubt, is all right," he continued, "and of course you can work a ship when she is all ataunto. But suppose you belonged, let us say, to a frigate, and at the end of an engagement you found yourself in command, and your ship unrigged, what is the first thing you would do?"

I considered for a moment, and then proceeded to describe the steps I should take under such circumstances, the admiral listening all the time intently, but uttering no word and giving no sign of any kind to indicate whether my reply was satisfactory or not, until I had finished, when he said—

"Very good, Mr. Courtenay, very good indeed—on the whole. Have you ever helped to fit out a ship?"

"Yes, sir," answered I, "I was aboard the poor old *Althea* during the whole time that she was in the hands of the riggers."

"Ah!" he exclaimed, "and you heartily wished yourself anywhere else than there, I'll be bound. But it has done you good, young gentleman; you have profited by your experience, I can see, and will perhaps some day be deeply thankful for the knowledge you then gained. Now, supposing that you found yourself on a lee shore, in a heavy gale of wind, with all your masts gone, what steps would you take for the preservation of the ship and the lives of your crew?"

Again I replied at length, stating that I should anchor the moment that the ship drifted into a suitable depth of water, letting go both bowers, backing them up with the sheet anchors, and shackling the remainder of the bower cables on to those of the sheet anchors, which latter I should then veer away upon to within a few fathoms of the clinch.

"And suppose that, having done this, your ship dragged, or parted her cables, what then?" persisted the admiral.

"Then, sir," said I, "we could only trust in God's mercy, while standing by to take care of ourselves and each other as soon as the ship should strike."

"Good!" exclaimed the admiral; "a very excellent

and proper answer, Mr. Courtenay. Now," he continued, "I have been asking you these questions with a purpose. I wanted to ascertain for myself whether I should be justified in sending you away in command of that little schooner that you took so cleverly, and I think I shall. I believe you will do exactly for the work I have in my mind for you. Sickness and casualties together have played havoc among the officers on this station of late, to such an extent that I have not nearly as many as I want; consequently I am only too glad to meet with young gentlemen like yourself, who have made good use of their opportunities. These waters are swarming with the enemy's privateers,—with a sprinkling of pirates thrown in, it would appear, from what the skipper of the unfortunate *Wyvern* says,—and they must be put down—sunk, burned, destroyed by any means that can best be compassed, or, better still, captured. I therefore propose to fit out that little schooner of yours, and to place you in command of her, for the especial purpose of suppressing these pests, and incidentally capturing as many of the enemy's merchantmen as you can fall in with. Now, how d'ye think you'll like the job?"

I replied, delightedly, that nothing could possibly suit me better; that I was inexpressibly grateful for the confidence he was about to repose in me, and that I would leave nothing undone to prove that such confidence was justified.

"Very well, then, that is settled," observed the

admiral genially. "We will have the schooner overhauled at once, and made ready for sea as quickly as may be. Then you can go to sea for a month; there will be an examination next month, for which you must arrange to be in port, and then—having passed, as I feel certain you will—you shall have your commission, and be off to sea again to win your next step."

## CHAPTER VIII

### WE CAPTURE A SPANISH INDIAMAN

THE schooner was turned over to the dockyard people that same afternoon, and duly surveyed; and on the following day, when I presented myself at the admiral's office, the old boy handed me a list, as long as the main bowline, setting forth the several alterations deemed necessary to fit the little craft for His Majesty's service.

"Here, Mr. Courtenay, just run your eye over that list, and tell me what you think of it," he cried, as he passed it to me across the table.

I "ran my eye over it." "New gang of rigging fore and aft—new bulwarks, six feet high, fitted with hammock rail, etc., complete—deck strengthened by doubling the deck-beams—new coamings to hatchways,"—and so on, and so on, until my imagination had conjured up a picture of the trim little *Susanne* transmogrified out of recognition, and so stiffened and hampered by her extra deck-beams and new rigging, that we should have reason to deem ourselves fortunate should we ever succeed in screwing six knots out of her on a bowline.

The admiral must have beheld my face growing ever longer as I worked my way through this precious list to the end of it, for when I had finished it, and looked up at him blankly, he laughed aloud, as he exclaimed—

"Why, boy, what is the matter with you? Your face is as long as a fiddle!"

"Oh, sir," I exclaimed, in accents of despair, "you surely will not allow those—those—dockyard people to completely ruin the poor little hooker by making all these alterations and additions to her? She is a new vessel, sir—I understood from the mate of her that this was her first voyage. She is as sound and strong as wood and iron can make her, and any attempt to further strengthen her can only result in the destruction of her sailing powers. Then, as to those high bulwarks, sir, what will be the use of them? They will not afford us an atom of protection, while they will make her sag away to leeward like a barge! And this new gang of rigging"—

The admiral again burst out laughing. "There, there," he said soothingly, as he held up his hand to stop me, "don't distress yourself any further, Mr. Courtenay; I'll go aboard her myself this afternoon, and see how much of this she really requires before signing the order. Meanwhile, go aboard yourself and draw up a list of such alterations and additions as *you* may think needful, and hand it to me when I come down to have a look round."

I did so, and the upshot of it all was that I eventually wheedled the admiral into consenting that the schooner should remain absolutely untouched above the deck, the only alterations made in her consisting in an extension of the cabin and forecastle accommodation, the enlargement of the magazine, and the substitution of iron ballast for the stones which the Frenchmen had considered good enough to keep the little hooker on her feet. I had some difficulty in gaining my patron's consent to the retention of the low, light bulwarks with which the craft was fitted, the admiral being strongly of opinion that they ought to be high enough and stout enough to shelter us from musketry fire. Moreover, I think he considered that we looked altogether too rakish and piratical as we then were; but I represented to him that under certain conditions this might be advantageous rather than otherwise, and in the end the kind-hearted old fellow indulgently let me have my way. The result of this was that within a fortnight of our arrival we were at sea again, with the little ship—rechristened by the name of the *Tern*— smelling outrageously of fresh paint, to the unmitigated disgust of the thirty-six stout fellows who were quartered in her forecastle. Young Lindsay, with many apologies to Captain Harrison, elected to unite his fortunes with mine, rather than turn over to the *Minerva*; and I was also given another lad—a very quiet, lady-like young fellow named Christie—to bear us both company and do duty as master. Black Peter, also came to the conclusion that there would be more scope for his talents aboard the schooner than in the frigate, and without asking anybody's leave, installed himself, unceremoniously and as a matter of course, in the position of cabin servant.

We weighed about five o'clock in the evening, with the last of the sea breeze,—a very smart, handsome privateer schooner named the *Coquette* being in company,—and just managed to sneak through the narrow channel between Gun and Rackum Cays, when the wind dropped dead, and left us in the East Channel in the midst of a glassy calm, rolling our rails under to the furious swell that came sweeping along past Plum Point. The *Coquette* was within biscuit-toss of us, and she too was rolling and tumbling about to such an extent that I every minute expected to see her roll her sticks away. This lasted for close upon two hours, during which the sun went down in a blaze of splendour and lavish magnificence of colour such as I have never beheld outside the limits of the West Indian waters. Then, just as the burning glories of the west were fading into sober grey, while Hesperus beamed softly out with momentarily increasing effulgence in the darkening blue of the eastern sky, a gentle breeze came stealing to us off the land, to which both schooners, with a mutual challenge to each other, gladly trimmed their canvas, and away we both went, hugging the Palisades closely, for the sake of the smoother water, until Plum Point was passed, when we gradually drew away from each other, the *Coquette* shaping a course for Morant

Point, while I edged away for the island of Martinique, having formed the opinion that some of the more knowing of the enemy's homeward-bound merchant skippers might endeavour to slip out of the Caribbean between the islands of Martinique and Dominica, in the hope of thereby eluding our cruisers and privateers, most of which chose the neighbourhood of the Windward Passages for their cruising-ground. By the end of the second dog-watch the breeze had freshened so much that it became necessary to hand our royal and topgallant sail; and soon afterwards the wind hauled gradually round until it became the true trade wind, piping up to the strength of half a gale, and compelling us to haul down a single reef in our big mainsail and two reefs in our topsail, under which the little beauty lay down and thrashed through it with all the life and go of a thorough-bred racer. The *Coquette* was still in sight, some eight miles away to windward, and, famous as she was for her speed, I had the supreme delight of observing that we had headreached upon her to the extent of quite two miles. And now we began to discover the great advantage of having exchanged our stone ballast for iron, the schooner being not only much stiffer under her canvas, but also more lively than before. It was grand sailing weather, the breeze, although strong, being perfectly steady, while the sea was long and regular, allowing the little hooker plenty of time to rise to each as it came rushing down upon her with hissing crest all agleam with sparkling sea-fire. And it was exhilarating to stand right away aft, close by the weather taffrail, and watch the little beauty as she tore along with breathless speed through the dusky night. The sky was clear as a bell, save for a few detached fleeces of trade-cloud that came swooping along at frequent intervals athwart the stars, so that there was plenty of light to see by; and it was as intoxicating as wine to merely stand abaft there, as I did, feeling the strong rush of the wind past me, and drinking in its invigorating freshness and coolness, as the deck heaved and plunged beneath my feet, and the bending masts swayed and reeled to and fro, the trucks sweeping long arcs among the dancing stars, and the wind piping high and shrill through the rigging, as the schooner leaped and plunged irresistibly forward, with a storm of spray flashing in over her weather cat-head and blowing aft as far as the mainmast at every buoyant upward leap of her to meet the sea, while a whole Niagara of hissing foam — with an under-stratum of whirling clouds of lambent green sea-fire — went swirling past the lee rail at a speed that made one giddy to look at. Five bells in the first watch saw us fairly abreast at Morant Point, and then, as the night was clear and the breeze steady, I went below and turned in.

Nothing of any importance occurred during the next few days, and, carrying on upon the schooner to the last stitch that she could stagger under, we arrived off the northern extremity of the island of Martinique exactly at midnight on the fifth night after leaving Port Royal. I considered that we had now reached our cruising-ground, and that there was consequently no need for any further hurry. We therefore shortened sail to double-reefed mainsail, fore staysail, and jib,—furling all our square canvas,—and leisurely passed through the channel between Martinique and Dominica until we were some sixty miles to windward of both islands, when we headed the little hooker to the northward and *ratched* as far as the latitude of Antigua, then heaving about and returning over the same ground again.

The first two days of our cruising proved utterly barren of results, but the time was by no means wasted, for, having sedulously exercised the crew in the working of the guns and in cutlass drill every day during our passage across from Port Royal, I now rigged up a floating target and gave them a little firing practice, taking care to have a man on the royal yard to give us timely notice of the appearance of any sail that perchance might be frightened away by the sound of firing; and I was soon gratified at the discovery that I numbered among my crew several very fairly clever marksmen.

It was within a few minutes of sunset, on the evening of the third day of our cruise, that, being again off the northern extremity of Martinique, and heading to the southward, the lookout aloft reported the upper canvas of what looked like a large ship standing out close-hauled between that island and Dominica. I immediately got the ship's telescope and went aloft with it, being just in good time to catch a glimpse of the royals and heads of the topgallant sails of a ship steering a course that would carry her some six miles to the northward of us. Having made as sure as I could of her bearing, distance, and course, I descended to the deck, and gave orders to wear ship, after executing which manœuvre we hauled down all our canvas and lay in wait for the approaching craft, the schooner, although under bare poles, headreaching at the rate of about two miles per hour. I estimated that the distance of the stranger from us was then some twenty-five miles, and if she was making a speed of eight knots—which was a fairly liberal allowance—it would afford us ample time to drift fairly athwart her hawse; and this I hoped to do undiscovered, as I believed that, from the cut of her canvas, she was a merchantman belonging to one or another of our enemies, and I was most anxious that she should not take fright and bear up for either of the islands, involving us in a long stern-chase, with possibly a cutting-out job at the end of it if she should succeed in reaching the refuge of a harbour.

The evening was fine, with a moderate breeze from about east-north-east, and not very much sea running. The swell, however, was high enough to hide us for at least half the time, and although the stars soon beamed forth brilliantly, while a thin silver sickle of moon hung high aloft, the conditions generally seemed fairly promising for success. Of course I gave the most stringent orders that no lights whatever should be permitted to show aboard the schooner, and I was careful to remain on deck myself to see that these orders were rigorously observed. The canvas of the stranger seemed to grow upon the horizon very slowly, and the time of waiting for her approach appeared long; but at length, by four bells in the first watch, she had drawn up to within about three miles of us, and I gave the word to see all clear for sheeting home and hoisting away at a moment's notice; for the time had now arrived when, if anything like a proper lookout was being kept on board her, we might be discovered at any instant. But minute after minute passed, and she still came steadily on, heeling slightly to the steady trade wind, and bowing solemnly over the undulating swell, with a curl of white foam under her bluff bows that made her appear to be travelling at about three times her actual speed. We had by this time forereached athwart her fore-foot, and were edging along at a pace that promised to place us about half a mile to windward of her by the time that she would be crossing our stern, and now I kept the night-glass immovably bearing upon her, watching for the sudden yaw that should indicate the discovery of a possible enemy in her path. I had by this time made up my mind that she was a Spaniard, and the mere fact of her adventuring herself thus alone, instead of availing herself of a convoy, was to me sufficient assurance that she went heavily armed and manned. It also suggested the possibility that she might be carrying an exceptionally rich freight, it sometimes happening that the skipper of such a ship, especially if he chanced to be a man of daring and courage, preferred to take his chance of making the voyage alone rather than risk being cut off from the convoy by the swarm of privateers and picaroons that hovered upon its skirts almost from the moment of its sailing to that of its arrival.

Our people were by this time all at their stations, with sheets and halliards in their hands, ready to sway away at the first word of an order from me; and it was not so dark but that I was able to see, out of the corner of my eye, the nudges and gestures of delight which they interchanged as the great, stately Indiaman swept at length athwart our stern, dark and silent as a phantom.

"Up helm and wear her round," I shouted, all necessity for further concealment being now at an end; "sheet home and hoist away for'ard—hold on aft with your peak and throat halliards until we are fairly round! Starboard braces round in! trim aft the starboard head-sheets! *Now* hoist away your mainsail! Ah, they see us at last! There she bears away. Steady there with your lee helm, my man; do not let her come to just yet. Keep the chase upon your weather bow; she must not be allowed to get to leeward of us. Mr. Lindsay, just pitch a shot athwart her hawse as a hint that we wish her to heave-to."

The shot was fired, and another, and yet a third, but the stranger took no notice whatever, the object of her captain being apparently to bear away across our bows and so get before the wind, when, of course, the cloud of studding-sails that her rig allowed would afford her a very important advantage over the schooner. But I was not going to permit that if I could help it, and it soon became perfectly clear that we could, the schooner having the heels of the ship, although we were soon under the lee of the latter, with her sails partially becalming ours. At length, finding that we could outsail the Indiaman, I luffed close in under her lee and hailed, in the best Spanish that I could muster—

"Ho, the ship ahoy! Heave-to, and strike, sir, to His Britannic Majesty's schooner *Tern*!"

The only reply to this was a rattling volley of musketry, evidently aimed at me as I stood on the weather rail, just abaft the main rigging, for I heard the bullets whistling all round my head.

"If you don't heave-to, sir," I exclaimed angrily, "by heaven, I will fire into and sink you!"

"Schooner ahoy! who are you?" now came a hail, in very indifferent English, from the ship; and in the dim starlight I could just make out the shape of a shadowy figure standing by the mizzen rigging.

"This schooner, sir, is His Britannic Majesty's schooner *Tern*, as I have already had the honour to inform you. Do you intend to heave-to, sir, or will you compel me to fire into you?" I retorted, in English this time.

The figure vanished from the lee rail of the ship without making any reply to my question; and, annoyed

## WE CAPTURE A SPANISH INDIAMAN 153

at being treated in this curious fashion, I turned my face inward and shouted—

"Let her go off a little, Mr. Lindsay,—just far enough to enable us to fire at his rigging,—and then see whether a broadside will bring the fellow to his senses."

I leapt down off the rail, and turned to walk aft, when the figure suddenly popped into view again aboard the Indiaman, and shouted—

"No, no, señor; do not fire, for the love of God! We have several ladies aboard here, and I will surrender, rather than that they should be hurt! I surrender, sir, I surrender!"

And the next instant I heard the same voice shouting, in Spanish, an order for the crew to lay aft and back the mainyard.

As the broad mainsail of the ship collapsed and shrivelled into massive festoons to the hauling of the crew upon the clew-garnets, buntlines, and leechlines, preparatory to backing the maintopsail, we too shortened sail in readiness to heave-to at the same moment as the prize; and five minutes later I found myself, with my sword drawn and a dozen stout fellows, armed to the teeth, at my heels, standing upon the quarter-deck of the stranger, with a little crowd of well-dressed men — evidently Spaniards — curiously regarding me and my following by the light of a couple of lanterns that someone had placed on the capstan-head.

"Bueno!" exclaimed a fine, sailorly-looking, elderly

man, "all is well; they are undoubtedly English, and we have therefore nothing to fear!"

And so saying, he stepped forward and handed me his sheathed sword.

As I doffed my hat and held out my hand to receive the weapon, I could not help saying—

"Pardon, señor, but may I be permitted to ask an explanation of that remark?"

"Assuredly, noble sir," answered the Spaniard, returning my bow, with a dignified grace that excited my keenest envy; "the explanation is perfectly simple. The fact is, that when your schooner suddenly appeared just now, as though she had risen from the bottom of the sea, my first impression was that we had been unfortunate enough to stumble across the path of my detested countryman, Pedro Morillo; and I was determined to sink with my ship and all on board her rather than surrender to him."

"And pray, señor, who is this man Pedro Morillo, of whom you speak? and why should he require a countryman of his own to surrender to him? and why should you be so very strongly averse to falling into his power?" demanded I.

"Ah, señor, it is easy to see that you are a stranger to these waters, or you would not need to ask for information respecting that fiend Morillo," answered the Spaniard. "He is a cruel, avaricious, and bloodthirsty pirate, sparing neither man nor woman, friend nor foe. But little is really known about him, señor, for those who meet him rarely survive to tell the tale; but there have been one or two who, by a miracle, have escaped him, and it is from them that we have gained the knowledge that it is better to perish by his shot than to fall alive into his hands."

"Is the vessel by means of which he perpetrates his piracies a brigantine, very handsome, and wonderfully fast?" I inquired, suddenly bethinking me of poor Captain Tucker and his story.

"Certainly, señor, that answers perfectly to the description of the accursed *Guerrilla*. Have you seen her of late? But no, of course you have not, or you would not now be here; for Morillo is said to be especially vindictive against the English, inflicting the most atrocious tortures upon all who fall into his hands. In the dim light we at first mistook your schooner for the *Guerrilla*, and that is why we fired upon you as we did. Permit me, señor, to express my profound regret at my so unfortunate mistake, and my extreme gratification that it was not followed by a disastrous result."

At this compliment we of course exchanged bows once more; after which I took the liberty of addressing to this very polite and polished skipper a few questions with regard to his ship, coupled with a hint that I was anxious to complete without delay my arrangements for placing a prize crew on board and bearing up for Jamaica.

Our prize, I then learned, was the *Doña Dolores* of Cadiz, a Spanish West Indiaman of eleven hundred and eighty-four tons register, homeward bound from Cartagena,

Maracaibo, and La Guayra, with a very valuable general cargo and twenty-eight passengers, ten of whom were ladies. Captain Manuel Fernandez—the skipper—was most polite, and anxious to meet my views in every way; at least, so he informed me. He conducted me into the ship's handsome saloon and introduced me to his passengers,—the female portion of which seemed to be frightened nearly out of their wits,—and was kind enough to promise me that, if it would be agreeable to me, the whole of his people should assist my prize crew to work the ship. This suggestion, however, did *not* happen to be agreeable to me, so I was compelled to explain, as politely as I could phrase it, that my duty compelled me not only to decline his magnanimous offer, but to secure the whole of his crew, officers and men, below, and also to remove all arms of every description from the ship; after which, if he would give me his parole, it would afford me much pleasure to receive him as a guest on board the schooner. I could see that this was a bitter pill for the haughty don to swallow, but I was politely insistent, and so of course he had to yield, which he eventually did with the best grace he could muster; and an hour later the *Dolores*, with Christie, the master's mate, in command, and ten of our lads as a prize crew, was bowling along before the wind with studding-sails set aloft and alow, while the *Tern* followed almost within hail; it being my intention to escort so valuable a prize into port, and thus take every possible precaution against her recapture.

# CHAPTER IX

WE ENCOUNTER AND FIGHT THE *GUERRILLA*

ON the morning but one succeeding the capture of the *Dolores*,—the schooner and her prize then being some two hundred and forty miles to the westward of Dominica,—a sail was discovered at daybreak some twelve miles to the southward and westward of us, beating up against the trade wind, close-hauled upon the starboard tack; and a few minutes later she was made out to be a brigantine. We paid but scant attention to her at first, craft of her rig being frequently met with in the Caribbean, trading to and fro between the islands; but when the stranger, almost immediately after her rig had been identified, tacked to the northward, as though with the intention of getting a closer look at us, I at once scented an enemy, and, possessing myself of the telescope, forthwith made my way into the fore crosstrees for the purpose of subjecting her to a rigorous examination, wondering, meanwhile, whether by any adverse chance the stranger might eventually turn out to be the notorious pirate

Morillo in his equally notorious brigantine the *Guerrilla*. I had no sooner got the craft fairly within the field of the instrument than I discovered my conjecture to be correct, a score of trifling details of rig and equipment becoming instantly recognisable as identical with similar peculiarities already noticed by me when I before saw the pirate vessel.

Such is the perversity of blind fortune! Under ordinary circumstances nothing would have pleased me better than to meet this audacious outlaw and his cut-throat crew in a clear sea, and to try conclusions with them. But now I was hampered with the possession of a valuable prize which I was most anxious to take safely into port, while my little force was seriously weakened by the withdrawal of the prize crew which I had been obliged to put on board the *Dolores*. It was therefore not wholly without apprehension that, under these untoward circumstances, I witnessed the approach of the formidable brigantine. I would have preferred to have met her, if possible, upon somewhat more equal terms; but there she was, doubtless bent upon the capture of the *Dolores*, and there was nothing for it but to prepare for her as warm a reception as it was in our power to give. I therefore descended to the deck and gave orders to call all hands and clear for action, at the same time signalling to Christie that the stranger in sight was a pirate, and that he was to keep out of harm's way during the impending action, keeping on upon his course, and leaving us in the schooner to deal with the intruder.

Our preparations were soon complete, but none too soon; for, approaching each other as we were at a good pace, the space between the brigantine and ourselves narrowed very rapidly. Nevertheless there was time, when all was done, to say a few words to the men; so, as I anticipated that the struggle upon which we were about to engage would be a tough one, I called them aft and said—

"My lads, you have all heard of the atrocious pirate Morillo who haunts these waters; you have heard something of his doings from those poor fellows belonging to the *Wyvern* who were picked up by us when we were searching for the *Althea's* boats, and you saw for yourselves a specimen of his handiwork in the blazing hull of the *Kingston Trader*, the unfortunate crew of which ship only too probably perished with her. The scoundrel and his gang of cold-blooded murderers are aboard that brigantine; and after what you have heard and seen, I need not tell you what is likely to be the fate of any of us, or of those aboard the *Dolores*, should we be so unfortunate as to fall into their hands. They are undoubtedly about to attempt the capture of the Spaniard. Now, it is for *you* to say whether they shall do so, or whether you will send them all to the bottom of the sea instead. Which is it to be, men?"

"Put us alongside of her, Mr. Courtenay, sir, and we'll

soon show you—and them too—which it's to be," answered one of the men, the rest instantly corroborating the remark by such exclamations as, " Ay, ay ; we'll give 'em their gruel, never fear." " Well spoke, Tommy ; true for you, my son," and so on.

"Very well," said I, "that is the answer I expected. Now go to your guns, men ; and see that you make every shot tell."

While clearing for action we had also made sail and shot ahead of the *Dolores* ; and within five minutes of the moment when the crew went back to their guns, we were within half a mile of the brigantine, which craft was then crossing our bows, tearing through the long, low swell like a racing yacht, with a storm of diamond spray flashing up over her weather bow at every graceful plunge of her into the trough. She was a beautiful vessel, long and low, with enormously taunt, raking masts and a phenomenal spread of canvas—a craft well worth fighting for ; and I thought what a proud day it would be for me if perchance I should be fortunate enough to capture and take her triumphantly into Port Royal harbour. She was now well within range, so I sang out to Lindsay, who was looking after matters on the forecastle, to know whether the nine-pounder pivot gun was ready.

"All ready, sir, and bearing dead on the brigantine," was the answer.

"Then heave a shot across the rascal's fore-foot at once," shouted I ; "and you, my man, hoist away the ensign at the flash of the gun," I continued to the fellow who was standing by the peak signal halliards.

As the words left my lips there was a ringing report and a smart concussion; and, springing upon the weather rail, I was just in time to see the shot neatly strike the water immediately under the brigantine's figure-head, the spray from it leaping up and leaving a dark stain upon the foot of her foretopmast staysail.

"Well aimed!" exclaimed I exultantly; "if you will all do as well as that throughout the fight, lads, you will soon give a good account of her."

While I was still speaking there came an answering flash from the brigantine, which at the same moment boldly ran up a *black* flag at her gaff-end; and ere the report had time to reach us, a nine-pound shot crashed fair into our bows, raking us fore and aft, and carrying off the top of our unfortunate helmsman's head as it flew out over our taffrail. The poor fellow sank to the deck all in a heap, without a groan, without a quiver of the body, and I sprang to the wheel just in time to save the schooner from broaching-to.

"Anyone hurt there, for'ard?" I shouted; for I saw two or three men stooping as though to help someone.

"Yes, sir," answered one of the men; "poor Tom Parsons have had his chest tore open, and I doubt it's all over with him!"

"You must avenge him, then," I shouted back. "Load again, and give it her between wind and water if you can."

They were already reloading the gun, even as I spoke, and a minute later the piece again rang out, the shot striking the brigantine's covering-board fair and square, close to her midship port, and making the splinters fly in fine style. We were now so close to her that we could see that her decks seemed to be full of men, and I thought I heard a shriek as our shot struck. Her reply was almost instantaneous, her whole starboard broadside being let fly as she shot into the wind in stays; and once more the shot—*five* nine-pounders—came crashing in through our bulwarks, filling the air with a perfect storm of splinters, but happily hurting no one but myself. A large jagged splinter struck me in the left shoulder, lacerating the flesh rather badly; but one of the men sprang to my assistance and quickly bound it up.

"Up helm, my man, and let her go off until our starboard broadside bears," said I to the man who now relieved me at the wheel, adding in a shout to the crew—

"Stand by your starboard guns, and fire as they come to bear upon her!"

Bang! bang! bang! Our modest broadside of *three* six-pounders spoke out almost simultaneously. I did not see the shot strike anywhere, but almost immediately afterwards down came her maintopmast and the peak of her mainsail. Her mainmasthead had been shot away, and the *Dolores* at least was safe; for the pirates, having lost their after sail, would now be compelled to make a running fight of it before the wind, which would enable

Christie to haul his wind and get out of danger. Our men raised a cheer at their lucky shot, and I, determined not to throw away the least advantage, gave orders to port the helm and bring the schooner to the wind on the starboard tack, so getting the weather-gage of the brigantine. As we rounded-to our antagonist fell off, the two craft thus presenting their larboard broadsides to each other; and, both being ready, we fired at precisely the same moment, the report of the two discharges being so absolutely coincident that I did not know the brigantine had fired until her shot came smashing in through our bulwarks, wounding five men and rendering one of our six-pounders useless by dismounting it. So close were we to each other by this time that before we could load again the brigantine had passed astern of us, and none of our guns would bear upon her or hers upon us. Her crew were doing their utmost to keep her close to the wind, but with the peak of her mainsail down she would not lay any higher than within about eight points; and I determined to take the utmost advantage of her comparatively helpless position while I might, for a lucky shot on her part might make her case ours at any moment. I therefore signed to the helmsman to put down his helm, and at the same moment gave the order—

"Ready about! helm's a-lee!"

The nimble little schooner spun round upon her heel as smartly as a dancing girl, presenting her starboard broadside to the brigantine.

"Stand by your starboard broadside, and fire as your guns bear!" shouted I; and as we swept round almost square athwart our antagonist's stern the six-pounders once more spoke out, one shot striking the stern of her fair amidships and smashing her wheel to pieces, while the other two took her in the larboard quarter at an angle that must have caused them to traverse very nearly three-quarters of the length of her deck before they passed out through her starboard bulwarks.

The brigantine, no longer under the control of her helm, fell off until she was running dead before the wind, when the pirates trimmed their yards square; and a moment later I saw a number of her hands in the fore rigging swarming aloft. The moment that her starboard broadside could be brought to bear upon us she fired; and the next moment our bowsprit and foretopmast both went, the former, with the flying-jib, towing under the bows, while the latter dangled to leeward by its rigging, with the royal towing in the water alongside. Our lads, having by this time reloaded the starboard guns, again fired, hulling the pirate, and then, by my orders, left their guns to clear away the wreck; for, encumbered as we now were, with the jib under the bows and the square canvas hanging over the side, the schooner was gradually coming-to, although her helm was hard a-weather.

This ended the fight, for when I next found time to look at the brigantine she had studding-sail booms rigged out on both sides and her people were busy getting the studding-sails upon her, while the straight wake that she was making showed that they had already contrived to rig up some temporary contrivance for steering her. Seeing this, I at once hove the schooner to, and went to work to repair damages; for, now that I had had the opportunity to discover the stuff of which Señor Morillo was made, it struck me as by no means improbable that the moment he had repaired his damages he would return and attack us afresh.

Altogether the fight had not lasted longer than some eight or ten minutes at the utmost, but during that short time we had lost two men, killed outright, while six—including myself—were wounded, four of them severely. Christie, recognising that his duty was to take care of the prize, had hauled his wind when we passed ahead of him, and was now about a mile to windward, with his main-topsail to the mast; but when he saw that the fight was over he filled away and came booming down to us, sweeping close athwart our stern and heaving-to close to leeward of us. As he bore down upon us I saw him in the mizzen rigging, speaking-trumpet in hand; and when he was within hailing distance he hailed to ask if he could be of any assistance, adding that one of the passengers professed to be a doctor and had chivalrously offered his services, should they be required. This was good news to me indeed, for, being a small craft, we carried no surgeon, and but for this proffered help our poor wounded lads would have been obliged to trust pretty much to chance and such unskilled help as we could have afforded them among ourselves. I hailed back, expressing my thanks for the offer, and at once sent away a boat for the medico, not caring that Christie should run the risk of sending away a boat's crew out of his own scanty company.

In about ten minutes the boat returned, bringing in her a little, swarthy, burnt-up specimen of a Spaniard, and a most portentous-looking case of surgical instruments. But, although by no means handsome, Señor Pacheco soon proved himself to be both warm-hearted and skilful, ministering to the wounded with the utmost tenderness and with a touch as light and gentle as a woman's. When he had attended to the others I requested him to oblige me so far as to bind up my shoulder afresh, which he at once did, informing me at the same time that it was an exceedingly ugly wound, and that I must be particularly careful lest gangrene should supervene, in which case, if my life could be saved at the expense of my arm, I should have reason to esteem myself exceptionally fortunate. He remained on board, chatting with me for about an hour, after he had coopered me up, and very kindly promised to visit me and his other patients again in the afternoon, if I would send a boat for him; but he declined my invitation to breakfast, upon the plea that he had already taken first breakfast, while it was still too early for the second. He was full of polite compliments and congratulations upon our having beaten off such a desperado as Morillo was known to be, and graphically described the consternation that had prevailed in the cabins of the *Dolores* when the brigantine was identified as the notorious *Guerrilla*.

Contrary to my expectations, and greatly to my relief, the pirates did not return to attack us; and as a measure of precaution,—in case the idea should occur to Morillo later on,—as soon as our damages were repaired I stood to the northward and westward all that day, shaping a fresh course for Morant Point at sunset that evening. The sun went down in a heavy bank of clouds that had been gathering on the western horizon all the afternoon and slowly working up against the wind,— an almost certain precursor of a thunderstorm,—and as the dusk closed down upon us the wind began to grow steadily lighter, until by the end of the first dog-watch the air was so scant as to barely give us steerage-way. The night closed down as dark as a wolf's mouth—so dark, indeed, that, standing at the taffrail, I could only barely, and with the utmost difficulty, trace the position of the main rigging against the intense blackness of the sky. As for the *Dolores*, we lost sight of her altogether, and could only determine her position by the dim, uncertain haze of light that faintly streamed above her high bulwarks from the skylight of her saloon, or by the momentary gleam of a lantern passing along her decks and blinking intermittently through her open ports. This intense darkness lasted only about half an hour, however, when sheet-lightning began to flicker softly low down upon the western horizon, causing the image of the ship—now some two miles astern of us—to stand out for an instant like a cunningly wrought model in luminous bronze against the ebony blackness of the sky behind her.

With the setting in of the lightning the last faint breathing of the wind died away altogether, leaving us and the Spaniard to box the compass in the midst of a glassy calm, the sweltering heat of which was but partially relieved by the flapping of our big mainsail as the schooner heaved languidly upon the low swell that came creeping down upon us from the north-east. The night seemed preternaturally still, the silence which enveloped us being so profound that the noises of the ship—the occasional heavy flap of her canvas, accompanied by a rain-like pattering of reef-points; the creak of the jaws of the mainboom or of the gaff overhead on the mast; the jerk of the mainsheet tautening out suddenly to the heave of the schooner; the kicking of the rudder, and the gurgling swirl of water about it and along the bends—only served to emphasise while they broke in upon it with an irritating harshness altogether disproportionate to their volume. So intense was the silence *outside* the ship that one seemed constrained to listen intently for some sound, some startling cry, to come floating across the glassy water to break it; and the suspense and anxiety of waiting, despite one's better judgment, for such a sound, caused the discordant noises inboard to quickly become acutely distressing. At least such was *my* feeling at the time, a feeling that possibly may have grown out of the increasing smart of my wound, which was now giving me so much pain that I had little hope of getting any sleep that night, especially as the heat below was absolutely stifling.

Gradually—so gradually that its approach was scarcely perceptible—the storm worked its way in our direction, the brighter glimmer and increasing frequency of the sheet-lightning alone indicating that it was nearing us, until just about eight bells in the dog-watch the first faint mutterings of distant thunder became audible, while the vast piles of sooty cloud that overhung us seemed momentarily to assume new and more menacing shapes, as the now almost continuous quivering of the lightning revealed them to us. Anon, low down in the western sky there flashed out a vivid, sun-bright stream of fire that, distant as it was, lighted up the whole sea from horizon to horizon, tipping the ridges of the swell with twisted lines of gold, and transfiguring the distant *Dolores* into a picture of indescribable, fairy-like beauty, as it brought sharply into momentary distinctness every sail and spar and delicate web of rigging tracery. A low, deep rumble of thunder followed, which was quickly succeeded by another flash, nearer and more dazzlingly brilliant than the first; and now the storm seemed to gather apace, the lightning-flashes following each other so rapidly that very soon the booming rumble of the thunder became continuous, as did the blaze of the sheet-lightning, which was now flickering among the clouds in half a dozen places at once, bringing out into powerful relief their titanic masses, weirdly changing shapes, and varied hues, and converting the erstwhile cimmerian darkness into a quivering, supernatural light, that caused the ocean to glow like molten steel, and revealed every object belonging to the ship as distinctly as though it had been illuminated by a port-fire. So vivid and continuous was the light that I not only distinctly saw the fin of a shark fully half a mile distant, but was also able to watch his leisurely progress until he had increased his distance so greatly as to be no longer distinguishable. The continuous quivering flash of the sheet-lightning among the clouds afforded, of itself, a superbly magnificent spectacle, but the beauty of the display was soon still further increased by a wonderfully rapid coruscating discharge of fork-lightning between cloud and cloud, as though the fleecy giants were warring with each other and exchanging broadsides of jagged, white-hot steel; the thunder that accompanied the discharge giving forth a fierce crackling sound far more closely resembling that of an irregular volley of musketry than it did the deep, hollow, booming crash that followed the spark-like stream of fire that lanced downward from cloud to ocean.

A few minutes more and the storm was right overhead, with the lightning hissing and flashing all about us, and the thunder crackling and crashing and booming aloft with a vehement intensity of sound that came near to being terrifying. The whole atmosphere seemed to be aflame, and the noise was that of a universe in process of disruption.

Suddenly the schooner seemed to be enveloped in a vast sheet of flame, at the same instant that an ear-splitting crash of thunder resounded about us; there was a violent concussion; and when, a few seconds later, I recovered from the stunning and stupefying effect of that terrific thunderclap, it was to become aware that the foremast was over the side, and the stump of it fiercely ablaze. There was no necessity to pipe all hands, for the watch below now came tumbling up on deck, alarmed at the shock; and in a few minutes we had the buckets passing along. Fortunately we were able to effectively attack the fire before it had taken any very firm hold, and a quarter of an hour of hard work saw the flames extinguished; but it was a narrow escape for the schooner and all hands of us. The most serious part of it was the loss of our foremast, which completely disabled us for the moment. We went to work, however, to save the sails, yards, rigging, and so on, attached to the shivered mast; and before morning we had got a jury-lowermast on end and secured, by which time the storm had cleared away, the wind had sprung up again, and the *Dolores* had borne down and taken us in tow. Fortunately the wind was fair for us, and it held; and, still more fortunately, no enemy hove in sight to take advantage of our crippled condition. We consequently arrived safely in Port Royal harbour, in due course, on the eighth day after the occurrence of the accident, and forthwith received our full share of congratulations and condolences from all and sundry, from the admiral downward ; the congratulations, of course, being upon our good luck in having effected the capture of so valuable a prize as the *Dolores*, while the condolences were offered pretty equally upon our having met with the accident, and our having failed to capture Morillo and his wonderful brigantine.

# CHAPTER X

## SEÑOR JOSÉ GARCIA

MEANWHILE, my wounded shoulder had been giving me a great deal of trouble, becoming very inflamed, and refusing to heal; so that upon my arrival in Port Royal I was compelled to at once go into the hospital, where for a whole week it remained an open question whether it would not be necessary to amputate the arm. Fortunately for me, the head surgeon—Sandy M'Alister—was a wonderfully clever fellow, of infinite patience and inflexible determination; and, having expressed the opinion that the limb could be saved, he brought all the skill and knowledge of which he was possessed to the task of saving it, with the result that, in the end, he was successful. But it meant for me three weeks in the hospital, at the end of which time I was discharged, not as cured, but as in a fair way to be, provided that I took the utmost care of myself and strictly adhered to the regimen which the worthy M'Alister prescribed for me.

By the time that I was free of the hospital the saucy little *Tern* was beginning, under the hands of the repairers, to look something like her old self again, and I was kept busy from morning to night attending to a hundred and one details connected with her refit. Nevertheless I found time to present myself for examination, and, having passed with flying colours, next day found myself a full-fledged lieutenant, thanks to the very kindly interest taken in me by my genial old friend the admiral. To that same kindly interest I was also indebted for the friendly overtures made by, and the hospitable invitations without number received from, the planters and other persons of importance belonging to the island; but I had my duty to attend to and my wound to think of, and I therefore very sparingly accepted the invitations that came pouring in upon me. Nevertheless I made many new friends, and enjoyed my short spell ashore amazingly.

The admiral was, as I have already said, particularly kind to me in every way, and in nothing more so than in the unstinting commendation which he bestowed upon my conduct during my first brief cruise in the *Tern*. Yet, despite all this, it was not difficult for me to perceive that the reflection that Morillo and his gang were still at large greatly nettled him, and that I could not find a surer way to his continued favour than by finding and capturing or destroying the audacious pirate.

Accordingly I made what inquiries I could relating

to the whereabouts of the fellow's headquarters, and also instructed Black Peter to try his luck in the same direction; but, up to within twenty-four hours of the time when the schooner would again be ready for sea, neither of us had met with the slightest success. When, however, the twenty-four hours had dwindled down to ten, I received the welcome intimation that Black Peter had at length contrived to get upon Morillo's trail. The information was brought to me by Black Peter himself, who, having secured an afternoon's liberty, which he broke by coming aboard about ten-thirty instead of at six o'clock p.m., presented himself—considerably the worse for liquor, I regret to say—at my cabin door, beaming hilariously all over his sable countenance as he stuttered—

"We-e-ll, M-mistah Cour'-nay, I g-got him a' las', sah!"

"Got who, you black rascal? And what do you mean, sir, by breaking your leave, and then presenting yourself in this disgraceful condition? You are drunk, sir; too drunk to stand steadily, too drunk to speak plainly; and I should only be giving you your deserts if I were to turn you over to the master-at-arms. What have you to say for yourself, eh, sir?" I fiercely demanded.

"Wha' have I to s-s-say for 'shelf, Mistah C-Cour'-nay? Ha! ha! I has p-plenty to s-s-shay. Why, sah, I—I—I've *g-got* him, sah!"

"Got who, you villain? Got who?" I reiterated.

"Why—why—M-M-Mor—the pirate!" blurted Peter,

finding himself unable to successfully pronounce Morillo's name.

"Do you mean to say that you have succeeded in obtaining news of Morillo, Peter?" I demanded eagerly, my anger at the fellow's condition at once giving way to the keenest curiosity.

"I—just dat, sah; no less," answered Peter, nodding his head as he leered at me with a drunken look of preternatural smartness.

"Then," said I, "go and get somebody to pump cold water upon your head until you are sober, after which you may come back here and tell me all about it. And if you fail to give a good account of yourself, stand clear, my man! I fancy a taste of the cat will do you no harm."

Peter regarded me with horror for a moment as the sinister meaning of this threat dawned upon his muddled senses; then he drew himself up to his full height, saluted with drunken gravity, and vanished into the outer darkness, as he stumblingly made his way up the companion ladder and for'ard.

About a quarter of an hour later he returned, comparatively sober, and, saluting again, stood in the doorway, waiting for me to question him.

"So there you are again, eh?" remarked I. "Very well. Now, Peter, if you are sober enough to speak plainly, I should like to know what you meant by saying that you have 'got' Morillo, the pirate. Do you mean that you have actually found and *captured* the fellow?"

"Well, no, Mistah Courtenay, I don't dissactly mean that; no such luck, sah! But I'se got de next best t'ing, sah; I'se got a man who says he knows where Morillo's to be foun'," answered Peter.

"Um! well that is better than nothing—if your friend is to be trusted," said I. "Who is he, and where did you run athwart him?"

"He ain't no friend ob mine," answered Peter, virtuously indignant at so insulting an insinuation; "he's jus' a yaller man—a half-breed—dat I met at a rum shop up in Kingston. I heard him mention Morillo's name, so I jined him in a bottle ob rum,—*which I paid for out ob my own pocket*, Mistah Courtenay,—and axed him some questions. He wouldn't say much, but he kep' on boastin' dat he knew where Morillo could be found any time—excep' when he was at sea. So I made him drunk wid my rum, Mistah Courtenay, and den brought him aboard here instead ob puttin' him aboard his own footy little felucca in Kingston harbour."

"I see. And where is the fellow now, Peter?" inquired I.

"Where is he now, sah?" repeated Peter. "Why, sah, he is on deck, comfortably asleep between two ob de guns, where I put him when I come aboard."

"Very good, Peter; I begin to think you were not so very drunk after all," answered I, well pleased. "But it will not do to leave him on deck all night," I continued; "he will get sober, and give us the slip. So, to make quite sure of him, stow him away down below, and have a set of irons clapped on him. When we are fairly at sea to-morrow, I will have him up on deck, and see what can be made of him. Meanwhile, Peter, he is your prisoner, remember, and I shall hold you responsible for him. Now go and turn in, and beware how you appear before me drunk again."

Early next morning I presented myself at the admiral's office, timing myself so as to catch the old gentleman immediately upon his arrival from Kingston, when, having reported the *Tern* as ready for sea, I received my orders to sail forthwith, and also written instructions in reference to the especial object of my cruise. These, I was by no means surprised to find, indicated that, while doing my utmost to harass the enemy, I was to devote myself especially to the task of hunting down and cutting short the career of Morillo the pirate and his gang of cut-throats.

We weighed shortly before noon, beating out against a sea breeze that roared through our rigging with the strength of half a gale; and when we were fairly clear of the shoals I gave orders for Black Peter's prisoner of the previous night to be brought on deck. A minute or two later the fellow—a half-caste Spanish negro—stood before me; and when I beheld what manner of man he was, I could readily believe him to be on terms of friendly intimacy not only with Morillo but with all the human scum of the Caribbean. The rascal presented a not altogether unpicturesque figure, as he stood in the brilliant sunlight, poising himself with the careless, easy grace of the practised seaman upon the heaving, lurching deck of the plunging schooner; for he was attired in a white shirt, with broad falling collar loosely confined at the neck by a black silk handkerchief, blue dungaree trousers rolled up to the knee and secured round the waist by a knotted crimson silk sash, and his head was enfolded in a similar sash, the fringed ends of which drooped upon his left shoulder. But it was the fellow's countenance that riveted my attention despite myself; it was of itself ugly enough to have commanded attention anywhere, but to its natural ugliness there was added the further repulsiveness of expression that bespoke a character notable alike for low, unscrupulous cunning and the most ferocious cruelty. But for the fact that he had been encountered upon ground whereon neither Morillo nor any of his gang would have dared to show themselves, I could readily have believed that he not only had a pretty intimate knowledge of the movements and haunts of the pirates, but that he was probably a distinguished member of the gang.

"Well, my fine fellow, pray what may your name be?" I demanded in English, as he was led up and halted before me.

"Too mosh me no speakee Anglish!" he promptly replied, shrugging his shoulders until they touched the great gold rings that adorned the lobes of his ears, and spreading out his hands, palms upward, toward me.

"What *do* you speak, then?" I demanded, still in English, for somehow I did not for a moment believe the rascal's statement.

"Me Español," he answered, with another shrug and flourish of his hands.

"Good, then!" remarked I, in Spanish; "I will endeavour to converse with you in your own tongue. What is your name?"

"I am called José Garcia, señor," he answered.

"And you were born—?" I continued interrogatively.

"In the city of Havana, thirty-two years ago, señor," was the reply.

"Then if you are a Spaniard—and consequently an enemy of Great Britain—what were you doing in Kingston?" I demanded.

"Ah no, señor," he exclaimed protestingly; "I am no enemy of Great Britain, although born a Spaniard. I have lived in Jamaica for the last fifteen years, earning my living as a fisherman."

"Fifteen years!" I repeated. "Strange that you should have lived so long among English-speaking people without acquiring some knowledge of their language; and still more strange that you should have spoken English last night in the grog shop in the presence and hearing of my steward! How do you account for so very singular a circumstance as that?"

The fellow was so completely taken aback that for a few seconds he could find no reply. Then, seemingly convinced that further deception was useless, he suddenly gave in, exclaiming, in excellent English—

"Ah, sir, forgive me; I have been lying to you!"

"With what purpose?" I demanded.

"Instinct, perhaps," he answered, with a short, uneasy laugh. "The moment I was brought on deck I recognised that I was aboard a British ship-of-war, and I smelt danger."

"Ah," I remarked, "you afford another illustration of the adage that 'a guilty conscience needs no accuser.' What have you been doing that you should 'smell' danger upon finding yourself aboard a British man-o'-war?"

"I have been doing nothing; but I feared that you intended to impress me," answered the fellow.

"So I am," returned I, "but not for long, if you behave yourself. And when you have rendered the service which I require of you, you shall be richly rewarded, according as you serve me faithfully or otherwise."

"And—and—what is this service, sir?" demanded he, with some slight uneasiness of manner.

"You last night boasted that you could at any time find Morillo—unless he happened to be at sea," I said. "Now, I want to find Morillo. Tell me where I may meet with him, and you shall receive fifty pounds within an hour of the moment when I shall have carried his ship a prize into Port Royal harbour."

"Morillo? who is Morillo?" he demanded, trying unsuccessfully to assume an air of ignorance and indifference at the mention of the name.

"He is the pirate of whom you were speaking last night," I answered sharply, for I suspected that he was about to attempt further deception with me.

"I must have been drunk indeed to talk about a man of whom I have never heard," he exclaimed, with a hollow pretence at a laugh.

"Do you mean to tell me that you do not know Morillo, or anything about him?" I demanded angrily. "Now, take time to consider your answer. I want the truth, and the truth I am determined to have by one means or another. You have attempted to deceive me once, beware how you make such an attempt a second time. Now, what do you know of Morillo the pirate?"

"Nothing!" the fellow answered sullenly. But there was a shrinking of himself together, and a sudden grey pallor of the lips, that told how severe a tax upon his courage it was—under the circumstances—to utter the lie.

"Think again!" I said, pulling out my watch. "I will give you five minutes in which to overhaul your memory. If by the end of that time you fail I must endeavour to find means to refresh it."

"What will you do?" demanded the fellow, with a

scowl that entirely failed to conceal the trepidation which my remark had caused him.

I made no reply whatever, but rose, walked to the binnacle, took a squint at the compass, and then a long look aloft as I turned over in my mind the idea that had suggested itself to me, asking myself whether I should be justified in carrying it into action. I believed I now pretty well understood the kind of man I had to deal with; I took him to be a treacherous, unscrupulous, lying scoundrel, and a coward withal,—as indeed such people generally are,—and it was his cowardice that I proposed to play upon in order to extort from him the information I desired to obtain. In a word, my plan was to seize him up and threaten to flog him if he refused to speak. My only difficulty arose from a doubt as to how I ought to proceed in the event of my threat failing to effect the desired result. Should I be justified in actually carrying my threat into execution? For, after all, the fellow really might *not* know anything about Morillo; his remarks to Black Peter on the previous night might be nothing more than boastful lies. And if they were, all the flogging I might give him could not make him tell that of which he had no knowledge. But somehow I had a conviction that he *could* tell me a great deal that I should be glad to know, if he only chose; so I finally decided that if he continued contumacious I would risk giving him a stroke or two, being guided in my after conduct by his behaviour under the lash.

By the time that I had fully arrived at this resolution the five minutes' grace had expired, and I returned to where the fellow still stood, guarded by a Jack with drawn cutlass.

"Well," I demanded, "which is it to be? Will you speak freely, or must I compel you?"

"I have nothing to say; and I demand to know by what authority I have been kidnapped and brought aboard this accursed schooner?" was the reply.

"Did I not tell you a few minutes ago that you are impressed?" I answered. "You have been brought aboard here in order that you may render me a service, which I am convinced you *can* render if you will. When that service has been faithfully performed, I will not only set you free again but I will also handsomely reward you. You know what the service is that I require of you. Once more, will you or will you not render it?"

"I repeat that I have nothing to say. Put me in irons again if you choose; you cannot make a man tell that which he does not know," answered Garcia; and as he spoke he turned away, seeming to consider that the dialogue was at an end.

"Here, not so fast, my joker," interrupted the seaman who had the fellow in charge, seizing Garcia unceremoniously by the back of the neck and twisting him round until he faced me again, "it ain't good manners, sonny, to turn your back upon your superiors until they tells you that they've done with you, and that you can go."

The half-breed turned upon his custodian with a snarl, and a drawing back of his upper lip that exposed a whole row of yellow fangs, while his hand went, as from long habit, to his girdle, as though in quest of a knife; but the look of contemptuous amusement with which the sailor regarded him cowed the fellow, and he again faced me, meekly enough.

"Now," said I, "your little fit of petulance being over, let me ask you once more, and for the last time, will you or will you not afford me the information I require?"

"No, Señor Englishman, I will *not*! I am a Spaniard and Morillo is a Spaniard, and nothing you can do shall induce me to betray a fellow-countryman! Is that plain enough for you?"

"Quite," I answered, "and almost as satisfactory as though you had replied to my question. You have as good as admitted that you can, if you choose, tell me what I want to know; now it remains for me to see whether there are any means of compelling you to speak. Take him away for'ard, and keep a sharp eye upon him," I continued, to the sailor who had him in charge. "And as you go pass the word for the carpenter to rig the grating. Perhaps a taste of the cat may loosen this gentleman's tongue."

"The cat?" exclaimed the half-breed, wheeling suddenly round as he was being led away; "do you mean that you are going to flog me?"

"Certainly, unless you choose to speak of your own free will," answered I.

"Very well, then, I *will* speak; and your blood be on your own head!" he hissed through his clenched teeth. "I will direct you how to find Morillo, and when you have found him he will amply avenge your insult to me, and your audacity in seeking him; he will make your life such an unendurable torment to you that you will pray him, with tears of blood, to put you out of your misery. And I shall be there to see you suffer, and to laugh in your face as he refuses to grant you the boon of a speedy death."

"That is all right," I answered cheerfully, "I must take the risk of the fate you have so powerfully suggested. And now, that matter being disposed of, I shall be glad to hear from you how I am to find your friend."

The fellow regarded me in stupid surprise for a moment, as though he could not understand his failure to terrify me by his vaguely awful threat; then, with a gesture that I interpreted as indicative of his final abandonment of me to the destruction that I seemed determined to court, he said—

"Do you know anything of the Grenadines, señor?"

"No," I answered, "nothing, except that they exist, and that they form a practically unbroken chain of islets stretching between the islands of St. Vincent and Grenada."

"That is so," he assented. "One of the most important of these islets is situate about thirteen miles to the northward of Grenada, and is called Cariacou. It is supposed to be uninhabited, but it is nothing of the kind; Morillo has taken possession of it, and established quite a little settlement upon it. There is a snug harbour at its south-western extremity, affording perfect shelter and concealment for his brigantine, and all round the shore of the harbour he has built storehouses and residences for himself and his people. I pray only that he may be at home to give you a fitting reception."

"I am much obliged for your kind wish," I replied drily. "And now, just one question more—is this harbour of which you speak difficult of access? Are there any rocks or shoals at its entrance or inside?"

"No, none whatever; it can safely be entered on the darkest night," was the answer.

"Good," I returned; "that will do for the present, Señor Garcia, and many thanks for your information. You will observe that I have accepted as true every word that you have spoken; but I should like you to think everything over again, and satisfy yourself that you have made no mistake. Because I warn you that if you have *you will be shot on the instant.* You may go!"

He was forthwith marched away and placed in close confinement below,—for my interview with him had convinced me that the fellow was as malignantly spiteful as a snake, and would willingly destroy the ship and all hands if an opportunity were afforded him,—after which I retired to my cabin, got out the chart, and set the course for the island of Cariacou, a course which we could just comfortably lay with yards braced taut against the lee rigging and all sheets well flattened in. The trade wind was blowing fresh enough to compel us to furl our topgallant sail, but it was steady, and under a whole topsail and mainsail the little hooker drove ahead over the long, regular ridges of swell at a good, honest, nine-knot pace hour after hour, as steadily as the chronometer itself. We sighted the island, some sixteen miles distant, on the evening of our fourth day out, and I at once shortened sail and hove-to, in order that I might carry out a little plan which I had concocted during our run across.

## CHAPTER XI

### CARIACOU—AND AFTERWARD

AS soon as the darkness had closed down sufficiently to conceal our movements, I filled away again upon the schooner, and stood in until we were within two miles of the southern extremity of the island,—which also forms the southern headland of the harbour mentioned by Garcia,—when, having run well in behind the head, I again hove-to and, launching the dinghy, proceeded toward the harbour's mouth; my crew being two men who, like myself, were armed to the teeth.

We pulled in with muffled oars, and in due time arrived within a stone's throw of the shore. The coast here proved to be precipitous and rocky, the swell which set round the southern extremity of the island breaking with great violence upon the shore and rendering landing absolutely impossible; moreover, the night was so dark that—although in every other respect admirably suited for my purpose—it was impossible to clearly see where we were going, and two or three times we inadvertently got so close to the rocks that we narrowly and with the utmost difficulty avoided being dashed upon them. At length, however, we rounded the southernmost head and entered the harbour, and almost immediately afterwards made out a narrow strip of sandy beach, upon which I landed without difficulty, leaving the two men to look after the dinghy and lay off a few yards from the shore, ready to pull in again and take me aboard at a moment's notice if necessary.

Having landed, I ascended a rather steep, grassy slope, some seventy or eighty feet high, and stood to look about me. The harbour was quite a spacious affair, the entrance being about half a mile wide, while the harbour itself seemed—so far as I could make out in the darkness—to be quite two miles long. The general shape of this inlet immediately suggested to me the conviction that if, as Garcia had informed me, Morillo really had established his headquarters here, he would be almost certain to have constructed a couple of batteries—one on each headland —to defend the place; and I at once set about the task of ascertaining how far my conjecture might happen to be correct. Toward the eastward from where I had halted the land continued to rise in a sort of ridge, culminating in what had the appearance of a knoll, and it struck me that, if a battery really existed on that side of the harbour, I ought to find it not far from this spot. I accordingly wended my way toward it as best I could, forcing a passage for myself through the grass and scrub, with a most unpleasant conviction that I might at any moment place my hand or foot upon a venomous snake or reptile of some sort; and finally, after about twenty minutes of most unpleasant scrambling, found myself alongside the "knoll," which, as I had more than half suspected, now proved to be nothing less than a rough earthwork, mounting four thirty-two pounders.

My devious path had brought me to the face of the battery, so I had to clamber up the steep face of the slope before I could get a view of the interior. This I did, entering the battery through one of the embrasures, when I found myself standing upon a level platform constituting the floor of the battery. Keeping carefully within the deep shadow of the gun, and crouching down upon my hands and knees, I at once proceeded to reconnoitre the place, and presently made out a couple of huts, the smaller of which I concluded must be the magazine, while the larger probably accommodated the garrison. Both were in utter darkness, however, and my first impression was that they were untenanted; but, to make quite certain, I crept very softly up to the larger building, and, finding a closed door, listened intently at it. For a few seconds I heard nothing save the sough of the night breeze through the branches of some cotton-wood trees that grew close at hand, but presently I detected a sound of snoring in the interior, which, as I listened, grew momentarily more distinct and unmistakable. The sounds certainly emanated from more than one sleeper; I thought that there were probably at least three or four of them at work, but my hearing was not quite keen enough to enable me to accurately differentiate the sounds and thus arrive at the correct number of those who emitted them. They were, however, sound asleep, and therefore not likely to be disturbed by a slight noise. Moreover, the hut was well to windward, and the sough and swish of the wind through the cotton-woods seemed powerful enough to drown such slight sounds as I might be likely to make; so I stole softly across the open area to the nearest gun, which I at once proceeded to carefully spike with the aid of some nails and a leather-covered hammer with which I had provided myself. Despite the deadening effect of the leather the hammer still made a distinct "clink," which to my ears sounded loud enough to wake the dead; but a few seconds' anxious work sufficed to effectually spike the first gun, and as nobody appeared to have heard me, I then proceeded to spike the next, and the next, until I had rendered all four of them harmless. This done, I slipped out of the same embrasure by which I had entered, and successfully made my way back to the beach and to the spot off which the dinghy lay awaiting me.

The presence of a battery on the south head of the harbour entrance convinced me that there must also be a similar structure on the north head. As soon, therefore, as I found myself once more aboard the dinghy, I headed her straight across the mouth, reaching the northern side in about twenty minutes. Half an hour's search enabled me to find the battery which I was looking for,—which proved to be a pretty exact counterpart of the one I had already visited,—and here again I succeeded in spiking all four of the guns without discovery. This I regarded as a fairly successful night's work; so, as we should have to be stirring pretty early in the morning, I now returned to the schooner, and, having hove her to with her head off shore, turned in and had a good night's rest.

At daybreak on the following morning I was called by Black Peter, and within ten miuntes I was on deck. We were then some eight miles off the land, with the schooner heading to the eastward; but we at once wore round and bore straight away for the harbour's mouth, clearing for action and making all our arrangements as we went.

An hour's run, with the wind well over our starboard quarter, brought us off the mouth of the harbour, which we at once entered; and as soon as we were fairly inside, the schooner was hove-to, and two boats were lowered, each carrying eleven men armed to the teeth, in addition to the officer in command. One of the boats was commanded by Christie and the other by Lindsay; and their mission was to capture the two batteries commanding the harbour's mouth, and blow them up before the spiked cannon could be again rendered serviceable. I brought the telescope to bear upon the batteries as soon as we were far enough inside the harbour to get a sight of them, and was amused to observe that there was a terrible commotion going on in both. Our presence had been promptly discovered, and the first attempt to open fire upon us had resulted in the discovery that their guns were all spiked. Of course it was by no means an easy matter to estimate the strength of the garrisons of these batteries, but I calculated that it would probably total up to about thirty men to each battery; and as they would be nearly or quite all Spaniards, I felt that the boats' crews which I had sent away would be quite strong enough to satisfactorily account for them. Nor was I disappointed; for although the pirates opened a brisk musketry fire upon our lads the moment that they were fairly within range, the latter simply swarmed up the hill and carried the two batteries with a rush, the pirates retreating by the rear as the *Terns* clambered in through the embrasures. The moment that the boats shoved off from the schooner's side I saw that the spirit of emulation had seized upon the two crews, for they both went away at a racing pace, and their actions throughout were evidently inspired by this same spirit; the result of which was that the two batteries were destroyed within five minutes of each other, while the whole affair, from the moment when the boats shoved off to the moment when they arrived alongside again, was accomplished within an hour and a quarter, and that, too, without any loss whatever on our side, or even a wound severe enough to disable the recipient. The pirates were less fortunate, their loss in the two batteries amounting to five killed, and at least seven wounded severely enough to render them incapable of escaping. These seven were brought on board by our lads, and secured below immediately upon their arrival.

Meanwhile I had not been idle, for while the boats were away I had employed my time in making, with the aid of the telescope, a most careful inspection of this piratical stronghold; and I was obliged to admit to myself that it would be difficult to imagine—and still more difficult to find—a spot more perfectly adapted in every way for its purpose. The harbour itself was spacious enough to hold a fleet, and almost completely land-locked, so that, once inside, a ship was perfectly concealed; while the fact that the opening faced in a south-westerly direction rendered it absolutely safe in all weathers. And, so far as enemies were concerned, the two batteries at the harbour's mouth were so admirably placed that they *ought* to have proved amply sufficient for the defence of the place; and no doubt they *would* have so proved in other hands, or had a proper lookout been kept. That they had fallen so easily to us was the fault, not of Morillo, but of the man whom he had left in command.

At the bottom of the bay or inlet—for it partook of the nature of the latter rather than of the former — lay the settlement that Morillo had established, consisting of no less than seventeen buildings. There was also a small wharf, with a brig lying alongside it.

The moment that the boats arrived alongside I ordered the men out of them, and had them dropped astern, when sail was made and we stood down toward the settlement, with our ensign flying at the gaff-end. As we drew near I was able to make out that here too our presence was productive of a tremendous amount of excitement; and presently fire was opened upon us from a battery of six nine-pounders that had been constructed on the rising ground immediately to the rear of the wharf, while the black flag was boldly run up on a flagstaff close at hand. It did not suit my purpose, however, to engage in a running fight; I therefore bore down upon the brig—discharging our port broadside at the battery when we were within pistol-shot of it—and, running alongside, grapnelled her. This done, every man Jack of us swarmed ashore, Lindsay holding the wharf with a dozen of our lads, while Christie and I, with the remainder of the crew, made a rush for the battery and took it. Ten minutes sufficed us to spike the guns and blow up the magazine, which done, we found ourselves masters of the whole place, the inhabitants having taken to flight the moment that this third battery fell into our hands.

We now proceeded to make a leisurely inspection of the place, with the result that we discovered it to be quite a miniature dockyard, with storehouses, mast-houses, rigging and sail-lofts all complete; in fact, there was every possible convenience for repairing and refitting a ship. Nor was this all; there was also a large magazine full of ammunition, quite an armoury of muskets, pistols, and cutlasses, and several dismounted guns, ranging from six-pounders to thirty-two pound carronades; while the storehouses were well stocked with provisions and stores of every possible description. One large building immediately facing the wharf was apparently used as a receptacle for plunder, for we found several bales of stuff that had evidently formed part of a cargo, or cargoes, but there was surprisingly little of it, which was accounted for, later on, by the discovery that the brig was full of plunder to the hatches. In addition to the buildings which were in use as stores, there were two most comfortably fitted up as barracks, while at the back of the settlement and well up the side of the hill stood a little group of seven handsome timber dwelling-houses, each standing in its own garden and nestling among the lofty trees that clothed the hillside.

Having secured complete possession of the place, my first care was to have the small amount of plunder that lay in the storehouse, and the guns, conveyed on board the *Tern* and sent down her main hatchway. This job took us about two hours, during which a few shots were occasionally fired at us from the woods; but as the bullets all fell short, we did not trouble ourselves to go in pursuit of the individuals who were firing upon us. Our next act was to blow up the magazine, thus destroying the whole of the pirates' stock of ammunition; and when this had been successfully accomplished, we went systematically to work, and set fire to the whole of the storehouses and barracks, one after the other, until the whole place was in flames. Finally, we turned our attention to the seven dwelling-houses on the hillside. These proved, to our astonishment, to be most elegantly and sumptuously furnished in every respect, the only peculiarity noticeable being a lack of uniformity among the articles contained in some of the houses, plainly showing that they had been gathered together at different times and from different places. Evidences of female influence were abundantly present in all these houses, from which we assumed that they formed the abode of Morillo and his most important subordinates during their short sojourns in port. The six largest of these buildings we set fire to, leaving the seventh as a refuge for the unfortunate women, who were doubtless concealed at no great distance in the adjacent woods.

The burning of these houses completed the destruction of the settlement, which was accomplished absolutely without casualties of any kind on our side. We waited until the houses were well ablaze, and then retreated in good order to the harbour, a few shots being fired at us here and there from ambush as we went; but as we were well out of range I took no notice of them, and in due time we arrived once more on the wharf.

Our next business was to take possession of the brig, which we did forthwith, Christie, with eight hands, going on board her as a prize crew. She was a beamy, bluff-bowed, motherly old craft named the *Three Sisters*, hailing out of Port-of-Spain, and was evidently British built, her whole appearance being that of a sober, honest, slow-going trader, such as one constantly meets with, doing business among the islands. Her hold, however, was full of booty; and I conjectured that Morillo had, through his agents, purchased her in a perfectly straightforward manner for use in the conveyance of booty from Cariacou to such ports as afforded opportunity for its disposal without the asking of too many inconvenient questions.

It was the work of but a few minutes for the prize crew to transfer their few belongings from the schooner to the brig; and, this done, we got both craft under way and stood out to sea—the brig under every stitch of canvas that she could show to the breeze, while the schooner, under topsail, foresail, and jib, had to heave-to at frequent intervals to wait for her.

My first intention was to send the brig to Port Royal in charge of the prize crew alone, remaining off the island in the *Tern* until Morillo should appear—as he would be certain to do, sooner or later—in his brigantine. A little reflection, however, caused me to alter my plans and to determine upon escorting the *Three Sisters* to her destination, lest she should haply encounter Morillo on the way, in which case the fate of her defenceless prize crew would probably be too dreadful to bear thinking about. As soon, therefore, as we were clear of the harbour I set the course for Jamaica, and away we both went, cheek by jowl, the brig—with a roaring breeze over her starboard quarter—reeling off her six and a half knots per hour with as much fuss and splutter as though she were going fifteen!

For the first two days nothing of any importance occurred. On the third night out from Cariacou, however, —or, to be strictly accurate, about two o'clock in the morning,—it being my watch on deck, the night dark and somewhat overcast, two sails were sighted on our starboard bow, heading to the eastward on the port tack, and steering a course which would bring them close to us. One of them was a craft of considerable size, the other a small vessel; and from the moment that these two facts became apparent, I made up my mind that one was the prize of the other, though which of the two was the captor, there was just then no means of ascertaining. The smaller craft was perhaps a privateer, and the big one her prize; or —quite as likely—the big craft might be a frigate, and the small craft her prize. In either case, however, it behoved me to be very careful; for one of the two was almost certain to be an enemy, and if she happened to be also the captor of the other it was more than probable she would tackle us. From the moment, therefore, when we first sighted them, I never allowed the night glass to be off them for more than a few seconds at a time.

When first discovered, they were hull down, and only just distinguishable in the darkness as two vague blots of black against the lowering gloom of the night sky; but the trade wind was piping up rather stronger than usual that night, while we and the strangers were approaching each other on a nearly straight line. We consequently closed each other rapidly, and within about twenty minutes from the moment of their discovery we were able to make out that one of the twain was a full-rigged ship, while the other seemed to be a large brigantine; and a few minutes later I discovered that the ship was showing a much broader spread of canvas than the brigantine, thus proving the latter to be the faster craft of the two. It was scarcely likely, therefore, that the ship was a frigate; and if not that, she must be a merchantman, and doubtless the prize of the brigantine.

At this point, the question suggested itself to me: Might not the brigantine be Morillo's craft? She appeared to be about the same size, so far as it was possible to distinguish in the darkness; and if so, it would fully account for the boldness with which she held on upon her course, instead of heaving about and endeavouring to avoid a possible enemy—for doubtless they had made us out almost if not quite at the same time as we had discovered them. I most fervently hoped it might be as I surmised, for, if so, I should have the fellow at advantage, inasmuch as he would doubtless have put a fairly strong prize crew on board the ship, which would proportionately weaken his own crew. Full of the hope that this Ishmael of the sea might be about to place himself within my power, I caused all hands to be called, and, having first made sail, sent them to quarters, the gunner at the same time descending to the magazine and sending up a plentiful supply of powder and shot. By the time that we were ready, the brigantine and her consort had neared us to within a couple of miles, the two craft closing meanwhile, doubtless for the purpose of communicating instructions. That they were quite prepared to fight aboard the brigantine was perfectly evident, for we could see that her deck was lit up with lanterns, the light of which, shining through her ports, enabled me to ascertain that she mounted six guns of a side. Both craft held their luff, but it was now quite clear that the brigantine was much the faster and more weatherly of the two, she walking away out to windward of the big fellow as though the latter had been at anchor the moment that she made sail in answer to our challenge.

And now ensued a little bit of manœuvring on both sides, with the twofold object of discovering whether the stranger happened to be an enemy, and if so, to secure the weather-gage of him. We had the advantage, however, as we were running free and could haul our wind at any moment; and this advantage I kept by hauling up on the starboard tack and then heaving in stays with the topsail aback, waiting for the brigantine to close; which she presently did, ranging up within biscuit-toss of our lee quarter. She was now so close to us that, despite the darkness, it was quite possible to make out details; and it was with a feeling of mingled disgust and disappointment that I discovered that, whatever she might be, she certainly was not Morillo's beautiful but notorious brigantine.

She was, however, in all probability an enemy,—it seemed to me that, so far as I could make out in the uncertain light of the partially clouded stars, she had a French look about her,—so, with the idea of securing the advantage of the first hail, I sprang upon the rail as she ranged up alongside, and hailed, in Spanish—

"Ho, the brigantine ahoy! What vessel is that?"

"The *Belle Diane*, French privateer. What schooner is that?" came the reply, also in Spanish of the most execrable kind, uttered with an unmistakable French accent.

"His Britannic Majesty's schooner *Tern*, monsieur, to which ship I must request you to surrender, or I shall be under the painful necessity of blowing you out of the water," answered I, firmly persuaded of the policy of rendering oneself as formidable as possible to one's enemy.

But my well-meant endeavour proved to be a signal failure; the enemy was not in this case to be so easily frightened.

"Les Anglais! mille tonneres!" I heard the Frenchman in the brigantine's main rigging exclaim, as he waved his clenched fist in the air. Then he retorted, in what he doubtless believed to be the purest English—

"Vat is dat you say, Monsieur Angleeshman? If I do not surrendaire, you vill blow me out of de vattar? Ha, ha! Sacre! It is *I*, monsieur, who vill blow dat footy leetle schooner of yours into ze sky, if you do not surrendaire yourshelf plus promptement, eh!"

"All right, monsieur; blaze away, then, as soon as you like!" retorted I, in the best attempt at French I could muster. Then, to my own people, who were at quarters—

"Stand by, starboard guns! Wait until she rolls toward us. Now, *fire*!"

Our imposing broadside of three guns rang out at the precise moment when the brigantine rolled heavily toward us, exposing her deck to our fire; and I heard the shot go crashing through her bulwarks to the accompaniment of sundry yells and screams, that told me they had not been altogether ineffective. Almost at the same instant *three* of her guns replied; but their muzzles were so deeply depressed, and she was just then rolling so heavily toward us, that the shot struck the water between her and ourselves, and we neither saw nor felt any more of them. Meanwhile, our square canvas being aback, our antagonist swept rapidly ahead of us; seeing which, I filled upon the schooner and bore up under the brigantine's stern, raking with our port broadside as we crossed her stern, immediately hauling my wind and making a half-board across her stern again to regain my position upon her weather quarter. Our starboard guns were by this time reloaded, and we gave her the three of them, double-shotted, as we recrossed her; and the tremendous clatter, with the howls and shrieks that followed this discharge, showed that we had wrought a considerable amount of execution among the Frenchmen.

"There's *something* gone aboard of him, but what it is I can't make out," exclaimed Lindsay, who was standing close beside me. "Ah!" he continued, "I see what it is now; it is her mainboom that we have shot away. I can see the outer end of it towing overboard. And see, she is paying off; with the loss of their after-sail they can no longer keep their luff!"

It was even as Lindsay had said; we had shot away the brigantine's mainboom, and thus rendered her big, powerful mainsail useless; so that, despite the lee helm that they were giving her, she was gradually falling off, until within a minute or two she was nearly dead before the wind. This placed her almost completely at our mercy, for we were now enabled to sail to and fro athwart her stern, raking her alternately with our port and starboard guns, and with our nine-pounder as well, while she could only reply with two guns which her people had run out through her stern ports. Still, although disabled, she was by no means beaten, her plucky crew keeping up a brisk fire upon us from these two guns until by a lucky broadside we dismounted them both. But even then they would not give in; despite the relentless fire that we continued to pour into them, they contrived after a time to get two more guns into position, with which they renewed their fire upon us as briskly as ever. This sort of thing, however, could not continue for very long; our fire was so hot and our guns were so well aimed, that we fairly drove the plucky fellows from the only two guns that they could bring to bear upon us, and within a couple of minutes of the cessation of their fire, a lantern was waved aboard the brigantine, and someone hailed that they surrendered, while at the same moment all sheets and halliards were let go and her canvas came down by the run, as a further intimation that they had had enough of it.

Upon this we of course at once ceased firing, and ranged up alongside the prize, hailing her that we would send a boat aboard. Then, for the first time, we discovered that both our large boats were so severely damaged that neither of them would float; whereupon Lindsay offered to board the prize in the dinghy, with two hands, and take possession. Accordingly, the little cockle-shell of a craft was dropped over the side, and in less than two minutes my chum hailed to say that he was safely aboard, and that the execution wrought by our fire had been terrible, the brigantine having lost nearly half her crew, both the captain and the chief mate being among the killed. He added that the brigantine's long-boat was undamaged, and that he proposed to hoist her out, with the assistance of the prisoners, and send her to us by the two hands who had manned the dinghy, if we would look out to pick her up in the event of their being unable to bring her alongside. To this I of course agreed; and a quarter of an hour later the boat was safely alongside us, with a prize crew of twelve picked men tumbling themselves and their traps into her.

Meanwhile, what had become of the *Three Sisters* and the big ship? I looked round for them, and behold! there they both were, about half a mile to windward, and bearing down upon us *in company*! "Phew!" thought I, "here is a nice business! While we have been playing the game of hammer and tongs down here, the big ship—doubtless manned by a strong prize crew—has run alongside the old brig and taken her! And yet—can it be so? Christie has eight hands with him, and I believe the fellow would make a stout fight for it before giving in. I cannot understand it; but we shall soon see. If they have captured him we shall have to recapture him, that is all!" Then, turning to the men, who were busy securing the guns and repairing such slight damage as had been inflicted upon our rigging, I said—

"Avast, there, with those guns! Load them again, lads, for we may have to fight once more in a few minutes. Here is the big ship running down upon us, and it looks very much as though she had taken the brig. Fill your topsail, and let draw the headsheets!"

Getting sufficient way upon the schooner, we tacked and stood toward the new-comers, passing close under the stern of the ship, with the intention of hailing her. But before I could get the trumpet to my lips, a figure sprang into the ship's mizzen rigging, and Christie's well-known voice hailed—

"*Tern* ahoy! is Mr. Courtenay aboard?"

"Ay, ay," I answered; "I am here, Mr. Christie. What are you doing aboard there?"

"Why," answered Christie, "I am in charge, you know. Seeing you busy with the brigantine, I thought I might as well try my luck at the same time; so I managed somehow to put the brig alongside this ship, and—and—well, *we just took her.*"

"Well done, Mr. Christie!" I shouted; but before I could get out another word, my voice was drowned in the roaring cheer that the *Terns* gave vent to as they heard the news, told in Christie's usual gentle, drawling tones; and by the time that the cheers had died away the two craft had drawn so far apart that further conversation was, for the moment, impossible.

## CHAPTER XII

I BECOME THE VICTIM OF A VILLAINOUS OUTRAGE

TAKING room, Christie presently hauled to the wind and hove-to; and some ten minutes later he presented himself on board the schooner—brought alongside by the ship's gig, manned by four of the ship's crew—to report his own share in the incidents of the night. From this report I gathered that, like myself, at first he had mistaken the French privateer for Morillo's brigantine, and had also arrived at the conclusion that the ship was a prize of the latter. He had kept a keen watch upon the movements of the schooner until it had become apparent that we intended to attack the supposed pirate, when he at once turned his attention to the ship, with the object of ascertaining whether, with such a phenomenally slow craft as the *Three Sisters*, anything could be done with her. He believed that, with luck, it could, as he felt pretty certain that the attention of the ship's prize crew would be fully occupied in watching the manœuvres of the brigantine and the schooner; and, trusting to this, he hauled his wind until he had placed the brig in position the merest trifle to windward of the course that the ship was steering, when, taking his chance of having thus far escaped observation, he clewed up and furled everything, afterwards patiently awaiting the development of events.

And now ensued a very curious and amusing thing, it having transpired that the French prize crew of the ship *had* seen the brig, and had at once jumped to the conclusion that she was a prize to the schooner. The curious behaviour of the *Three Sisters* had puzzled them not a little at the outset, but when we opened fire upon the brigantine they knew at once that we must be an enemy; and, supposing that the prize crew of the brig— whom they rashly judged to be their own countrymen— had taken advantage of our preoccupation to rise and recapture their vessel, they immediately bore down to their assistance. This lucky mistake enabled Christie to fall alongside the ship without difficulty, when, laying aside for the nonce his gentle, lady-like demeanour, he led his eight men up the ship's lofty sides and over her high bulwarks on to her deck, where the nine of them laid about them with such good will that, after about a minute's resistance, the astounded Frenchmen were fain to retreat to the forecastle, where, in obedience to Christie's summons, they forthwith flung down their arms and surrendered at discretion. Then, clapping the hatch over them, and stationing two men with drawn cutlasses by it

## I BECOME THE VICTIM OF AN OUTRAGE

as a guard, Christie proceeded to liberate the imprisoned crew of the ship,—which he discovered to be the British West Indiaman *Black Prince*, homeward bound at the time of her capture, two days previously, with an exceedingly valuable general cargo,—and then sent his own men back to the *Three Sisters*, which had all this time been lying alongside, secured to the Indiaman by grapnels. The brig then cast off, and the two craft forthwith bore down upon us to report, the fight between ourselves and the brigantine being by that time over.

By the time that our own and the brigantine's damages had been repaired it was daylight, and we were all ready for making sail once more. But before doing so I caused the whole of the Frenchmen to be removed to the schooner, where they were first put in irons and then clapped safely under hatches; after which I visited first the *Belle Diane* and then the Indiaman. I must confess I was astonished when I beheld the effect of our fire upon the former; I could scarcely credit that so much damage had been inflicted by our six-pounders in so short time, her stern above the level of the covering-board being absolutely battered to pieces, while the shot had also ploughed up her decks fore and aft in long, scoring gashes, so close together and crossing each other in such a way as showed what a tremendous raking she had received. She began the action with fifty-seven men, all told, out of which eighteen had been killed outright, and the remainder, with one solitary exception, more or less seriously wounded. Looking upon the paths our shot had ploughed along her deck, I was only surprised that any of her people were left alive to tell the tale. In addition to this, five of her twelve guns were dismounted, and her rigging had been a good deal cut up; but this was now of course all knotted and spliced by Lindsay's people. She was a very fine vessel, of three hundred and forty-four tons measurement, oak built, copper fastened, and copper sheathed to the bends, very shallow—drawing only eight feet of water—and very beamy, with most beautiful lines. Her spars looked enormously lofty compared with our own, as I stood on her deck and gazed aloft, and her canvas had evidently been bent new for the voyage. She had only arrived in West Indian waters a week previously, from Brest, and the *Black Prince* was stated to be her first prize.

Having given the *Diane* a pretty good overhaul, and satisfied myself that her hull was sound, I gave Lindsay his instructions, and then proceeded on board the *Black Prince*, where I arrived in good time for breakfast, and where I made the acquaintance, not only of her skipper—a fine, grey-headed, sailorly man named Blatchford—but also of her thirty-two passengers, eighteen of whom were males, while the remainder were of the gentler sex, the wives and daughters mostly of the male passengers. There were no young children among them, fortunately. My appearance seemed to create quite a little flutter of excitement among the petticoats, and also not a little astonishment, apparently; for I overheard one of the matrons remark to another, behind her fan, " Why, he is scarcely more than *a boy*!"

The *Black Prince* was a noble ship, of twelve hundred and fifty tons, frigate-built, and only nine years old, splendidly fitted up, and full to the hatches of coffee, tobacco, spices, and other valuables; she also had a reputation for speed, which had induced her skipper to hazard the homeward voyage alone, instead of waiting for convoy. The poor old fellow was of course dreadfully cut up at his misfortune—for, having been in the enemy's hands more than twenty-four hours, she was a recapture in the legal sense of the term, and, as such, we were entitled to salvage for her. However, unfortunate as was the existing state of affairs, it was of course vastly better than that of a few hours before, and he interrupted himself in his bemoanings to thank me for having rescued him out of the hands of those Philistines, the French privateersmen. I informed him that it would be my duty to take him into Port Royal, but he received the news with equanimity, explaining that even had I not insisted on it, he should certainly, after his recent experience, have availed himself of my escort to return to Kingston, and there await convoy. I breakfasted with him and his passengers, and then, leaving Christie aboard as prize master, returned to the schooner; and we all made sail in company, arriving at Port Royal five days later, without further adventure.

The admiral was, as might be expected, immensely

pleased at our appearance with *three* prizes in company, and still more so when I reported to him the discovery and destruction of Morillo's headquarters.

"You have done well, my boy, wonderfully well; better even than I expected of you," said he, shaking me heartily by the hand. "Go on as you have begun, and I venture to prophesy that it will not be long before I shall feel justified in giving you t'other 'swab,'" pointing, as he spoke, to my single epaulet.

To say that I was delighted at my reception but very feebly expresses the feelings that overwhelmed me as the kind old fellow spoke such generous words of appreciation and encouragement. Of course I knew that I had done well, but I regarded my success as due fully as much to good fortune as to my own efforts, and I was almost overwhelmed with joy at so full and complete a recognition of my efforts. So astonished indeed was I, that I could only stammer something to the effect that our success was due quite as much to the loyalty with which Christie and Lindsay had seconded me, and the gallantry with which the men had stood by me, as it was to my own individual merits.

"That's right, my boy," remarked the admiral; "I am glad to hear you speak like that. No doubt what you say is true, but it does not detract in the least from the value of your own services. I always think the better of an officer who is willing to do full justice to the merits of those who have helped him, and your promotion will not come to you the less quickly for having helped your shipmates to theirs. You have *all* done well, and I will see to it that you are all adequately rewarded—Christie and Lindsay by getting their step, and you by getting a somewhat better craft than the little cockle-shell in which you have already done so well. I am of opinion that all you require is opportunity, and, by the Piper, you shall have it."

And the old gentleman kept his word; for when I went aboard the *Tern* on the following day—I dined and slept at the house of some friends a little way out from Kingston that night—Christie and Lindsay met me with beaming faces and the information that the former had got his step as master, while Lindsay had received an acting order as lieutenant pending his passing of the necessary examination. The only drawback to this good news was the intelligence that the man Garcia had mysteriously disappeared during the night, leaving not a trace of his whereabouts behind him.

An hour or two later I went ashore and waited upon the admiral at his office, in accordance with instructions received from him on the previous day; and upon being ushered into his presence, he at once began to question me relative to the qualities of the *Diane*. I was able to speak nothing but good of her; for indeed what I had seen of her, during the passage to Port Royal, had convinced me that she was really a very fine vessel in every respect, a splendid sea-boat, wonderfully fast, and, I had no doubt, a thoroughly wholesome, comfortable craft in bad weather.

"Just so," commented the admiral, when I had finished singing her praises; "what you have said quite confirms my own opinion of her, which is that, in capable hands, she may be made exceedingly useful. Moreover, she is more nearly a match for Morillo's brigantine than is the little *Tern*, eh? Well, my lad, I have been thinking matters over, and have made up my mind that she is good enough to purchase into the service; so I will have it seen to at once, and of course I shall give you the command of her. She will want a considerable amount of attention at the hands of the shipwrights after the mauling that you gave her, but you shall supervise everything yourself, and they shall do nothing without your approval; so see to it that they don't spoil her. I notice that she mounts six sixes of a side. Now I propose to alter that arrangement by putting four long nines in place of those six sixes, with an eighteen-pounder on her forecastle; and with such an armament as that, and a crew to match, you ought to be able to render an exceedingly good account of yourself. What do you think of my idea?"

I replied truthfully that I considered it excellent in every way; and we then launched into a discussion of minor details, with which I need not weary the reader, at the end of which I went aboard the *Tern* and paid off her crew, preparatory to her being turned over to the shipwrights, along with her prize.

## I BECOME THE VICTIM OF AN OUTRAGE

It happened that just about this time there was an exceptionally heavy press of work in the dockyard; for there had been several frigate actions of late, and the resources of the staff were taxed to the utmost to effect the repairs following upon such events and to get the ships ready for sea again in the shortest possible time; with the result that such small fry as the *Diane* and the *Tern* were obliged to wait until the heaviest of the work was over and the frigates were again ready for service. It thus happened that, although I contrived to worry the dockyard superintendent into putting a few shipwrights aboard the *Diane*, three weeks passed, and still the brigantine was very far from being ready for sea. During this time I made my headquarters at " Mammy " Wilkinson's hotel in Kingston,—that being the hotel especially affected by navy men,—although I was seldom there, the planters and big-wigs of the island generally proving wonderfully hospitable, and literally overwhelming me with invitations to take up my abode with them. But about the time that I have mentioned it happened that certain alterations were being effected aboard the brigantine, which I was especially anxious to have carried out according to my own ideas; I therefore spent the whole of the day, for several days in succession, at the dockyard, going up to Kingston at night, and sleeping at the hotel.

It was during this interval that, one night about ten o'clock, a negro presented himself at the hotel, inquiring for me; and upon my making my appearance in the entrance-hall, the fellow—a full-blooded African, dressed very neatly in a white shirt and white duck trousers, both scrupulously clean, for a wonder—approached me, and, ducking his head respectfully, inquired—

"You Massa Courtenay, sar, cap'n ob de man-o'-war schoonah *Tern*?"

"Well, yes," I replied, "my name is Courtenay, and I commanded the *Tern* up to the time of her being paid off; so I suppose I may fairly assume that I am the individual you have been inquiring for. What is it you want with me?"

"You know a genterman, nam'd Lindsay, sar?" asked the negro, instead of replying to my question.

"Certainly I do," answered I; "what of him?"

"Why, sar, he hab got into a lilly scrape down on de wharf, and de perlice hab put him into de lock-up. Dey don' beliebe dat he am man-o'-war bucra, and he say, 'Will you be so good as to step down dere an' identerfy him an' bail him out?'"

"Lindsay got into a scrape?" repeated I incredulously. "I cannot believe it! What has he been doing?"

"Dat I cannot say, sar," answered the black; "I only know dat a perliceman come out ob de door ob de lock-up as I was passin' by, and asked me if I wanted to earn fibe shillin'; and when I say 'yes,' he take me into de lock-up and interdooce me to young bucra, who say him name am Lindsay, and dat if I will take a message to you he will gib me fibe shillin' when I come back wid you."

## I BECOME THE VICTIM OF AN OUTRAGE 219

"It is very extraordinary," I muttered; "I cannot understand it! But I will go with you, of course. Wait a moment until I fetch my cap."

So saying, I left the fellow and hastened to my room, where, closing the door, I opened my chest and furnished myself with a supply of money, and then, closing and locking the chest, I hastened away to where the negro was waiting for me. As I passed through the hall several men of my acquaintance were lounging there, smoking, and one of them hailed me with—

"Hillo, Courtenay! whither away so fast, my lad?"

It was on the tip of my tongue to explain to them my errand, but I bethought me just in time that if Lindsay had been doing anything foolish he might not care to have the fact blazoned abroad; so I kept my own counsel, merely replying that I was called out upon a small matter of business, and so effected my escape from them into the dark street.

"Oh, here you are!" exclaimed I, as the negro emerged, at my appearance, from the deep shadow of the hotel portico. "Now, then, which way? Is Mr. Lindsay in the town jail?"

"No, sar, no; he am in de harbour lock-up," answered my guide. "Dis way, sar; it am not so bery far."

"The *harbour* lock-up?" queried I. "Where is that? I didn't know that there was such a place."

"Oh yes, sar, dar am. You follow me, sar; I show you de way, sar," answered the negro.

"All right, heave ahead then," said I; and away we went a little way down the main street, and then turned to the right, plunging into one of the dark, narrow side streets which then intersected the town of Kingston.

"Keep close to de wall, sar," cautioned my guide; "dere am a gutter in de middle ob de road, and if you steps into dat you go in ober your shoes in muck."

I could well believe this, for although it was too dark in this narrow lane to see anything, the abominable odour of the place told me pretty well what its condition must be. We plodded on for nearly ten minutes, winding hither and thither, and penetrating deeper and deeper into the labyrinth of dark, crooked lanes, but gradually edging nearer to the harbour, while, as I thought, working our way a considerable distance to the westward. Presently my guide, who had been humming some negro melody to himself, lifted up his voice in a louder key and began to chant the praises of a certain "lubly Chloe, whose eyes were like the stars, and whose 'breaf' was like the rose!" The fellow had a wonderfully melodious voice, and in listening to him as he strode easily along at a swinging pace, improvising verse after verse in honour of the unknown Chloe, I lost my bearings as well as my count of time, and was only brought back to a consciousness of the present by suddenly finding my head closely enveloped in what seemed to be a blanket, while at the same instant my feet were tripped from under me, so that I should have fallen forward but for the restraining

## I BECOME THE VICTIM OF AN OUTRAGE

influence of the blanket and of a pair of arms that gripped mine tightly behind my back, so that I was instantly overpowered and effectually precluded from making the slightest effort to free myself. Then, before I had time to realise what was happening, I was lifted off my feet, and, despite my desperate struggles and ineffectual efforts to shout for assistance, carried in through an open doorway and flung upon my face upon the ground, where someone at once knelt upon me and securely lashed my hands behind my back, some other individual at the same instant lashing my ankles firmly together.

"Dere, dat will do, Peter; I t'ink him cannot do much harm now," remarked the voice of my whilom guide; and as the fellow spoke I was relieved of the very considerable weight that had been pressing upon me and holding me down. Then I was rolled over on my side, and, as the blanket that enveloped my head and very nearly suffocated me was cautiously removed, I felt the prick of something sharp against my left breast, and the same voice that had spoken before observed—

"Massa Courtenay, we hab no wish to hurt you, sah; but it am my painful duty to warn you dat, if you sing out, or make de slightest attempt to escape, I shall be obleeged to dribe dis lilly knife ob mine home to yo' heart, sar. So now you knows what you hab to expec'. Does you understan' what I say, sah?"

"Certainly I do," answered I, with suppressed fury, "your meaning is clear enough, in all conscience. But beware what you do, my fine fellow.  You were seen by several of my friends at the hotel, who will have no difficulty in identifying you; and I warn you that you will be made to pay dearly for this outrage to a British naval officer.  What is the meaning of it all?  Have you any idea of the enormity of your offence?"

"Oh yes, sah," answered my guide cheerfully, "we hab a very clear idea ob dat, haben't we, Peter?" addressing another big, powerful negro of somewhat similar cut to himself, but attired in much less respectable garments.

Peter grinned affirmatively, but said nothing; whereupon his companion continued—

"Now, Peter, where am dat gag?  Just bring it along, and let us fix it up, so as to make all safe.  It would be a most drefful misfortune if Massa Courtenay was to sing out, and force me to split him heart wid dis knife ob mine; so we will just make it onpossible for him to do any such foolis' t'ing."

All this time the knife—a formidable dagger-shaped blade fully a foot long—was kept pressed so firmly to my breast that it had drawn blood, the stain of which was now dyeing the front of my white shirt, so the moment was manifestly inopportune for any attempt at escape or resistance even; I therefore submitted, with the best grace I could muster, to the insertion of the gag between my teeth, reserving to myself the right to make both ruffians smart for their outrage upon me at the first available opportunity.  But before the gag was placed between

## I BECOME THE VICTIM OF AN OUTRAGE

my teeth, I contrived to repeat my inquiry for an explanation.

"Nebber you mind, Massa Courtenay; you will find out all about dat in good time, sah," answered the leading spirit of the twain; and with that reply I was perforce obliged to be content for the moment.

Having made me perfectly secure, the two negroes squatted down upon their haunches, and, with much deliberation, produced from their pockets a short clay pipe each, a plug of tobacco, and a knife; and, after carefully shredding their tobacco and charging their pipes, proceeded to smoke, with much gravity and in perfect silence. It struck me that possibly they might be waiting for someone, whose appearance upon the scene would, I hoped, throw some light upon the cause of this extraordinary outrage, and give me an inkling as to what sort of an end I might expect to the adventure. Meanwhile, having nothing else to do, I proceeded to take stock of the place, or at least as much of it as I could command in my cramped and constrained position.

There was little or nothing, however, in what I saw about me of a character calculated to suggest an explanation of the motive for my seizure. The building was simply one of those low, one-storey adobe structures, thatched with palm leaves, such as then abounded in the lower quarters of Kingston, and which were usually inhabited by the negro or half-breed population of the place. The interior appeared to be divided into two apartments by an unpainted partition of timber framing, decorated with cheap and gaudy coloured prints, tacked to the wood at the four corners; and as a good many of these pictures were of a religious character, in most of which the Blessed Virgin figured more or less prominently, I took it that the legitimate occupant of the place was a Roman Catholic. The furniture was of the simplest kind, consisting of a table in the centre,—upon which burned the cheap, tawdry, brass lamp that illumined the apartment,—a large, upturned packing-case, covered with a gaudy tablecloth, and serving as a table against the rear wall of the building, and three or four old, straight-backed chairs, that had evidently come down in the world, for they were elaborately carved, and upholstered in frayed and faded tapestry. A few more cheap and gaudy coloured prints adorned the walls; a heavy curtain, so dirty and smoke-grimed that its original colour and pattern was utterly unrecognisable, shielded the unglazed window; two or three hanging shelves—one of which supported a dozen or so of dark green bottles—depended from the walls; and that was all. The floor upon which I lay was simply the bare earth, rammed hard, thick with dust and swarming with fleas,—as I quickly discovered,—and the whole place reeked of that hot, stale smell that seems to pervade the abodes of people of uncleanly habits.

The two negroes smoked silently and gravely for a full half-hour, about the end of which time my captor slowly and with due deliberation knocked the ashes from

# I BECOME THE VICTIM OF AN OUTRAGE

his pipe, and, rising to his feet, yawned and stretched himself. In so doing his eye fell upon the shelf upon which stood the bottles, and, sauntering lazily across the room, he laid his hand upon one of the bottles and placed it on the centre table. Then, lifting up the cloth which covered the packing-case, he revealed a shelf within the interior, from which he withdrew a water monkey, two earthenware mugs, and a dish containing a most uninviting-looking mixture, which I presently guessed, from its odour, to be composed of salt fish and boiled yams mashed together, cold. These he placed upon the table, and, still without speaking, the pair drew chairs up to the table and, seating themselves opposite each other, proceeded to make a hearty meal, helping themselves alternately, with their fingers, from the central dish, and washing down the mixture with a mug of rum and water each.

They were still thus agreeably engaged when the distant sound of rumbling wheels and clattering hoofs became audible, rapidly drawing nearer, and accompanied by the persuasive shouts and ejaculations of a negro driver.

"Dat am de boy Moses wid de cart, I 'spects," remarked the negro whose name I had not yet learned. "What a drefful row de young rascal makes! Dat nigger won't nebber learn discreshun," he continued, wiping his fingers carefully on a flaming red handkerchief which he drew from his breeches pocket.

Peter grunted an unintelligible reply, and the next moment the vehicle pulled up sharply at the door; the cessation of its clatter being immediately followed by the entrance of a negro lad, some eighteen years of age.

"I'se brought de cart, as you tole me, Cæsar," he remarked. "Am it all right?"

"It am, sar," remarked Cæsar—the hitherto unnamed negro—loftily; "when did you ebber know me to fail in what I undertooken, eh, sar?"

"Nebber, sah, nebber," answered Moses appreciatively. "An' so dat am de gebberlum, am it?" pointing at me with his chin, as I lay huddled up on the floor.

"Yes, sar, it am," answered Cæsar curtly, in a tone of voice which was evidently intended to cut short all further conversation. "An' now, Peter," he continued, "if you has finished yo' supper we better be movin'. Nebber mind about puttin' de t'ings away; de ole 'oman will see to dat when she comes home in de mornin'. Now den, Peter, you take hold ob de genterman's legs, and help me to carry him out; does you hear?"

Peter the Silent grunted an affirmative, stooping as he did so and seizing my legs, while Cæsar raised me by the shoulders in his powerful arms, remarking, as he did so—

"Massa Courtenay, jus' listen to me, if you please, sah. We am goin' to take you for a nice, pleasant lilly dribe in a cart, and I am goin' to sit on you, so dat you may not fall out. Now I still has my knife wid me, and if I feels you begin to struggle, I shall be under de mos'

# I BECOME THE VICTIM OF AN OUTRAGE

painful necessity ob drivin' it into you to keep you quiet; so I hope dat you will lie most particular still durin' yo' little journey. You sabbe?"

I nodded my head.

"Dat's all right, den," resumed Cæsar. "Now, Peter up wid him, and away we goes."

And therewith the two black rascals raised me carefully, and carrying me into the open, placed me in a mule cart, covered me with a thick layer of green forage, and—Cæsar coolly carrying out his threat to sit upon me—drove away.

# CHAPTER XIII

## IN THE POWER OF THE ENEMY

OUR drive was a most unpleasant one for me, for the cart had no springs, and the boy Moses, like Jehu, drove furiously. It fortunately lasted only some five-and-twenty minutes or so, however; and at the end of that period we pulled up on what I guessed, from the running of the vehicle and the sound of rippling water, to be a sandy beach. My conjecture proved to be correct, for when presently I was hauled out from underneath the forage, and stood upon my feet, more dead than alive, I found that we were on the margin of a tiny creek or cove, about three-quarters of a mile to the westward of the outskirts of Kingston. A small canoe lay hauled up on the sand, and in the bottom of this craft I was carefully deposited; after which she was run down into the water, when Cæsar and Peter sprang lightly into her, giving her a final shove to seaward as they did so, and paddled away, leaving Moses and his cart to make the best of their way back to the town.

Lying upon my back in the bottom of the canoe, with my face turned upward to the stars, I was able to see that we were heading eastward toward Kingston harbour; and about half an hour later the canoe glided up alongside a small felucca, of some thirty tons burden and was made fast by her painter. The canoe secured to his satisfaction, the negro Cæsar climbed over the felucca's low bulwarks, and I heard his bare feet pattering along the deck until, as I supposed, he reached the companion, when the sounds became muffled, and were presently lost. Then I caught the sound of voices,—Cæsar's and others' —but so indistinctly that I was unable to distinguish what was being said. The conversation, however, was brief, for in three or four minutes the tread of Cæsar's bare feet again became audible, accompanied by that of others; and I then discovered that a conversation, of which I was the subject, was being conducted in Spanish! This seemed to suggest that I had fallen into the hands of the enemy, though why the Spaniards should wish to kidnap so very unimportant a personage as myself I could not for the life of me imagine, unless they had adopted some new system of warfare, one element of which consisted in kidnapping as many of the enemy's officers as possible, without much reference to their importance or otherwise! But of course I should soon see; for as I lay there in the bottom of the canoe, cogitating to this effect, I became aware, from the remarks interchanged by those on deck, that I was about to be transferred to the felucca; and if the Spaniards had adopted the novel system of kidnapping British officers, I should doubtless find some of my fellow-officers on board in the same plight as myself.

Presently Cæsar swung himself over the felucca's bulwarks and down into the canoe, when he at once seized me by the shoulders, and, calling upon his friend Peter to lend him a hand, proceeded to pass me up over the felucca's rail to the three Spanish-speaking individuals who stood on deck stretching out their arms to receive me. They were very careful not to hurt me unnecessarily during the process of transfer, from which circumstance I derived a certain amount of comfort; the inference being that, whatever might be their motive in thus seizing me, no bodily harm to me was intended. Having safely transferred me from the canoe to the deck of the felucca, my abductors next conveyed me below to the hot, stuffy little cabin of the craft, where, outstretched upon a locker that was barely long enough to accommodate my length, they left me without a word, and returned to the deck, carefully closing the doors and drawing over the slide at the head of the companion ladder, and then as carefully closing both flaps of the hitherto open skylight. This done, their conversation with Cæsar and his satellite was continued in a leisurely, desultory fashion for about half an hour,—the burden of it being unintelligible to me through the closed skylight,—when I heard the two negroes descend into their canoe and shove off, wishing the others a quick and pleasant passage. Then followed some leisurely movements on deck, accompanied by the throwing down of a rope or two, the creaking of blocks and parralls, a few quiet ejaculations as of men pulling and hauling, the clink of windlass pawls, the loud slatting of loose canvas in the strong land-breeze that was blowing; and finally—as the latter sounds ceased—I felt the felucca heel strongly over to port, and heard the increasing gurgle and wash of water along the bends and under the counter of the little craft, accompanied by an occasional call from for'ard to the helmsman, by which I knew that we were under way, and standing down the harbour toward Port Royal.

By and by I felt the felucca come upright, there was a warning cry on deck, a sudden, violent flap of canvas overhead, and the felucca heeled slightly over to starboard; by which I knew that she had squared away, jibed over, and was running out of the harbour. A few minutes later I felt her beginning to rise and fall over the gathering seas as she skimmed away off the land; the motion steadily grew stronger, merging into a swift, floating, forward rush, as the seas came up astern of her, followed by a long, dragging pause as the crest swept past; and presently the companion slide was pushed back, the doors at the head of the ladder were flung open, and a man— one of those who had helped to convey me below— descended into the cabin.

"Phew! señor, you are warm down here!" he exclaimed, in perfect English, as he stood gazing thoughtfully down upon me. I could of course make no reply, as I was still gagged; but he probably observed the dreadful condition that the gag and the lashings round my wrists and ankles had reduced me to, for he continued, as he stooped over me—

"We are now at sea; and as it is therefore impossible for you to raise an alarm, or effect your escape, I think I may safely make you a little more comfortable. You look terribly distressed, amigo; and my orders are imperative that you are to be delivered safe and sound. There!" as he removed the gag and cast off the lashings, "that ought to be more to your liking."

"For pity's sake," I ejaculated, "give me something to drink! That horrible gag has all but suffocated me!"

"Something to drink? With pleasure, señor. What shall it be—plain water or 'grog,' as you English call it? I think it had better be grog, for I cannot recommend the water we carry in our scuttle-butt."

So saying, he went to a little cupboard alongside the companion ladder, and produced therefrom a water monkey, two tin pannikins, and a bottle of rum, all of which he placed on the cabin table.

"There, señor, help yourself freely; the little *Josefa* and all that she contains is yours!"

"Thanks, señor," I replied, as I poured out with a shaking hand and benumbed fingers a generous modicum of rum, filling up the pannikin with evil-smelling water, "I drink to our better acquaintance."

## IN THE POWER OF THE ENEMY 233

So saying, I emptied the pannikin at a gulp, and set it down upon the table. "And now, señor," I continued, as my companion, in turn, proceeded to help himself and to pledge me, "perhaps you will kindly inform me, first, whom I have the honour to address; secondly, why I have been brought aboard this felucca; and, thirdly, to what place you propose to convey me?"

"Assuredly, señor," answered the Spaniard; "it will afford me much happiness to gratify so very natural and reasonable a request. In the first place, señor, I am your Excellency's most humble servant, Juan Dominguez, captain of this felucca. In the next place, you are here by order of my excellent friend and patron, Don Pedro Morillo, captain of the brigantine *Guerrilla*; and, in the third place, I am conveying you—also by Don Pedro's orders—to Cariacou, an island which I understand you have already visited, under certain memorable circumstances."

So that was it, was it? I was kidnapped, not in accordance with some wild scheme of the Spaniards to cripple our too active navy by robbing it of every officer that they could lay hands upon, but in order that a cowardly, bloodthirsty pirate might at leisure, and in safety, wreak his revenge upon me for the injury that I, in the exercise of my duty, had done him. Speaking in all frankness, I do not believe I am a coward; but I confess that the information thus calmly communicated to me by this Spaniard — who was most probably a naturalised British subject—caused my blood to run cold; for I had heard quite enough of Morillo to feel tolerably well assured that if his motive in causing me to be kidnapped was revenge, he would not be satisfied with merely shooting me, or stabbing me to the heart; he would undoubtedly exercise his utmost ingenuity to render my passage out of this world as lingering and painful as possible; and, from all accounts, he was quite an adept in the art of torture!

"You seem disturbed at my intelligence, amigo," remarked my companion, gazing upon me with a smile of amusement. "Well," he continued, "perhaps you have cause to be; who knows? I have heard that it was you who, taking advantage of my friend's absence at sea, visited Cariacou and destroyed poor Morillo's batteries and buildings there, carrying off his brig and everything else that you and your crew could lay hands upon. I hope, for *your* sake, that Morillo was misinformed, and that you will be able to demonstrate to his complete satisfaction your entire freedom from all complicity in that very ill-advised and malicious transaction; he may then be content to simply hang you at his yardarm. But if you fail to convince him—phew! I sincerely pity you; I do indeed, señor."

"Thanks, very much," retorted I, with the best attempt at sarcasm that I could muster,—for I began to perceive that this fellow was amusing himself by endeavouring to frighten me, and I did not intend to afford him very much gratification in that way,—"your pity is infinitely comforting to me, especially as it is evident to me that the feeling is genuine. May I ask whether your share in this present transaction is undertaken purely out of friendship for Morillo, or is it being carried out upon a business basis?"

"Well, to be strictly truthful, there is a little of both," answered Dominguez. "Why do you inquire, if it is not an indiscreet question?"

"Now," thought I, "I wonder whether this question of his is intended to indicate that he is open to a bribe—a bribe to put me ashore again, safe and sound, provided that I make him a sufficiently liberal offer. Perhaps the attempt may be worth making; it will, at all events, enable me to judge what are my chances, so far as he is concerned." So I replied—

"To be candid with you, friend Dominguez, it occurred to me that you had undertaken this little adventure as much with the object of turning a more or less honest penny as for any other reason. Now, supposing that I should experience any difficulty in satisfying Morillo upon the point that you just now referred to, what do you imagine will be the result? Something exceedingly unpleasant for me, I assume, since you were good enough to express pity for me."

"Something exceedingly unpleasant?" he repeated, with a laugh. "Well, yes, that is one way of putting it, certainly, but it is a very mild way; so ridiculously mild that it suggests no idea of what was in my mind when I said I pitied you. Flaying alive is unpleasant, so is being roasted alive over a slow fire, so is gradual dismemberment—a finger or a toe at a time, then a hand or a foot, and so on until only the trunk remains,—all these are unpleasant, *exceedingly* so, I should imagine, from what I have seen of the behaviour of those who have undergone those operations at my friend's hand; but in the contingency you just now suggested, I fancy that Morillo would do his best to devise something considerably better—or worse, whichever you please to call it—for *you*."

I shuddered, and a feeling of horrible sickness swept over me. Strive as I would, I could not help it, as this inhuman wretch spoke, with evident gusto, of the torments to which I might—failing Morillo's ability to devise still greater refinements of cruelty—be subjected. But by the time that he had finished speaking, I had succeeded in rallying my courage sufficiently to remark—

"Thanks; your reply to my question leaves nothing to be desired in the way of lucidity. Now, supposing I should happen to feel some repugnance to those delicate attentions on Morillo's part that you have just alluded to, what inducement would be sufficient to persuade you to 'bout ship, and land me on the wharf at Kingston, instead of at Cariacou?"

"Ah," replied Dominguez, "that is a question that is not to be answered off-hand; there are several points that occur to me as requiring careful consideration before I could name the sum that would induce me to act as you wish. Of course you will understand that I have no personal animus against you; you have never injured me, and therefore I have no feeling of revenge to gratify by delivering you into Morillo's power. But, on the other hand, Morillo is my friend, and I am always glad to oblige him when I can, particularly when, as in the present case, I am well paid for it. Now, if I were to act as you suggest, I should be thwarting, instead of obliging him; I should convert him from a friend into an enemy; and I think that you are now in a position to understand what that means. It means that I should be compelled to *disappear* as completely as though the ground had opened and swallowed me; because it is one of Morillo's characteristics that, while he is a staunch and generous friend, he is also a bitter and relentless enemy. He *never* forgives; so long as his enemy lives, he will never rest until he has been revenged upon him. And this reminds me that if you and I should succeed in coming to an arrangement, you must not regard the matter between yourself and Morillo as settled; I warn you that you will have to maintain a ceaseless watch, for so long as you and he live he will never relax his efforts to get you into his power. Afloat, and with a greatly superior force, you *may* reckon yourself to be reasonably safe; but *ashore*— no! Very well. Now, what I have told you will enable you to understand my position in relation to this matter:

at present I am his friend, but I have his enemy in my power; and if I aid and abet that enemy to escape I become his enemy, which will necessitate my prompt retreat to the other side of the world, to begin life afresh, with the haunting feeling that, go where I will and do what I may, I am *never safe*! That alone points to a necessary demand on my part of a considerable sum—a *very* considerable sum—from you as compensation for the many serious inconveniences and dangers that must inevitably follow upon my falling in with your proposal. But that is not all. There is my mate, Miguel, and the lad Luis, for'ard; both of them would require some very substantial inducement to lead them to fall in with our views. Altogether, I should say that what you propose would probably cost you—well, at least, ten thousand pounds."

"Ten thousand pounds?" I ejaculated. "Nonsense, man; you must be dreaming. Why, I could no more raise ten thousand pounds than I could fly."

"No?" he queried coolly; "not even to save yourself from "—

"Not even to save myself from the utmost refinement of cruelty that your friend Morillo is capable of devising," I answered decisively.

"Pardon me, señor, but I can scarcely believe you," retorted Dominguez, with that hateful, sneering smile of his. "You have been exceptionally fortunate in the matter of prizes since your arrival in these waters, and I feel convinced that in prize money alone you must now have a very handsome sum standing to your credit. Then, if I am correctly informed, you have made many friends. You are, for instance, a great favourite with the admiral, who would doubtless be willing to advance a very considerable sum to help you out of your present exceedingly disagreeable predicament; and I have no doubt there are others who would be equally willing to help you if your position were clearly laid before them."

"But, man alive, I cannot do it," I exclaimed angrily. "So far as prize money is concerned, I suppose three thousand pounds is the very utmost that I possess. And as for the admiral, I am no more to him than any other officer, and I am certain that he would absolutely refuse to advance a single penny-piece for such a purpose as you suggest; to do so would simply be offering an inducement to you—and others like you—to kidnap officers, and then hold them to ransom. But I tell you what it is," I continued; "you may rest assured of this, that if any harm befalls me,—if, in short, you deliver me into Morillo's power,—the admiral will make you suffer as severely for it as Morillo himself could possibly do. So there you are, between two fires; and, if you care for my opinion, it is that the admiral is likely to prove a worse enemy to you than even Morillo over this business."

"That, possibly, might be the case if the admiral happened to discover that I have been implicated in it," replied my companion, with exasperating composure. "But then, you see, he never will! I have taken every possible precaution against that."

"How about Cæsar and Peter, the two negroes who brought me aboard here?" I inquired.

"Pshaw!" answered Dominguez impatiently, "do you suppose they would inform against me? Not they. Why, they are both—well, never mind what they are, except that I feel perfectly safe, so far as they are concerned."

"Very well," I retorted, "time will show whether your confidence in them is well founded or not. Meanwhile, my position is such that three thousand pounds is the outside figure I can offer you as my ransom, and you may take it or leave it as you please."

"Then I fear, amigo, that your days are numbered," replied Dominguez composedly, as he rose from his seat preparatory to returning on deck. "I am sorry for you," he continued, "very sorry; but I *must* think of myself before all else, and three thousand is not nearly tempting enough. Possibly when you have had a little longer to think it over you will be able to see your way to make a very considerable advance upon that sum. There is plenty of time; the *Josefa* is a grand little ship, but she has one fault, she is slow, and I do not expect that we shall reach Cariacou in less than a full week. You have therefore six or seven days before you in which to consider the matter; and should you see your way to raise the ten thousand, at any time before we sight the island, I shall be happy to talk with you again. Meanwhile, there is your bunk. Will you turn in at once, or would you prefer to take a turn on deck first?"

"Thanks," answered I, with alacrity, delighted to discover that I was not to be confined to the cabin. "I think I will go on deck for half an hour or so, to get a breath of fresh air; it is rather close down here."

"As you will," returned Dominguez, amicably enough; "I have no fear of your attempting to escape. You are scarely likely, I think, to go overboard and offer yourself as a meal to the sharks. Do you smoke? I can recommend these," as he drew from a locker a box of cigars.

I helped myself to one mechanically, and lit it, Dominguez following my example, and then politely offering me precedence up the companion ladder. I accepted the courtesy, and made my way somewhat stiffly up the steep steps; for my limbs were still cramped from the compression of the ligatures wherewith I had been bound. After what I had passed through it was an inexpressible relief to me to find myself once more breathing the free, pure air of heaven, with the star-spangled sky arching grandly overhead.

It was a brilliantly fine night,—or morning rather, for it was by this time past two o'clock a.m.,—the sky cloudless save for a small shred of thin, wool-like vapour skimming rapidly athwart the stars; the trade wind was blowing a moderate breeze, and the felucca was bruising along on an easy bowline with long, swinging plunges and soarings over the low, jet-black, glistening surges at a pace of some five and a half knots perhaps, with a perfect thunder of roaring, breaking seas under her bluff bows, and a belt of winking, sparkling sea-fire, a couple of fathoms wide, sweeping past her lee rail and swirling into the broad, short wake that she trailed behind her. The land was still clearly in sight on our port quarter, the range of the Liguanea Mountains towering high into the star-lit sky and gradually sloping away to the eastward in the direction of Morant Point. Beside Dominguez and myself there was but one other figure visible on deck, that of the man at the helm—a long, thin, weedy-looking figure, so far as I could make out in the ghostly starlight, but one who had evidently used the sea for some time, if one might judge by the easy, floating poise of his figure on the plunging deck as he stood on the weather side of the tiller, with the tiller rope lightly grasped in his right hand, swaying rhythmically to the leaps and plunges of the little hooker. As Dominguez followed me out on deck he stepped aft to the small, dimly lighted binnacle, glanced into it, made some brief remark in a low tone to the silent helmsman, walked forward and took a long look ahead and on both bows, and then, returning aft, excused himself to me for turning in, upon the plea that it would soon be his watch on deck, and so dived below and left me.

Left thus to myself, I fell to mechanically pacing the short deck of the felucca for a few minutes, smoking thoughtfully the while and turning over in my mind the disquieting conversation that had just passed between Dominguez and myself; then, my gaze happening to wander aft to the solitary figure at the tiller, I sauntered aft and endeavoured to strike up a conversation with him. The fellow, however, proved to be so boorish and saturnine in his manner that I quickly abandoned the attempt and, pitching my half-smoked cigar over the rail, retired below and tumbled, "all standing," into the bunk that Dominguez had indicated as mine, where, despite the food for serious reflection that the occurrences of the night afforded me, I soon fell into a sound sleep.

The week that succeeded my abduction was so utterly barren of events that it may be passed over with the mere remark that throughout the whole of the time we had perfect weather, with a steady, moderate trade wind, under the impulsion of which the felucca bruised along upon her proper course, reeling off her five to six knots per hour with the regularity of a clock; and during the whole of that time, strange to say, we sighted not a single sail. I had been by no means idle during this time, however, as may well be supposed; for every day at noon saw the little hooker a hundred and thirty to a hundred and fifty miles nearer the spot where, if nothing happened in the interim to prevent it, I was to be delivered into the hands of a fiend in human form, whose hatred of me was so intense and vindictive that he had taken a considerable amount of trouble, and put himself to considerable expense, merely to get me into his power and wreak a blood-curdling revenge upon me.

But to tamely submit to be thus handed over to Morillo's tender mercies was the very last thing that I contemplated. I had every reason to believe that the picture drawn by Dominguez of the form which Morillo's revenge would probably take was a tolerably truthful one; and while I was prepared to face death in any form at a moment's notice in the way of duty, I had not the remotest intention of permitting myself to be tortured to death merely to gratify the ferocity of a piratical outlaw, if I could possibly help it. So for the first three or four days I devoted myself wholly to the task of endeavouring to bribe my custodians to forego their intention of handing me over to Morillo, and to land me upon the nearest British territory instead. But I by and by made the discovery that my efforts in this direction were doomed to failure; Dominguez was clearly so profoundly impressed with Morillo's power, and with his tenacious memory for injuries, that the conviction had borne itself in upon him that if he yielded to my persuasions it would be absolutely necessary to his safety, not only to buy over the whole of those engaged upon the business of my abduction, but also to place the whole width of the globe between himself and Morillo; and to execute these little matters satisfactorily would, according to his own calculations, necessitate the disbursement on my part of the modest amount of ten thousand pounds sterling, a sum which, as I explained to him over and over again, it was utterly beyond my power to raise. It was not that Dominguez was grasping or avaricious; it was simply that he regarded a certain course of action necessary to his own safety and well-being, in the event of his consenting to yield to my wishes; and as he had no intention of suffering any pecuniary or other loss or damage by so yielding, it appeared to him that the thing could not be done under the sum he had named, and there was the whole matter in a nut-shell.

The attempt at bribery having thus resulted in failure, there remained to me but one other alternative, that of a resort to force—myself against Dominguez and the two men who formed his crew. For, come what would, I was firmly resolved never to suffer myself to be delivered alive into Morillo's hands; if it was my doom to die at the end of this adventure, I would die fighting. So, while feigning to yield to the inexorable force of circumstances, I began to meditate upon the most promising means whereby to escape from the exceedingly unpleasant dilemma in which

I found myself involved; and after giving the whole matter my most careful attention, I came to the conclusion that my simplest plan would be to take—or attempt to take—the felucca from Dominguez and his associates, and, having done so, make for the nearest British harbour.

# CHAPTER XIV

## I SEIZE THE FELUCCA

HAVING come to this conclusion, the next thing was to devise a plan of some sort; but upon attempting to do this, I soon discovered that it was wholly impossible, so much depending upon circumstances over which I had no control whatever, that I might have formed a dozen plans with never a chance to carry any one of them through. The only thing, therefore, was to await an opportunity, and be prepared to seize it the moment that it presented itself. Perhaps the most difficult part of my task was to preserve all through this trying time such a demeanour as would effectually conceal from Dominguez the fact that I was alert and on the watch for something; but I managed it somehow, by leading him to believe that, rather than suffer torture, I had determined to provoke Morillo into killing me outright; a plan of which Dominguez highly approved, while expressing his doubts as to the possibility of its achievement.

In suggesting—as I find I have in the above paragraph — that I had no plan whatever, I have perhaps conveyed a wrong impression; what I intended the reader to understand was that I had no *finished* scheme, complete in all its details, to depend upon. A plan of a sort I certainly had, but it was of the vaguest and most nebulous kind, consisting in nothing more specific than the mere determination to seize the felucca at the first favourable opportunity, and sail her, single-handed, to the nearest British port; but of *how* this was to be accomplished I had not the most remote idea. The only point upon which I was at all clear was that it would be inadvisable, for two reasons, to make my attempt too early: my first reason for arriving at this conclusion being that, the longer I deferred action the nearer should we be to Barbadoes, for which island I intended to make; while my second reason was that, should Dominguez perchance suspect me of any sinister design, the longer the delay on my part the less suspicious and watchful would he be likely to become. Fortunately for my purpose, we were making rather a long passage of it, the little hooker not being by any means a particularly weatherly craft; consequently our first land-fall—on our sixth day out—was the curious shoal and accompanying group of rocky islets called Los Roques, or The Roccas, off La Guayra, close to which we hove about and stood to the northward on the starboard tack.

This occurred during the early morning, about an hour after sunrise. The trade wind was then blowing steadily but moderately, and the weather was, as usual, fine and clear. Toward noon, however, it became noticeable that the wind was very decidedly softening down; and when Dominguez took his meridian observation of the sun, we were not going more than four knots. It was the custom aboard the felucca to dine in the middle of the day, as soon as Dominguez had worked out his calculations, the skipper and I dining first, and then going on deck while Miguel, the mate, took his meal. While Miguel was below Dominguez usually took the tiller, but of late I had occasionally relieved him—with a vague idea that possibly it might, at some opportune moment, be an advantage for me to be at the helm. And, as it happened, I chanced to be first on deck on this particular day, and, without any premeditation, went aft and relieved Miguel; so that, when a few minutes later Dominguez came on deck, he found me in possession of the tiller, and staring intently at some floating object about a quarter of a mile away, and slightly on our weather bow, that kept rising into view and vanishing again as the long, lazy undulations of the swell swept past it.

"What are you staring at so hard, Señor Courtenay? Do you see anything?" demanded Dominguez, as he sauntered aft toward me from the companion, cigar in mouth.

"Yes," answered I, replying to his last question first, "there is something out there, but what it is I cannot for the life of me make out. There—there it is! You can see it now lifting on the back of the swell, about a point on the weather bow."

"Ay," he answered eagerly, "I see it, and, unless I am greatly mistaken, I know what it is. Keep her away a little, señor, if you please; let her go off a point. I do not want to pass too close to that object if it be what I imagine."

"And pray what do you imagine it to be, señor, if one may be permitted to ask the question?" inquired I, as I gave a pull upon the tiller rope and kept the felucca away, as requested.

"A turtle! a sleeping turtle, and an unusually fine one, too!" answered Dominguez, in a low voice, as he stood staring out away over the weather bow, with one hand shading his eyes while the other held his smouldering cigar.

As Dominguez spoke a little thrill of sudden excitement swept over me, for I thought, "Just so; I know what he means. He intends to make an effort to capture that turtle,—probably by means of the boat,—and, if he does, my chance will have come!" But I steadied myself instantly, and returned, in a perfectly nonchalant tone of voice—

"And supposing that it be, as you imagine, a sleeping turtle, what then, señor?"

"Hush, señor, I pray you!" replied Dominguez, in a low, excited whisper. "Keep silence; you will soon see!"

Presently the object lifted into view again, only some ten or a dozen fathoms away; and as it went drifting quietly past, we got so distinct and prolonged a view of it as to render its identity unquestionable. It was, as Dominguez had imagined, a sleeping turtle of enormous size.

"Holy Virgin, what a magnificent fellow!" ejaculated Dominguez, as the creature vanished in the trough on our weather quarter, "we *must* have him! Señor, if we lower the sail, so that the felucca cannot drift far, will you have any objection to being left by yourself for a few minutes, while Miguel and I and the boy go after that turtle with the boat?" he demanded eagerly.

So my chance *had* come, if I could but so demean myself for a few minutes as not to arouse the suspicions of this man by any ill-timed exhibition of eagerness or too earnest assent to his proposal. I took a second or two to steady my nerves, and then asked—

"Cannot we *all* go in the boat together? I have never yet seen a turtle captured, and should greatly like to witness the operation."

"No, señor; I am sorry, but it is out of the question," answered Dominguez hastily. ' The boat is but small, and I am very doubtful whether she will be capable of carrying three of us and that great brute—if we are so fortunate as to catch him. I would send Miguel and Luis only, but that I know they would not be able to secure him unaided. We shall not be gone long, señor, and the felucca *cannot* drift far in this light breeze and with so little swell running."

"N—o, I suppose not," I answered, with just the slightest imaginable show of reluctance. "All right, señor," I continued, "away with you, by all means; I should be sorry to spoil your sport for you. Shall I lower the sail?"

"Not just for a moment, señor," answered Dominguez; "we must creep far enough away that the flapping of the canvas may not wake our friend yonder, or we shall lose him." Then, poking his head through the open skylight, he called softly, in Spanish—

"Miguel! Miguel! come on deck at once, friend; there is a large turtle out here floating, fast asleep, and I want to catch him."

Miguel mumbled a reply of some sort,—what it was I could not tell,—and Dominguez briskly withdrew his head from the skylight and sprang upon the rail, looking away out on the weather quarter for the turtle. It was still visible, at intervals, but fully a quarter of a mile astern now.

"There, that will do; we are far enough away now, I think," he muttered, stepping lightly off the felucca's low rail to the deck. "Here, Miguel," as that worthy emerged from the companion, wiping his lips with the back of his hand, "help me to lower the sail, quick! And you, Señor Courtenay, will you do me the favour to haul taut the sheet as the sail comes down, so that it may not flap about and make more noise than we can help?"

"Certainly," I answered cheerfully, letting go the tiller rope and seizing the fall of the sheet. "Lower away whenever you like."

The single lateen sail, stretched upon its long, heavy, tapering yard, came sliding down the mast, rustling heavily, despite all that I could do to prevent it; and presently it lay quiescent, stretched along the deck, with the after yardarm projecting far over the taffrail. I sprang up on the companion slide to see whether the turtle was still visible, and was rejoiced to find that he *was*,—floating, an unconspicuous and unrecognisable object by this time,—nearly half a mile away, apparently quite undisturbed by the rustling sounds of the canvas.

"Is he still there, señor?" demanded Dominguez, in an eager half-whisper.

I nodded, pointing silently to where I could see the creature appearing at intervals on the ridges and backs of the swell.

"Good!" ejaculated Dominguez. "Now, where is Luis? Oh, here you are!" as that individual poked his head up through the fore scuttle to see what was going on, his still working jaws betraying that he too had been disturbed during the process of consuming the midday meal. "Just look into the boat, Luis, my son, and see that the oars and baler are in her, while Miguel and I unship the gangway. Can you still see him, Señor Courtenay?"

"Yes," I replied, "he is still there, but a long way off now. I think I had better keep my eye on him, and direct you by an occasional wave of the hand, as you pull down, or you will have a job to find him."

"Thank you," answered Dominguez; "if it will not be troubling you too much I shall be greatly obliged."

"Oh, no trouble at all," responded I. "I should stand here to watch the fun in any case."

Dominguez and Miguel soon managed, between them, to unship the gangway, which done, they lifted the boat—a mere dinghy—out of her chocks on top of the main hatchway, slued her bows round toward the gangway, and ran her over the side, fisherman fashion, the three of them immediately jumping in and shoving off from the felucca's side; Dominguez, who steered the boat, looking round at me from time to time for directions as to the way in which he was to head the boat.

Released now from the scrutiny of the Spaniard's eyes, it was no longer necessary for me to maintain that painful self-restraint which had cost me so severe an effort in order that I might not by look or gesture arouse the ghost of a suspicion as to my intentions; so, while I continued to mechanically wave the boat to the right or the left, as circumstances demanded, I now gave my mind to the task of determining the details of my proposed line of action.

To begin with, I was fully resolved that Dominguez and his companions having left the felucca, they should never again return to her, if I could possibly prevent it. At the right moment I would make sail upon the little craft and head her for Barbadoes, leaving them to get ashore as best they could. And here my conscience pricked me a little, for I had already had experience of a voyage in an open boat, and knew what it meant. On the other hand, however, my life was at stake; for it had by this time become perfectly apparent to me that unless I could raise the sum of ten thousand pounds demanded by Dominguez—which was a simple impossibility—that individual would most certainly deliver me over to Morillo; in which case there was every reason to believe that I should die a cruel and lingering death of torment—which I considered myself quite justified in avoiding by every means in my power. Moreover, we were not very far from the land. The Roccas were only some twenty-five miles away, at the utmost, and could easily be reached by Dominguez before midnight; and the weather was fine, and the water smooth. The voyage of the dinghy was therefore not likely to be of a very adventurous or dangerous character; so that, by taking possession of the felucca and turning the Spaniard and his companions adrift, I should only be inflicting upon them a very mild punishment for their unlawful seizure of my person, especially when the cruel object of that seizure came to be taken into consideration. I would not leave them, however, wholly without provisions and water, if I could help it. My first thought, therefore, was how I might be able to convey to them a small supply of each without affording them an opportunity to regain possession of the felucca; and after a few minutes' deliberation I thought I could see a way by which this might be accomplished.

Meanwhile the dinghy went drifting rapidly away astern, propelled by Miguel and Luis, who stood up at their oars, looking ahead, while Dominguez stood up in the stern-sheets, looking over their shoulders and occasionally glancing back at me for guidance. At length, however, he caught sight for himself of the turtle, and thenceforward kept his attention wholly fixed upon it. As soon as I became fully satisfied of this I jumped down off the companion, for the moment for action on my part had now arrived.

The first thing was to get sail upon the felucca again; and to masthead the long, heavy lateen yard, with its big sail, was no easy task for one man. There was, however, a little winch affixed to the fore part of the mast, chiefly used for this very purpose; so, upon jumping down off the companion, my first act was to assure myself that the mainsheet was securely belayed, after which I rushed forward, and, setting hand-taut the main halliard, threw two or three turns of the fall round the barrel of the winch. I then ran aft again and sprang once more upon the companion to see what was happening aboard the dinghy. She was by this time drawing pretty close up to the sleeping turtle, and the whole attention of the trio aboard her appeared to be absorbed in the effort to get alongside the creature without waking him. Now, therefore, was my time for action. I accordingly dashed forward to the mast, and, shipping the crank handle of the winch, hove away upon the halliard for dear life. The yard and sail crept slowly—oh, how *very* slowly —up the mast, the canvas rustling in the wind noisily enough to wake the dead, still more to reach the ears and give the alarm to those in the dinghy. But, having once begun, there was nothing now for it but to go on with the work, and get the yard mastheaded and good way upon the felucca before those in the dinghy could pull back and get alongside.

At length, after what seemed to be an interminable time,—although the rapid *click, click* of the pawls told me that in reality I was accomplishing my task very smartly, —I managed to get the yard some two-thirds of the way up the mast, when I took a turn with the halliards and once more rushed aft to get a look at the boat. As I had expected, the slatting of the canvas had reached and given them the alarm, and the boat was now round and heading back after the felucca, Miguel and Dominguez straining frantically at the oars, while Luis had taken the place of the latter at the tiller. The little craft was being pushed furiously along—as I could tell by the manner in which her nose dipped and the white foam boiled round it at every stroke of the oars; but the felucca was gathering way, and with the wind square abeam and her imperfectly hoisted sail ramping full, seemed to be quite holding her own. I seized the tiller and kept her away another point, carefully watching both her progress and that of the boat, and ten minutes later I experienced the satisfying conviction that she was steadily leaving her pursuers. Once fully assured of this, I lashed the tiller, and once more running forward, completed the setting of the sail, when I let the little hooker come up to "full and by."

The next matter demanding my attention was that of conveying a supply of food and water to the luckless occupants of the dinghy without permitting them to come alongside. There were several small breakers of fresh water on deck, constituting the supply of the felucca, and one of these would be ample for the occupants of the dinghy until they could get ashore or were picked up—indeed, the boat had not capacity for more than one. They were all carefully bunged with cork and canvas, so I could safely launch one of them overboard for the dinghy to pick up. I therefore proceeded to unlash one and roll it toward the still open gangway; and then came the question of provisions. There was a large wash-deck tub on the forecastle which I knew to be water-tight, and it struck me that this might be utilised to float the dry provisions until the dinghy could pick them up; so—first making sure of the position of the boat—I dived below and routed out of Dominguez' bunk a large canvas ditty-bag that I had often seen there, and, emptying out the clothing which it contained, proceeded to fill it with bread and such other provisions as I could most readily lay hands on. This, when full, I tied securely at the neck and took on deck, placing it in the wash-deck tub after I had dragged the latter conveniently close to the gangway. Then, going below again, I brought up three plates, some knives and forks, three tin pannikins, and a few other oddments that I knew would be useful, and placed them in the wash-deck tub with the provisions. Then, when I thought that all was ready, the boat's mast and sail caught my eye as it lay upon the hatchway,— having been flung there by Luis when he cleared out the boat,— and this I determined they should also have, as, while quite resolved to abandon them, I was most anxious that they should be afforded every opportunity to reach the shore alive and well. Then, everything being ready, I once more ran aft to see whereabout the boat now was.

She was a long way astern—quite two miles—and, as

I looked, it appeared as though Dominguez had already given up the pursuit, for the boat did not seem to be moving. Her occupants were, however, all on their feet, staring hard in my direction and waving their arms frantically. I therefore put the helm up, and, jibing round, proceeded to run down toward them. This was rather a risky thing to do, but I thought that with care I could accomplish what I wanted, and still evade recapture. When they saw me returning for them—as they doubtless thought—they started pulling again for a minute or two, then once more lay upon their oars, watching. On my part I also was careful to keep a keen watch upon their movements, my intention being to pass within hailing distance of them, if possible, without giving them a chance to dash alongside. That this was their intention I soon became aware, for as the felucca swept down toward them I could see that their oars were in the water and that they were quietly manœuvring to get the dinghy head-on and as close as possible to the spot over which they expected me to pass. But I was not to be quite so easily caught napping; so, carefully measuring the distance with my eye, I again put the helm up, just at the right moment, and, sweeping past the dinghy within half a dozen fathoms, hailed her discomfited occupants somewhat to this effect:—

"Dinghy ahoy! I am not going to allow you to come alongside again, so I would recommend you to make the best of your way to the Roccas, which, as you know, bear south-south-west, some twenty-five miles distant. I have no doubt that, if you can reach them, you are certain to be taken off sooner or later. Meanwhile, I do not wish you to starve, so I am going to launch overboard some provisions and water for you to pick up; also the boat's mast and sail. The weather promises to hold fine, so you ought to make a fairly good and quick passage of it."

Meanwhile, the moment that Dominguez became aware of what I was doing he swept the boat round with a couple of powerful strokes of his oar, and once again they gave chase with might and main, Dominguez at the same time shouting to me that if I would allow them to return on board they would land me wherever I pleased, and never ask so much as a penny-piece by way of ransom. Could I have trusted the fellow, I would willingly have acceded to his proposal; but I could not. He had already shown himself to be so coldly callous, so absolutely indifferent to the fearful fate to which he had undertaken to consign me, that I felt it would be the sheerest, most insane folly to place myself in his power again. I therefore kept the felucca away until I found that she was rather more than holding her own in the race, when I once more lashed the tiller, and, calling to Dominguez to look out for the things that I was about to launch overboard, ran to the gangway, and first successfully set the wash-deck tub afloat, then rolled the breaker of water out through the open gangway, and finally sent the mast and sail adrift; after which I returned to the tiller and watched the process of picking up the several articles, as I gradually brought the felucca to her former course, close-hauled upon the starboard tack.

## CHAPTER XV

### HEAVY WEATHER

THE provisions, water, and the mast and sail were all successfully secured by the occupants of the boat, after which Dominguez, to my great satisfaction, made sail to the southward, and in another hour his tiny speck of canvas had vanished beyond the horizon. This left me free to attend to my own necessities without further anxiety on the score of being boarded; I therefore once more lashed the tiller in such a position that the felucca would practically steer herself, and then, having first taken a good look round, to see if anything was in sight, proceeded below, found the chart which Dominguez had been using, and ascertained the bearing and distance of the island of Barbadoes. A careful study of this chart revealed the rather disconcerting fact that, taking into consideration the circumstance that Barbadoes was to windward, while Jamaica lay well to leeward of me, it would be almost as quick to return to the latter as it would be to beat out to the former. On the other hand, however, there was this to be taken into consideration, that, on a wind, the felucca might be made to practically steer herself, as I had already ascertained by experiment, while it was quite certain that she could not be persuaded to do any such thing while running *off* the wind. Moreover, by ratching far enough to the northward to enable the felucca to fetch Bardadoes on the next tack, I should be stretching away in a fairly promising direction for being picked up by one of the many British cruisers that were watching the principal outlets from the Caribbean to the Atlantic. After mature deliberation, therefore, I arrived at the conclusion that I could not do better than adhere to my original determination of trying for Barbadoes.

The next question was, how I was to dispose of my time, or rather, what portion of my time it would be best to devote to sleep. One fact stared me in the face at the outset, namely, that until I was once more safe ashore I should have to make shift with the smallest possible amount of sleep, the care of the felucca calling for my almost constant attention; consequently, I should have to so arrange my periods of rest that they would coincide with the times when the felucca could best be left to take care of herself. These periods would obviously occur during the hours of daylight, when it would be possible to take a good look round, and if nothing was in sight, or likely to approach within dangerous proximity for an hour or two, lie down on deck in the shadow of the sail, snatch a short nap, and then take another look round; repeating the process as often as possible throughout the day, in order that I might be fresh and lively for an unbroken watch through the hours of darkness. Having arrived at this conclusion, I forthwith proceeded to carry out my plan, and found it to act fairly well; the only drawback being, that, for want of watching, the felucca evinced a tendency to run a little off the wind, while, when I attempted to remedy this by lashing the helm an inch or two less a-weather, she erred to about the same extent in the other direction by gradually coming-to until her sail was all shaking, and I had to jump hurriedly to my feet and jam the helm hard up to prevent her from coming round upon the other tack. Little by little, however, I remedied both these defects, so that by sunset I had her going along just "full and by," almost as steadily as though I had been standing at the tiller and steering her.

Meanwhile, the wind, which had been very moderate all day, with a distinctly perceptible disposition to become still lighter, had gradually softened down until the little hooker was barely doing her three knots per hour, while the sea had dwindled away until only the long, regular undulations of the swell were left, these being overrun by a wrinkling of those small, uncrested wavelets that frequently precede the setting-in of a calm. Yet there was no reason why a calm should be anticipated, for I was in a region where the trade wind blows all the year round, except when, for a few hours, it gives place to one of the hurricanes that occasionally sweep over the

Caribbean with devastating effect. Could it be possible that such a phenomenon was about to happen? There was no especial reason why it might not be so, for it was the "hurricane season." But there was no sign in the heavens of any approaching atmospheric disturbance—unless, indeed, that faint, scarcely perceptible, hazy appearance up aloft had a sinister meaning!

When the sun had declined to within a few minutes of his setting, I shinned up the mast and took a good look round; but there was nothing in sight. Waiting, therefore, until the sun had sunk below the horizon,—which he did in the midst of a thin, smoky haze, through which the rayless luminary glowed like a ball of red-hot iron,—I descended to the deck and forthwith set to work to prepare myself such a supper as the meagre resources of the felucca permitted; after discussing which, as the stars were shining brilliantly overhead, and the little craft was steering herself, I again stretched myself out on deck to snatch another nap.

I this time slept for several hours, for when I was at length awakened by the rustling of the sail it was close upon midnight. Starting to my feet, I first glanced aloft and then around me; but there was nothing to be seen, the darkness being so profound that it needed but a very small stretch of the imagination to persuade me that it might absolutely be felt! It was the thick, opaque darkness that I remembered having once experienced when, as a boy, I went exploring some Devonshire caverns and clumsily allowed my candle to fall and become extinguished in a pool of water. It seemed to press upon me, to become palpable to the touch, to so closely wrap me about that my very breathing became impeded. And oh, how frightfully hot and close it was! The air was absolutely stagnant, and the slight draught created by the uneasy motion of the felucca seemed to positively scorch the skin. Moreover, there was no dew; the deck-planks, the rail, everything that my hand came into contact with, was dry and warm. I groped my way to the rail and looked abroad over the surface of the ocean, and it will perhaps convey—at all events to those who have used the sea—some idea of the intensity of the darkness when I say that not the faintest glimmer of reflected light came to me from the polished undulations of the slow-creeping swell. The water, however, was highly phosphorescent, for alongside the felucca, and all round her as she rolled and pitched with a quick, jerky, uneasy motion, there extended a narrow band or cloud of faint greenish-blue sea-fire, in the midst of which flashed and glittered millions of tiny stars, interspersed here and there with less luminous patches, in the forms of rings and discs, that vanished and grew into view again at quick intervals in the most weird and uncanny manner.

I groped my way to the companion, and from thence below into the little cabin, where I lighted the lamp and seated myself at the table, well under its cheerful if somewhat smoky beams; for the grave-like darkness of the deck had oppressed me with a feeling very nearly akin to horror, and even the dull yellow light of the lamp seemed inexpressibly cheerful in comparison with it. There was no barometer aboard the felucca, so I had nothing to guide me to the meaning of the weather portents, but I was convinced that something out of the common—something more than a mere thunder-squall—was brewing; and, if so, I should probably have my hands full in taking care of the felucca, with nobody to help me. Still, so awkward a condition of affairs was preferable to that of being delivered over to Morillo, for him to work his fiendish will upon me.

The cabin was much too hot to be comfortable, so, having quickly conquered the feeling of depression produced by the darkness that had preceded the lighting of the cabin lamp, I helped myself to one of Dominguez' excellent cigars, and, lighting it, went on deck, where the dull gleam of the lamp, issuing from the small glazed skylight, now made quite a pleasant little patch of yellow radiance on the deck and bulwarks immediately adjacent. I was by this time broad awake, having secured all the rest and sleep I just then needed; so I fell to pacing to and fro over the small patch of illuminated deck, determined to watch the matter out.

I might have been thus engaged for about an hour, when I became aware that the darkness was no longer so densely and oppressively profound as it had been; there was just the faintest imaginable gleam of light in the sky, whereby it was possible to barely distinguish that the firmament was packed with vast, piling masses of heavy, menacing cloud. Very gradually the light strengthened, assuming, as it did so, a lowering, ruddy tint, until in the course of half an hour the whole sky had the appearance that is seen when it reflects a great but distant conflagration. And now I knew of a surety that a hurricane was brewing; for that fearful ruddy light in the sky was the self-same appearance that I had once before beheld when in the *Althea's* gig I had been attempting to make my way to Bermuda. There was no mistaking the sign, for it was one that, once seen, could never be forgotten.

And now, the storm-fiend having unfurled his fiery banner, and thus given warning of impending war, my time of inaction was over; for there was plenty to do before the felucca could be considered as prepared to engage in the coming struggle. And, at the best, the preparation could only be a partial one; for the craft was not only small, she was old, crazy, and miserably weak for the ordeal that lay before her; and it was not in my power to remedy so serious a defect as that. All that I could do was to take in the great lateen sail and secure it, and substitute for it, if I could, some very much smaller piece of canvas, that, while sufficient to save her from being overrun by the furious sea, would not be too big for the felucca to carry. Fortunately, there was such a sail on board,—a small lug-sail made of stout canvas, and nearly new,—which was intended to be substituted for the lateen on those rare occasions when the little craft might be caught in heavy weather; and this sail I now proceeded to drag up from below and bend to its yard; after which I lowered away the lateen, laid it fore and aft the deck, and made it up, securing it as well as I could by passing innumerable turns of a light wharp round it; after which I firmly lashed it to the bulwarks with as many lashings as I could find pins or cleats for. My next job was to close-reef and set the lug, which I did with the aid of the winch; and this done, I went forward, and, beginning with the fore scuttle, proceeded to carefully batten down every opening in the deck, bringing the cabin lamp on deck in order that I might have a sufficiency of light to work by. The skylight I secured as well as I could by passing lashings over the cover to a couple of ring-bolts conveniently placed in the deck, and I finished up by backing the companion doors with a couple of stout pieces of timber, which I sawed to the proper length and wedged in between the uprights, rendering it practically impossible for the doors to be forced open by a sea, while, by drawing over the slide, I could at the last moment effectually close all access to the cabin. This completed my labours, with which I was fairly well satisfied, the only portion of my defences about which I had any serious doubt being the skylight, the glazed panels of which might easily be smashed by a sea; but I was obliged to take my chance of that, being unable to find anything with which to protect them.

And now, all that remained was to watch and wait.

Nor had I to wait very long; for when, having completed my preparations, I found time to again glance aloft at the frowning sky, I observed that the heavy masses of fiery cloud, that had hitherto seemed to be practically motionless, so stealthy were their movements, were now working with a restless, writhing motion, while ever and anon some small detached fragment of vapour would come sweeping rapidly out from the westward athwart the twisting masses, as though caught and torn off from the main body by some sudden, momentary, partial, but violent movement in the atmosphere. These small, scurrying fragments of cloud, the vanguard of the approaching tempest, rapidly increased in size and in number, while the twisting and writhing of the great cloud masses momentarily grew more rapid and convulsive, until it appeared as though the entire firmament were in the throes of mortal agony, the suggestion soon becoming intensified by the arising in the atmosphere of low, weird, moaning sounds, that at intervals rose and strengthened into a wail as of the spirits of drowned sailors lamenting the coming havoc. And as the wailing sounds arose and grew in volume, sudden stirrings in the stagnant air became apparent, first in the form of exaggerated cats'-paws, that smote savagely upon the glassy surface of the water, scourging it into a sudden flurry of foam, and then dying away again, and then in sudden gusts that swept screaming past the felucca hither and thither, sometimes high enough aloft to leave the water undisturbed, at other times striking it and, as it were, rebounding from the surface, leaving in its path streaks and patches of ruffled water that had scarcely time to subside ere another gust went howling past, to leave them more disturbed than before. These sudden scurryings of wind were the forerunners of the hurricane itself, and only sprang up a short five minutes before the low, hoarse murmur of the gale itself became audible. As this sound arose I looked away to the westward,—the quarter from which it came,—and saw, by the faint, sombre, ruddy light of the unnaturally glowing sky, a thin white line appear upon the horizon, lengthening and thickening as I watched, until it became a rushing wall of foam, bearing down upon the felucca at terrific speed, while behind it the heavens grew pitchy black, and the murmur became a low, deep roar, and the roar grew in volume to a bellow, and the bellow rose to an unearthly howl, and the howl to a yelling shriek, as the hurricane leapt at the felucca—which, happily, was lying stern-on to it—and seized her in its grip, causing the stout, close-reefed lug-sail to fill with a report like that of a cannon, and burying her bows deep in the creamy, hissing smother ere she gathered way, while the scud-water flew over her in blinding, drenching sheets. For a moment, as I gripped the tiller convulsively, I thought the little hooker was about to founder bows first, but after a shuddering pause of a few breathless seconds of horrible suspense, she gathered way, and in another instant was flying before the gale like a frightened thing, at a speed which I dare venture to say she had never before attained.

It was a wild scene in the midst of which I now found myself. With the outburst of the gale the supernatural, ruddy glow of the sky had suddenly faded, to be succeeded by a frightful gloom, which yet was not actual darkness, for the whole surface of the sea had in a few brief seconds become a level sheet of boiling foam, so strongly phosphorescent that it emitted light enough for me to see, with tolerable distinctness, the hull, mast, and sail of the felucca, and to make out the position and character of the principal objects about her deck; and this same weird, ghostly light it probably was that, reflected from the clouds, enabled me also to discern their forms and to distinguish that they were no longer the rounded, swelling masses that they had hitherto been, but were now rent and tattered and ragged with the mad fury of the wind that had seized upon them and was dragging them at headlong speed athwart the arch of heaven. The air, too, was full of spindrift, to perhaps double the height of the felucca's mast, and that too was luminous with a faint, green, misty light that imparted a weird, unreal aspect to everything it shone upon; an effect which was further heightened by the unearthly screaming and howling of the gale.

There was nothing for it but to keep the felucca running dead before the gale; and, fortunately for me, this was by no means a difficult feat, as the craft steered as easily as a boat,—indeed she almost steered herself. For the first half-hour or so nothing special occurred, the hurricane continuing to blow as furiously as at its first mad outfly, while the felucca sped before it as smoothly and steadily as though mounted on wheels and running upon a perfectly smooth and level road; my only fear just then being that the mast would go over the bows, or the sail be blown out of its bolt-ropes. The spar, however, was a good one, and well stayed, while the sail was practically new, and the gear was good; everything therefore held, although I could *feel* that the little craft was straining to an alarming extent. But about half an hour, or thereabout, after the gale first struck us, a movement of the hull—gentle and easy at first, but rapidly increasing—told me that the sea was beginning to rise; and soon after that my troubles commenced in earnest, for the sea got up with astounding rapidity, and as it did so the steering became increasingly difficult, especially when the stern of the little hooker was thrown up on the crest of a sea, at which periods, for a few breathless seconds, the rudder seemed to lose its grip on the water, and the felucca was hurled irresistibly forward, with her bows buried deep in the boiling foam, while she seemed hesitating whether to broach-to to starboard or to port, either alternative of which would have been equally disastrous, since in either case she must have assuredly capsized and gone down. But, by what seemed nothing short of a series of interpositions on the part of a merciful Providence, in every case, just at the moment when a broach-to seemed imminent and inevitable, I felt the rudder take a fresh grip on the water, and we were again safe until the next sea overtook us. And so it continued throughout the remaining hours of that dreadful night, with grim Death threatening me at every upward heave of the little craft, until at length—after what seemed to have been a very eternity of anxiety—the day broke slowly and sullenly ahead, by which time I had grown absolutely callous and indifferent. My nerves had been kept in a state of acute tension so long that they seemed to have become incapable of any further feeling of any kind, and I had ceased to care whether I survived or not; or rather, I had become so thoroughly convinced of the absolute impossibility of ultimate escape, that there seemed to be nothing left worth worrying about. Moreover, I was by this time utterly exhausted with the tremendous exertion of keeping the little craft running straight for so long a time; for at the critical moments of which I have spoken, the helm seemed to so nearly lose its power that it became necessary to jam the tiller hard over, first to this side and then to that, as the felucca seemed actually starting on a wild sheer that must have flung her broadside on to the sea, and so have abruptly finished her career and mine at the same moment.

Thus was it with me when the dull and sullen dawn at length came oozing through the mirky blackness ahead, gradually spreading along the horizon, grey, dismal, and lowering, bringing the tattered shapes and sooty hues of the wildly flying clouds into stronger relief, and revealing a horizon serrated with the frenzied leapings of the angry waters that hissed and roared around the straining felucca, chasing her like angry wolves about to leap upon their prey. At first I thought I was alone in this scene of mad turmoil; but presently, when the light grew stronger, as the felucca hung poised for an instant upon the crest of a foaming comber, that boiled in over both rails amidships and flooded the deck knee-deep, I caught a momentary glimpse of a large craft, some nine miles away on the larboard bow, running, like myself, before the gale. She was hull down, of course, and very probably in the hollow of a sea when first I caught sight of her; for I saw only the heads of her lower masts, with the three topmasts rising above them, the topgallant masts either struck or carried away. She was running under a close-reefed maintopsail and goose-winged foresail, and I took her to be a frigate, though whether one of our own or an enemy, she was too far off for me to be enabled to judge; but, of whatever nationality she may have been, she was undoubtedly a fast vessel, for she soon ran out of sight, although I estimated the speed of the felucca to be quite nine knots.

About an hour later I became sensible of a distinct abatement in the fury of the hurricane, which, in the course of another hour, had still further moderated, until it had become no more than an ordinary heavy gale. Yet so callous had I now become that the change afforded me scarcely any satisfaction; I had grown so utterly indifferent that I had long ceased to care what happened. But I was worn out with fatigue; my limbs ached as though I had been severely beaten, my hands were blistered and raw with the chafe of the tiller, and my eyes were smarting for want of sleep. Rest I felt that I *must* have, and that soon, come what might of it. So, as the gale had moderated somewhat, I determined to heave-to. I believed the felucca would now bear the weight of her small, close-reefed lug even when brought to the wind, and if she did not—well, it did not matter. *Nothing* mattered just then, except that I *must* have rest. So, the sail being set on the starboard side of the mast, I watched my opportunity, and, availing myself of a "smooth," brought the felucca to on the starboard tack, with no worse mishap than the shipping of a sea over the weather bow—as she came up with her head pointing to windward—that swept away the whole of the port bulwarks, from abreast the windlass to the wake of the companion. As she came to, the little craft laid over until the water was up to the lee coamings of her main hatchway, and for a second or two I thought she was going to turn turtle with me; but, once fairly round and head-on to the sea, she rode wonderfully well, especially after I had lashed the helm a-lee and got the mainsheet aft. The latter was a heavy job, but I managed it in about half an hour, with the assistance of the watch-tackle, and, that done, the craft could take care of herself. I therefore slid back the top of the companion, swung myself heavily in through the opening, stumbled down the ladder, staggered across the little cabin, and flung myself, wet to the skin as I was, into my bunk, where I instantly lost consciousness, whether in a swoon or only in a profound sleep I never knew.

## CHAPTER XVI

### THE LAST OF THE FELUCCA

I WAS awakened, some five hours later, by the sound of water washing heavily to and fro, and upon looking over the edge of the bunk I discovered that the cabin was all afloat, the floor being covered to a depth of nearly a foot, so that I looked down upon a miniature sea, violently agitated by the furious leaping and plunging and rolling of the felucca. I could tell, by the roar of the wind and the hissing of the sea, with the frequent heavy fall of water on deck, that it was still blowing heavily, and my first impression was that the water had come down through the companion,—the slide of which I had left open,—but a few minutes of patient observation convinced me that, although a slight sprinkling of spray rained down occasionally, it was not nearly sufficient to account for the quantity that surged and splashed about the cabin. The only other explanation I could think of was that the felucca had sprung a leak; and, leaping out of the bunk, I made my way on deck to ascertain the truth of this conjecture.

It was a dismal and dreary scene that presented itself when I swung myself out on deck through the companion top. It was still blowing with the force of a whole gale; the sky to windward was as black and threatening as ever; and the sea was running so high and breaking so heavily that, as every succeeding comber came sweeping down upon the felucca, with its foaming, hissing crest towering above her to nearly the height of her masthead, it appeared to me—new to the scene as I was—that the next sea must inevitably overwhelm her. Yet, deep in the water as I instantly noticed her to be, the little craft still retained buoyancy enough to climb somehow up the steep slope of each advancing wave, though not to carry her fairly over its crest, every one of which broke aboard her—usually well forward, as luck would have it; with the result that while I had been sleeping below the whole of the lee bulwarks and the forward half of them on the weather side had been swept away, leaving her deck open to the sea, which had swept away every movable thing, leaving nothing but the mast and the splintered ends of the stanchions standing

This constant sweeping of the deck by green seas rendered the task of moving about extremely dangerous, for the rush of water over the fore part of the deck was quite heavy enough to lift a man off his feet and carry him overboard. But I wanted to sound the well; so, securing the pump-rod, which, for convenience, was hung in beckets in the companion, I watched my opportunity, and, rushing forward, succeeded in dropping the rod down the well and getting a firm grip upon the fall of the main halliard before the next sea broke aboard. Then, as the water poured off the deck, I quickly drew the rod out of the well and dashed aft with it to the shelter of the companion in time to escape the next sea. An inspection of the rod then sufficed to realise my worst fears; the little craft had upwards of three feet of water in her hold! Evidently she was leaking badly, and the sooner I could devise some means of relieving her of the weight of water in her the better it would be for me. Had I made this discovery half a dozen hours earlier I should probably have regarded it with perfect indifference; but those five hours of death-like sleep had so greatly refreshed me that I now felt a new man. My state of indifference had passed away with the intensity of my fatigue, and the instinct of self-preservation was once more asserting itself.

My first idea was to rig the pump; but this was instantly discarded, for I had but to stand in the companion way for a couple of minutes, and watch the heavy rush of water athwart the deck, to be convinced of the absolute impossibility of maintaining my position at the pump; for, even if lashed there, my utmost efforts would barely suffice to prevent myself from being swept overboard, while to work the pump would be quite out of the question. Then I remembered that the lazarette hatch was situated immediately at the foot of the companion ladder; and I thought that, by raising the cover, I might get a sort of well from which to bale, and in this way at least keep the leak from gaining upon me, even if I found it impossible to reduce it. For *time* was what I now wanted. I had a conviction that the felucca's seams were opening, through the violent straining of her in the heavy sea and through the tremendous pressure of the wind upon her sail; and I felt tolerably confident that, if I could succeed in keeping her afloat until the gale had blown itself out, all would be well.

But at this point of my meditations it suddenly occurred to me that I was hungry and thirsty; so I descended the companion ladder and made my way to the small pantry, in search of something to eat and drink. It was a small place, scarcely larger than a cupboard, and very imperfectly lighted by a single bull's-eye let into the deck; but it had one merit, it was well provided with good wide shelves, upon which everything that could possibly spoil was stowed; and here I was lucky enough to find an abundance of food—such as it was—and several bottles of the thin, sour wine which Dominguez and his crew drank instead of coffee. I ate and drank there in the pantry, standing up to my knees in water, and when I had finished, went to work with a bucket and rope to bail the water out of the lazarette, standing out on deck, on the lee side of the companion, and drawing the water out of the lazarette as out of a well. I stuck doggedly to this work throughout the whole afternoon and well on into the night, until I could bail no longer for very weariness; and then—having convinced myself that I had succeeded in checking the rise of the water—I took a final look round to ascertain whether anything happened to be in sight, but could see nothing, the night being again dark as pitch, came to the conclusion that it was blowing a trifle less hard than it had been, and that the felucca would live through the night even though I should cease to bale; and so descended to the cabin and again flung myself into my bunk, where I dropped sound asleep as my head touched the pillow.

When I next returned to consciousness my awakening was brought about through the agency of water splashing in over the side of my bunk, the felucca having steadily filled during the period of my sleep until the cabin was fully three feet deep in water. It was broad day, and oh, blessed change! the sun was shining brilliantly down through the skylight, while the wind had evidently dropped to a pleasant breeze. A heavy sea, however, was still running,—as I could tell by the movements of the felucca,—and I could hear the water well and gurgle up the side of the little craft and go pouring across her deck from time to time, although not so frequently as before I turned in.

I rolled reluctantly out of my bunk—for I seemed to be aching in every joint of my body, and my head was burning and throbbing with a dull pain like what would be occasioned by the strokes of a small hammer—and waded, waist deep in water, to the companion ladder, up which I crawled, and so out on deck.

The gale had blown itself out, the wind having subsided to a very gentle breeze, that I soon discovered was fast dying away to a calm—although what little wind there was still came breathing out from the westward. The sky was perfectly clear, of a rich, deep, pure blue colour, without a shred of cloud to be seen in the whole of the vast vault; and in the midst of it, about two hours high, hung the morning sun, a dazzling globe of brilliance and heat. The sea, I now found, had subsided almost entirely, but a very heavy swell was still running, over which the felucca rode laboriously, the water in her interior occasionally pinning her down to such an extent that the quick-running swell would brim up over her bows and pour in a perfect cataract athwart her deck. This, however, I was not surprised at, for—as nearly as I could judge—the felucca showed barely nine inches of freeboard! Still the little hooker seemed surprisingly buoyant, considering her water-logged condition, and now that the seas no longer broke over her, there seemed to be no reason why, given enough time, I should not be able to pump her dry, and resume my voyage to Barbadoes.

So I rigged the pump and went to work, hoping that, as the gale had now abated and the sea had gone down, the straining of the hull and the opening of the seams had ceased, and that consequently the felucca was no longer in a leaky condition. I toiled on throughout the whole of that roasting morning, with the sun beating mercilessly down upon me, while the water swirled athwart the deck and about my legs, until noon, and then, utterly exhausted with my labour, my skin burning with fever and my hands raw and bleeding, I was fain to cry "spell ho!" and give up for a time, while I sought somewhat to eat and drink. I had worked with a good will, sanguinely hoping that when I felt myself compelled to knock off I should discover that I had sensibly diminished the amount of water in the felucca's interior; but this hope was cruelly disappointed, for when I reached the companion, on my way below, I found that there was no perceptible difference in the height of the water in the cabin from what it had been before I turned to; indeed the water seemed to have *risen* rather than diminished, a sure indication that the hull was still leaking, and that by no effort of mine could I hope to keep the craft much longer afloat.

And now, as I descended to the cabin, and noted the violence with which the water surged hither and thither with the rolling and pitching of the little vessel, a wild fear seized upon me that I might find all the provisions in the pantry spoiled. A moment later and my surmise was changed to certainty, for as I opened the door of the small, cupboard-like apartment, a recoiling wave surged out through the doorway, its surface bestrewed with the hard, coarse biscuits that sailors speak of as "bread." The water had risen high enough to flood the shelf upon which the eatables had been stowed, and everything was washed off and utterly spoiled. Worse still, there was no possibility of obtaining a further supply, for the lazarette, or storehouse, was beneath the cabin floor and had been flooded for hours. Moreover, it was unapproachable. Fortunately I did not feel very hungry; I was, however, consumed with a burning thirst which—all the water-casks having been washed overboard — I quenched by draining a whole bottle of the thin, sour wine of which I have before spoken. Then I went to work to collect all the biscuit I could secure, and carried it up on deck to dry in the sun, spreading it out on a cloth on the top of the companion; and while engaged upon this task, and also in removing my small stock of wine to the deck—for the cabin was by this time uninhabitable—I began to consider what I could do to save my life when the felucca should founder, as founder she must, now that I had demonstrated my inability to keep the leaks under. The question was not a very knotty one, or one demanding very profound consideration; obviously there was but one thing to do, and that was to build a raft with such materials as offered themselves to my hand. And just at this point the first difficulty presented itself in the shape of the question: what available materials were there? For, as I have already mentioned, the deck had been swept of every movable thing, including the big lateen yard, which had doubtless gone overboard when the bulwarks were carried away. There seemed to be absolutely *nothing*, unless I set to work to break up the felucca herself! Yet stay, there was the mast, the yard that spread and supported the lug-sail, the tiller—a good, stout, serviceable stick of timber—and—yes, certainly, the hatches—which could now be safely taken off, as the sea no longer swept over the deck heavily enough to pour over the coamings. Surely with those materials I ought to be able to construct a raft buoyant enough to support me, even although it would be obviously necessary for me to construct it on the deck, and then patiently wait until the felucca sank and floated it off—for it would be quite impossible for me to launch it.

So to work I went, my first task being to descend into the flooded forecastle and grope about for an axe that I knew was kept there somewhere; and I was fortunate enough to find it almost at once. Then, returning to the deck, I lowered away the lug-sail and cut the canvas adrift from the yard, carefully lashing the latter, that it might not roll or be washed overboard. Then I began to cut away the mast, chopping a deep notch in it close to the deck, and when I heard it beginning to complain, I cut the laniards of the weather rigging, when away it went over the side with a crash. This gave me a good deal of trouble, for I wanted the spar on deck, not overboard; so I had to go to work to parbuckle it up the side, which I managed pretty well by watching the lift of the seas. Then I cut the mast in halves, laid the two halves parallel athwart the deck, and secured the yard and the tiller to them, as cross-pieces, with good stout lashings. And finally, to these last I firmly lashed four of the main hatch covers, when I had a platform of some twelve feet long and eight feet wide to support me. All that now remained to be done was to secure my provisions and wine, which I did by stowing the whole in a double thickness of tarpaulin, the edges of which I gathered together and tightly lashed with spunyarn, finally securing the bundle to the raft by a short end of rope, so that it might not be washed away when the felucca should take her final plunge; and I had then done everything that it was possible for me to do.

By the time that my task was finished the sun had sunk to within a hand's breadth of the western horizon, while the wind had dwindled away until it had become the faintest zephyr, scarcely to be distinguished save by the slight ruffling of the water here and there where it touched, it being so nearly a flat calm that already great oily-looking patches of gleaming smoothness had appeared and were spreading momentarily through the faint blue ripplings that still betrayed a movement in the air. As for me, I was utterly exhausted with my long day's toil under the roasting sun; every bone in my body was aching; I was in a burning fever, and was sick with the smart of my raw and bleeding hands. The old feeling of callousness and indifference to my fate was once more upon me, and as I gazed at the crazy-looking raft which I had constructed with such a lavish expenditure of painful toil, I smiled in grim irony of myself that I should have done so much to preserve that life which now seemed of such little worth, and which promised soon to become an unendurable burden to me. A reaction from the excitement that had sustained me during my labours had set in, and I am persuaded that had any further exertion been necessary for the preservation of my life I should not have undertaken it.

Meanwhile the felucca had sunk nearly to her covering-board, and might be expected to founder at any moment. I climbed laboriously upon the top of the closed skylight and took a last, long look round to ascertain whether anything had drifted into my range of view while I had been engaged upon the raft, but there was nothing; the horizon was bare throughout its entire circumference; so I climbed down again, and, staggering to the raft, flung myself down upon it, with my bundle of provision as a pillow, and patiently awaited the evanishment of the felucca.

Poor little craft! what a forlorn, weather-beaten, sea-washed wreck she looked, as she lay there wallowing wearily and—as it seemed to me—painfully upon the long, creeping, glassy undulations of the swell! How different from the trim, sturdy little hooker that had sailed seaward so confidently and saucily out of Kingston harbour a few years—no, not *years*, it must be months, or—was it only *days*—a few *days* ago? It seemed more like years than days to me, and yet—why, of course it *could* only be days. Heaven, how my head ached! how my brain seemed to throb and boil within my skull! and surely it was not blood—it must be fire that was coursing through my veins and causing my body to glow like white-hot steel! A big, glassy mound of swell came creeping along toward the felucca, and, as she rolled toward it, curled in over her covering-board and poured in a heavy torrent across her deck, swirling round my raft and shifting it a foot or two nearer the side; and as it swept past I dabbled one of my hands in it, and was dully surprised that the contact did not cause the water to hiss and boil! Another mountain of water came brimming over the deck of the shuddering craft and shifted the raft so far that it fairly overhung the covering-board, so that when the felucca rolled in the opposite direction the end of the raft not only dipped in the water but actually lifted and floated, the heave of the water sucking it perhaps another foot off the deck. The next two or three undulations passed harmlessly by,—the swing and roll of the felucca was such that she just happened to meet them at the right moment, though lagging a little at the last,—and then came another great liquid hill, towering high above the horizon, until the sinking sun was utterly obscured. On it swept toward the felucca, which had now slewed so that she faced the coming swell nearly stem-on, the water in her meanwhile rushing forward as she sank down into the trough until her stem-head was completely buried. Now she was meeting the breast of the on-coming swell, her bows still pinned down by the rush of water in her interior, and now the glistening green wave was upon her, sweeping aft along and athwart her deck, mounting over the coamings of the main hatchway and pouring down the opening in a smooth, hissing, four-sided cataract, snatching up the raft in its embrace and shooting it half a dozen fathoms clear of the doomed craft, and rushing along the deck until even the companion and the skylight were submerged. By that time the hull was full, the curious rectangular hollow in the surface of the water that marked the position of the main hatchway was filled, the hull was completely hidden save for a splintered stanchion that projected above water here and there. Then, as the wave passed, the bows of the felucca emerged, gleaming and dripping with snowy, foaming cascades, that poured off the uncovered portion of the deck. Higher and higher rose the bows out of the water, until some ten feet in length of the felucca was revealed, the deck gradually sloping until it assumed an almost perpendicular inclination, when slowly, silently, and glidingly, without a sob or gurgle of escaping air, the wreck slid backward and downward until it vanished beneath the waters, now gleaming in gold and crimson with the last rays of the setting sun. A few seconds later the great luminary also vanished, a sudden grey pallor overspread the ocean, and I found myself alone indeed, swaying upon that vast, heaving expanse, with nothing between me and death save the clumsy structure that I had so laboriously put together, and which now looked so insignificantly small that I caught myself wondering why my weight did not sink it.

But it did not; on the contrary, the raft proved to be surprisingly buoyant, riding over the great, glassy, round-backed hills of swell as dry as a bone, with a gentle, swaying movement that somehow seemed to soothe my fever-racked frame, so that the condition of semi-delirium that had possessed me just before the felucca foundered passed away and left me sufficiently self-possessed to recognise the necessity for eating and drinking, if I was to survive and get the better of my misfortunes. So I carefully opened my bundle and extracted from it a small quantity of sun-dried biscuit — which, thanks to the curiously gentle manner in which the raft had been launched, had received no further wetting — and proceeded to make such a meal as I could, washing it down with a sparing draught of wine. But although the biscuit had dried superficially, it was still wet and pasty in the middle, and horribly nauseous to the palate, so that I made but a poor meal; after which I stretched myself at full length upon the raft, and endeavoured to find relief in sleep. But, exhausted though I was, sleep would not come to me; on the contrary, my memory and imagination rapidly became painfully excited. I thought of Dominguez, and wondered whether he and his companions had escaped the hurricane; then I thought of Morillo and his fiendish hatred of me; and so my thoughts and fancies chased one another until they became all mingled together in an inextricable jumble; and through it all I heard myself singing, shouting, laughing, arguing upon impossible subjects with wholly imaginary persons, and performing I know not what other mad vagaries, until finally, I suppose, I must have become so utterly exhausted as to have subsided into a restless, feverish sleep.

# CHAPTER XVII

## CAPTAIN LEMAITRE

CONSCIOUSNESS returned to me with the sensation of soft, delicate light impinging upon my closed eyelids, and I opened my eyes upon the picture of a sky of deepest, richest, purest blue, studded with wool-like tufts of fleecy cloud, opalescent with daintiest tints of primrose and pink as they sailed overhead with a slow and gentle movement out from the north-east. The eastern horizon was all aglow with ruddy orange light, up through which soared broad, fan-like rays of white radiance — the spokes of Phœbus' chariot wheels — that, through a scale of countless subtle changes of tincture, gradually merged into the marvellously soft richness of the prismatic sky.. A gentle breeze, warm and sweet as a woman's breath, lightly ruffled the surface of the sea, that heaved in long, low hills of deep and brilliant liquid sapphire around me; and here and there a sea-bird wheeled and swept with plaintive cries, and slanting, motionless pinions, in long, easy, graceful curves over the slowly undulating swell.

I sat up and looked about me vaguely and wonderingly, for the moment forgetful of the circumstances that had placed me in so novel a situation, and at the instant a glowing point of golden fire flashed into view upon the eastern horizon, as the upper rim of the sun hove above the undulating rim of the sea; and in a moment the rippling blue of the laughing water was laced with a long, broadening wake of gleaming, dancing, liquid gold, as the great palpitating disc of the god of day left his ocean couch, and entered upon his journey through the heavens.

My forgetfulness was but momentary; as the radiance and warmth of the returning sun swept over the glittering, scintillating, golden path that stretched from the horizon to the raft, the memory of all that had gone before, and the apprehension of what still haply awaited me, returned, and, as quickly as my cramped and aching limbs would allow, I staggered to my feet, flinging anxious, eager glances all around me in search of a sail. The horizon, however, was bare, save where the long, narrow pinion of a wheeling sea-bird swiftly cut it for a moment here and there; and I sighed wearily as I resumed my recumbent position upon the raft, wondering whether rescue would ever come, or whether it was my doom to float there, tossing hour after hour and day after day, like the veriest waif, until thirst and starvation had wrought their will upon me, or until another storm should arise, and the now laughing ocean should overwhelm me in its fury.

And indeed I cared very little just then what fate awaited me; for I was so ill, my frame was so racked with fever and my head so distracted with the fierce throbbing and beating of the wildly coursing blood in it, that the only thing I craved for was relief from my sufferings. It was a matter of the utmost indifference to me at that moment whether the relief came from death or from any other source, so long as it came quickly. My strength was leaving me with astounding rapidity, and I was quite aware that if I wished to husband the little that still remained to me I ought to eat; but the mere idea of eating excited so violent a repugnance, that it was with the utmost difficulty I resisted the almost overwhelming temptation to pitch my slender stock of sea-sodden biscuit overboard. On the other hand, I was consumed with a torturing thirst that I vainly strove to assuage by so reckless a consumption of my equally slender stock of wine, that at the end of the day only two bottles remained. Such recklessness was of course due to the fact that I was unaccountable for my actions; I was possessed of a kind of madness, and I knew it, but I had lost all control over myself, and cared not what happened. More than once I found myself seriously considering the advisability of throwing myself off the raft, and so ending everything without more ado; and I have often wondered why I did not do so; it was certainly not the fear of death that prevented me. As the day wore on my sufferings steadily increased in intensity; my brain throbbed and pulsated with pain so acute that it seemed as though a million wedges were being driven into my skull; a host of weird, outrageous, and horrible fancies chased each other through my imagination; I became possessed of the idea that the raft was surrounded and hemmed in by an ever-increasing multitude of frightful sea monsters, who fought with each other in their furious efforts to get within reach of me; day and night seemed to come and go with bewildering rapidity; and finally everything became involved in a condition of hopelessly inextricable confusion, that eventually merged into oblivion.

.    .    .    .    .    .    .    .

My next consciousness was that of a sound of gurgling, running water, and of a buoyant, heaving, plunging motion; of flashing sunshine coming and going upon my closed eyelids; of the vibrant hum of wind through taut rigging and in the hollows of straining canvas; of a murmur of voices, and of the regular tramp of footsteps to and fro on the planking overhead; and for the moment I thought that I was aboard the *Tern*, and just awaking from a sleep during which I had been haunted with an unusually long series of peculiarly unpleasant dreams. But as I opened my eyes and looked with somewhat languid interest upon my surroundings, I became aware that I was in a small, plain, but fairly snug cabin, of which I seemed to possess no previous knowledge; and at the same moment a confused but rapidly clearing memory of what had happened came to me, together with the knowledge that I had been rescued from the raft, and was feeling very much better. But an attempt to move, preliminary to turning out, revealed the disconcerting fact that I was as weak and helpless as a new-born infant, so I was perforce obliged to remain where I was; and in a short time I dozed off into a light sleep again, soothed thereto by the hum of the wind, the gurgling wash of water along the side of the ship, close to my ear, and the gentle heave and plunge of the fabric that bore me.

From this nap I was awakened by the somewhat noisy opening of my cabin door; and upon opening my eyes I beheld a swarthy and somewhat dirty-looking individual bending over me. From his appearance I at once set him down as a Frenchman; and as I gazed up into his face with mild curiosity, this impression became confirmed by his exclaiming in French—

"Ah, monsieur, so you have come to your senses at last, eh? Good! I knew I could save you, although François declared you to be as good as dead when he brought you aboard! And now, mon ami, what do you say; can you eat something?"

"Thank you," replied I, in the same language; "now that you come to mention it, I think I can."

"Good!" ejaculated the unknown; "rest tranquil for

but a short time, and I will see what that rascal cook of ours can do for you. Stay! another dose of quinine will do you no harm, just by way of precaution, you know, although I think I have driven the fever out of you at last. Permit me."

And, so saying, he laid a rather grimy hand upon my forehead for a moment, and then transferred it to my wrist, remarking—

"Good! the skin is cool and moist, the pulse normal again. Ha, ha, my friend, you will do, you will do; henceforth the cook must be your doctor. All you need now is plenty of good nourishing food to restore your strength. Now, drink this, and as soon as you have swallowed it I will away to the galley."

While speaking, this individual had been busying himself with a bottle, from which he extracted a small quantity of white powder, which he mixed with water and then handed me the mixture to drink.

"Thank you," said I, handing him back the glass. "And now, monsieur, do me the favour to tell me your name, in order that I may know to whom I am indebted for my preservation."

"My name?" he repeated, with a laugh. "Oh, that will keep, monsieur, that will keep. At present your most urgent necessity is food, which I am now going to get for you. When I return I will tell you all you may wish to know, while you are eating. For the present, adieu, monsieur. If you feel disposed to sleep again, do so;

sleep is nearly as valuable as food to you just now. When I have some of the latter ready for you I will wake you, never fear."

So saying, and before I could utter another word, he vanished, slamming the cabin door after him.

His retirement caused me a sensation of distinct relief, at which I was very greatly annoyed with myself; for had not this man doubly saved my life, first by rescuing me from the raft, and afterwards by nursing me through what I believed had been a serious illness? Yet, ingrate that I was, even in the brief interview that I have just described I had taken an unmistakable dislike to the man! It was not so much that he was unclean in person and attire,—it was possible that there might be a good and sufficient excuse for that,—but what had excited my antipathy, when I came to analyse the feeling, was a certain false ring in his voice, a subtle something in his manner suggestive of the idea that his friendliness and heartiness were not natural to him—were assumed for a purpose. Yet why it should be so, why he should have rescued me from the raft and afterwards troubled himself to fight and drive out the fever that threatened to destroy me, unless from a feeling of humanity and compassion for my pitiable condition, I could not imagine; yet there had been—or so I fancied—a fierce, shifty gleam in his coal-black eyes during the few brief minutes that he had bent over me as I lay there in my bunk, that seemed to reveal cruelty and treachery, rather than pity and goodwill. Let me describe the man. Standing there beside my bunk, he had conveyed to me the impression of an individual nearly six feet in height,—I afterwards found his stature to be five feet ten inches in his stockings,—broad across the shoulders in proportion, and big boned, but lean almost to the point of emaciation. His skin was dry, of an unwholesome yellow tint, and shrivelled, as though he had once been stout and burly of form but had now become thin, while his skin had failed to shrink in the same proportion as his flesh. His eyes were, as I have said, black, small, and deeply sunken in his head; his hair was a dull, dead black, and was worn cropped close to his head; his black beard was trimmed to a point; and he wore a moustache, the long ends of which projected athwart his upper lip like a spritsail yard. His hands were thin, showing the tendons of the fingers working under the loose skin at every movement of them, while the fingers themselves were long, attenuated, ingrained with dirt, and furnished with long, talon-like yellow nails, that looked as though they never received the slightest attention. Finally, his clothing consisted of a cotton shirt, that looked as though it had been in use for at least a month since its last visit to the laundress, a pair of grimy blue dungaree trousers, and a pair of red morocco slippers.

As I lay there in the bunk, recalling the appearance of my rescuer, and trying to evolve therefrom some definite impression of the man's character, I became aware that the duty of the ship seemed to be carried on with a very unnecessary amount of vociferation and contumelious language. An Englishman will sometimes, in critical or urgent moments, garnish his orders with an expletive or two by way of stimulus to the crew; but upon the occasion to which I am now referring there was not the slightest excuse for anything of the kind. The weather was fine, the wind moderate, and we were evidently not engaged upon the performance of some feat of complicated or difficult navigation; for the course remained constant, and there was neither making nor shortening of sail. It simply appeared that the officer of the watch happened to be one of those distressing and trouble-making individuals who regard it as incumbent upon themselves to continually "haze" the men; for he was constantly bawling some trifling order, and accompanying it with a running fire of abuse that must have been furiously exasperating to the person addressed.

After an absence of about half an hour, the man who had already visited me returned, this time bearing a large bowl of smoking broth, and a plate containing three large ship biscuits of the coarsest kind. The broth, however, exhaled a distinctly appetising odour, which had the effect of again reminding me that I was hungry; so, with my visitor's assistance, I contrived to raise myself into a sitting posture, and forthwith attacked the contents of the bowl, previously breaking into it a small quantity of biscuit. The "broth" proved to be turtle soup, deliciously made, and, taking my time over the task, I consumed the whole of it, my companion meanwhile giving an account of himself, his ship, and the circumstances attending my rescue.

"My name, monsieur," he said, in reply to a question of mine, "is Lemaitre—Jean Lemaitre; a native of Fort Royal, in the island of Martinique, and owner as well as Captain of *La belle Jeannette*—the schooner which you are now honouring with your presence. I am in the slave-trade, monsieur,—doing business chiefly with the Spaniards,—and exactly a month ago to-day I sailed from Havana for the Guinea coast. We came west and south about, round Cape San Antonio, stretching well over toward the Spanish Main, in order to avoid, if possible, those pestilent cruisers of yours, which seem to be everywhere, and are always ready to snap up everything that they can lay their hands upon. By great good fortune we managed to dodge them, and got through without being interfered with; but it threw us into the track of the hurricane, and necessitated our remaining hove-to for twenty-six hours. Four days later, as we were sailing merrily along, we saw something floating ahead of us, and ten minutes later we all but ran down your raft, on which we saw you lying face downwards, while the sharks were fighting each other in their efforts to get at you and drag you off. François, my mate, was for leaving you where you were,—asserting that you must surely be dead, and that to pick up a dead man would make the voyage unlucky,—but I am a humane man, monsieur, and I insisted upon heaving-to and sending away a boat to bring you aboard. The boat's crew had a hard job of it to drive off the sharks, and to get you safely into the boat, monsieur; and, even so, the creatures followed the boat alongside— to the number of seventeen, for I counted them myself. François suggested that we should throw you to them, declaring that you were as good as dead already, and that it was a shame to disappoint the sharks after they had waited so patiently for you; but I am a humane man, monsieur,—as I believe I have already mentioned,—and I would not listen to his proposal. So I had you brought down below and placed in this spare cabin, where I have attended to you ever since,—that was ten days ago,—and now, behold, the fever has left you, your appetite has returned, and in another week, please the good God we shall have you on deck again, as well as ever you were."

"Thank you, monsieur," said I. "I am infinitely obliged to you for the humanity that prompted you to pick me up — despite the dissuasions of your mate, François—and also for the trouble you have taken in nursing me through my illness. Fortunately, I am in a position to make substantial recognition of my gratitude; and upon my return to Jamaica—as to which I presume there will be no difficulty—it shall be my first business to take such steps as shall insure you against all pecuniary loss on my account."

"Ah, monsieur," exclaimed Lemaitre, "I beg that

you will say no more on that score; it hurts me that you should think it necessary to mention so mercenary a word as that of 'reward.' We are both sailors, and although we have the misfortune to be enemies, that is no reason why one brave man should not aid another in distress, without looking for a reward. As to your return to Jamaica, no doubt that can be managed upon our return voyage"—

"Your return voyage!" I interrupted. "Can you not manage it forthwith, captain? I can make it quite worth your while to up helm and run me back at once. It is of the utmost importance to me to return to Port Royal with the least possible delay, and"—

"Alas, monsieur, it cannot be done," interrupted Lemaitre, in his turn. "A cargo of slaves is even now awaiting me in the Cameroon River, and my patrons in Havana are impatiently looking forward to their delivery. If I were to disappoint them I should be ruined, for I have many competitors in the trade to contend with, especially since all this talk has arisen about making slave-trading illegal. No; I regret to be obliged to refuse you, monsieur, but there is no help for it."

"At least," said I, "you will transfer me to a British man-o'-war, should we chance to fall in with one?"

"And be myself captured, and lose my ship for my

pains!" exclaimed Lemaitre. "Oh no, monsieur; we will give your ships a wide berth, if we fall in with them, and trust to our heels."

"Nonsense, monsieur," I returned. "Surely you cannot suppose I would be so ungrateful as to permit any such thing. I am a British officer, and should, of course, make a point of seeing that, in such a case, you were held exempt from capture. My representations would be quite sufficient to secure that for you."

"Well, monsieur, we will see, we will see," answered Lemaitre; and therewith he took the empty soup bowl from my hand, and retired from the cabin, slamming the door, as usual, behind him.

For the next three days I continued to occupy my bunk, my strength returning slowly; but on the fourth I made shift, with Lemaitre's assistance, to get into my clothes, and crawl on deck; and from that moment my progress toward recovery was rapid. Meanwhile, the "hazing" of which I have spoken continued at regular intervals, day and night, and I soon ascertained that the individual responsible for it was none other than the François who so kindly suggested that I should be hove overboard to the sharks. This fellow was evidently a born bully; he never opened his mouth to deliver an order without abusing and insulting the men, and as often as not the abuse was accentuated with blows, the sounds of which, and the accompanying cries of the men, I could distinctly hear in my cabin. That, however, was hardly the worst of it; for I soon discovered that Lemaitre, the skipper of this precious craft in which such doings were permitted, was a drunkard; for every night, at about nine o'clock, I used to hear him come below, and order out the rum and water; after which he and François, or the second mate,—according to whose watch below it happened to be, — would sit for about an hour, drinking one against the other, until the language of both became incoherent, when the pair of them would stagger and stumble off to their respective staterooms.

This was my first experience of a slaver, and a most unpleasant experience it was. The vessel herself,—a schooner of one hundred and twenty tons register,—although superbly modelled, a magnificent sea-boat, and sailing like a witch, was rendered uncomfortable in the extreme as an abode by her filthy condition. Cleanliness seemed to be regarded by Lemaitre as a wholly unnecessary luxury, with the result that no effort was made to keep in check the steady accumulation of dirt from day to day, much less to remove that which already existed. Even the daily washing down of the decks—which, with the British sailor, has assumed the importance and imperative character of a religious function — was deemed superfluous. Nor were the crew any more careful as to their own condition or that of their clothing. It is a fact that during the whole period of my sojourn on board *La belle Jeannette* I never saw one of her people attempt to wash himself or any article of clothing; and, as a natural result of this steadfast disregard of the most elementary principles of cleanliness, the little hooker simply swarmed with vermin.

But, bad as it was, this was not the worst. The crew, from Lemaitre downward, were a low, brutal, quarrelsome gang, always wrangling together, and frequently fighting; while, as I have already mentioned, the one predominating idea of François, the chief mate, was that they could only be kept in order by constantly and impartially rope's-ending them all round. Possibly he may have been right; at all events, I found it far easier to excuse his behaviour after I had seen the crew than I had before.

All this time Lemaitre had been behaving toward me with a rough, clumsy, off-hand kindness that his personal appearance would have led no one to expect, and which, try as I would, I could not bring myself to regard as genuine, because, through it all, there seemed now and then to rise to the surface an underflow of repressed malignity, not pronounced enough to be certain about, yet sufficiently distinct to provoke in me a vague sensation of uneasiness and distrust. To put the matter concisely, although Lemaitre was by no means effusive in his expressions of goodwill toward me, and although there was a certain perfunctory quality in such attentions as he showed me, there was with it all a curious subtle something, so intangible that I found it utterly impossible to define or describe it, which yet impressed me with the feeling that it was all unreal, assumed, a mockery and a pretence ; though *why* it should be so, I could not for the life of me divine.

## CHAPTER XVIII

### A DOUBLE TRAGEDY

I HAD been up and about for a full week, and had during that period observed in Lemaitre's manner toward me not only a steadily decreasing solicitude for my welfare—which was perhaps only natural, now that my health was rapidly improving—but also a growing disposition to sneer and gibe at me, covert at first but more pronounced and unmistakable with every recurring day, that strongly tended to confirm the singular suspicion I have endeavoured to bring home to the mind of the reader in the preceding chapter. Then one night an incident occurred that in a moment explained everything, and revealed to me the unpleasant fact that, so far as my enemy Morillo was concerned, I was still in as great danger as when on board the felucca, although in the present case the danger was perhaps a trifle more remote.

I have already mentioned Lemaitre's habit of drinking himself into a state of intoxication every night. This habit, and the obscene language that the man seemed to revel in when in such a condition, was so disgusting to me that not the least-prized advantage afforded by my convalescence was the ability to remain on deck until the nightly saturnalia was at an end and Lemaitre and his companion had retired to their cabins. On the particular night, however, of which I am about to speak, a slight recurrent touch of fever caused me to slip quietly below and turn in before the orgie began; not that I expected to get to sleep, but simply because I believed the warmth and dryness of my bunk would be better for me than the damp night air on deck.

Punctually at nine o'clock Lemaitre and his chief mate came noisily clattering down the companion ladder, glasses and a bottle of rum were produced, and the carouse began. It had not progressed very far before it became apparent to me, as I lay there in my hot bunk, tossing restlessly, that Lemaitre was in an unusually excited and quarrelsome condition, and that François, the chief mate, was rapidly approaching a similar condition as he gulped down tumbler after tumbler of liquor. They were always argumentative and contradictory when drinking together, but to-night they were unusually so. At length François made some remark as to the extraordinary good fortune they had met with on this particular voyage, in having come so far without falling in with a British cruiser; at which Lemaitre laughed scornfully, declaring that there was not a British cruiser afloat that could catch *La belle Jeannette*; and that, even if it were otherwise, he should have no fear of them this voyage. "For," said he, "have we not a guarantee of safety in the presence of that simple fool Courtenay on board? Have we not saved his life by rescuing him from the raft? And do you suppose they would reward our humanity, ha, ha! by making a prize of the schooner? Not they! If there is one thing those asses of British pride themselves upon more than another it is their chivalrous sense of honour —a sentiment, my child, that they would not outrage for the value of fifty such schooners as this. All the same," he added, with an inflection of deep cunning in his voice, "I do not want to meet with a British cruiser at close enough quarters to be compelled to hand the dear Courtenay over to his countrymen; oh no!"

"Why not?" demanded François; "what advantage is it to you to keep him on board? Is it because you are so fond of his company? Pah! if you had eyes in your head, you would see that, despite his gratitude to you for saving his life, he despises you. What do you mean to do with him? Are you going to turn him adrift among the negroes when we arrive upon the coast? I never could understand why you insisted upon saving him at all."

"No?" queried Lemaitre, with a sneering laugh. "Ah, that is because you are a fool, François, *mon enfant*, a more arrant fool even than the dear Courtenay himself.

Do you suppose I did it out of pity for his condition, or because I love the British? No. I will tell you why, idiot. It is because he will fetch a good five hundred dollars at least in the slave-market at Havana."

"So *that* is what you intend to do with him, is it?" retorted François. "Well, Lemaitre, I always knew you for an ass, but, unless you had told me so with your own lips, I would never have believed you to be such an ass as to sell a man for five hundred dollars when you can just as easily get a thousand for him. Yet you call me fool and idiot! Pah, you sicken me!"

"Oh, I sicken you, do I?" growled Lemaitre, by this time well advanced toward intoxication. "Take care what you are saying, my friend, or I shall be apt to sicken you so thoroughly that you will be fit for nothing but a toss over the lee bulwarks. No doubt it is I who am the fool, and you who are the clever one; but I should like to hear by what means you would propose to get a thousand dollars for the fellow. True, he is young and stalwart, and will be in prime condition by the time that we get back to Havana,—I will see to that,—but I have known better men than he sold for less than five hundred dollars; ay, *white* men too, not negroes."

"Did I not say you are an ass?" retorted François. "Who talks of selling him at Havana? You, not I. Do you not know who this Courtenay is, then? I will tell you, most wise and noble captain. He is the youth who attacked and destroyed Morillo's settlement at Cariacou,—I remember the name perfectly well,—and I was told at Havana, by one who ought to know, that Morillo had given it out among his friends that he would pay one thousand dollars to anyone who should bring Courtenay to him alive And that is not all, either. You know what Morillo is; he has declared a feud against this miserable, meddlesome Englishman, and not only will he gladly pay a thousand dollars for the privilege of wreaking his vengeance upon him, but the man who delivers your friend Courtenay into his hands will be free to sail the seas without molestation from Morillo as long as he lives. What think you of that, Captain Lemaitre?"

"Is this true?" demanded Lemaitre.

"Ay," answered François, "as true as that you and I are sitting here in this cabin."

"Why did you not tell me of this before, François, my friend?" asked Lemaitre, in a wheedling tone.

"Why did I not tell you before?" echoed François. "Ask rather why I tell you now, and I will answer that it is because I am such a fool that I cannot keep a good thing to myself when I have it. Sac-r-r-r-e! what need was there for me to make you as wise as myself, eh? However, I am not going to let you have this choice little bit of information for nothing. I have told you how to make a clear five hundred dollars over and above what you could have earned without the information I have been idiot enough to give you, and you must pay me half the amount; do you understand?"

"Ay, I understand," answered Lemaitre, with a sudden return to his former sneering, aggressive manner; "but I should like to know—just for the satisfaction of my curiosity—how you propose to compel me to pay you that two hundred and fifty dollars that you talk about."

"Why, easily enough," snarled François, with sudden fury, as he realised that Lemaitre intended to evade the extortion if he could. "If you do not pay me immediately after receiving the reward from Morillo, I will denounce you to him. I will say that you intended to have yielded up your prisoner to the British, in order that you might curry favour with them and secure immunity from capture by them; and that you would never have given him up to Morillo at all but for my threats. And I suppose you know what that will mean for you, eh?"

"Oh, so that is what you would do, is it, my friend?" returned Lemaitre, with a harsh laugh. "Well, well, it will be time enough for you to threaten when I refuse to pay you the two hundred and fifty dollars. Until then, there is no need for us to quarrel; so fill up your glass, François, and let us drink to the health of the dear Courtenay, who, after all, was quite worth picking up off the raft, don't you think?"

Then followed a gurgling sound as the two topers filled their glasses. A gulping and smacking of lips, succeeded by a banging of the empty tumblers upon the table, came clearly to me through the latticed upper panel of my door; and then certain staggering sounds, as the two struggled to their feet, were followed by Lemaitre thickly bidding his companion good-night, as the pair reeled and stumbled away to their respective berths.

I slept badly that night, the fever, with the intelligence I had just acquired, combining to make me restless and wakeful; but after tossing from side to side, until about two bells in the morning watch, I gradually sank into a troubled sleep, from which I was startled by a sudden outbreak of loud, excited shouts, succeeded by a sound of fierce scuffling, accompanied by a volley of oaths and exclamations, the stamp of feet, a heavy fall, a rush of footsteps up the companion ladder, and a sudden, heavy splash alongside. Then followed a terrific outcry on deck, with the hurrying rush of feet on the planking overhead, the furious slatting of canvas as the schooner shot into the wind, more excited shouts, ending in a sort of groaning mingled with ejaculations of dismay, a sudden silence, and then a terrific jabbering, suggestive of the idea that all hands had incontinently taken leave of their senses.

I sprang out of my bunk and hurriedly proceeded to dress, rushing on deck bare-footed to see what was the matter; and as I emerged from the companion way I saw all hands gathered aft, most of them staring hard over the taffrail, while one man was busily engaged in binding up the left arm of the second mate.

"Hillo, Monsieur Charpentier!" I exclaimed, "what is the matter? Has anything happened?"

"Happened, monsieur? I should think so!" exclaimed the second mate, turning to me a white and ghastly face; "a most awful thing has happened. When I went below just now to call François I was unable to make him hear, although I called several times and knocked ever so hard at his door. So I ventured to turn the door handle and enter his cabin, and what do you think I saw, monsieur? Why, poor François lying dead in his bunk, his clothes soaked with blood, and a great gaping wound in his breast, right over his heart! I was so horrified, monsieur, that I scarcely knew what to do; but, collecting myself with a mighty effort, I went to call the captain; and when I reached his cabin I found the door wide open and Monsieur Lemaitre crouched in a corner of it, with a great bloodstained knife in his hand, his eyes glaring, and his lips mumbling and muttering I know not what. I saw that there was something wrong with him, monsieur, —I believed he had gone mad,—and I was about to turn away and call for help; but he saw me, and, before I was aware, sprang upon me, seizing me with one hand by the throat while with the other he aimed blow after blow at me with his terrible knife. I defended myself as well as I could, monsieur, fighting bravely for my life; but what can one do against a madman? The captain seemed to possess the strength of twenty men; he forced me irresistibly back against the bulkhead, and then drove his knife through my arm. Believing that he had killed me, I relaxed my hold upon him; whereupon he hurled me to the deck, sprang over my fallen body, and bounded up on deck, *and from thence overboard*! And now they tell me, monsieur, that he had scarcely struck the water when a shark rose, seized him, and dragged him under! See, monsieur, look astern! He is gone; there is nothing to be seen of him! What shall we do? oh, mon Dieu, what shall we do?"

"Are you *quite sure* that the captain was seized by a shark?" I demanded, looking round from one to another of the men, who had now turned their faces inboard and stood staring alternately at Charpentier and myself.

"Oh yes, monsieur," excitedly replied half a dozen of them all together, "we all saw it; it was a monster. And," continued one of them, "the captain had scarcely risen to the surface after his plunge overboard when the shark seized him by the middle and dragged him under. We all saw the blood dyeing the water,—did we not, shipmates?—but the captain never uttered a cry; just threw up his arms and vanished. Is not that it, my friends?"

"Yes, yes," they all exclaimed again, "that is it. Jules describes it exactly as it occurred."

"Then," said I, "it seems to me, Monsieur Charpentier, that, Captain Lemaitre and the mate being dead, nothing remains but for you to take command and navigate the schooner to her destination."

"But, monsieur, I cannot do that, for, unhappily, I am not a navigator," replied Charpentier, wringing his hands.

"Do you mean to say that you know *nothing whatever* about navigation!" demanded I.

"Alas, no, monsieur! nothing whatever," was the reply.

"And is there no one else among you who can navigate the schooner?" asked I.

The men looked at each other, shaking their heads and muttering, "Not I"; and finally Charpentier exclaimed, "You see, monsieur, there is not one of us who can navigate. What is to be done? *You*, monsieur, are an officer—at least so I understood François to say; perhaps you could"—

"Well," demanded I, seeing that the fellow hesitated, "perhaps I could—what?"

"Pardon, monsieur," exclaimed he, "I was in hopes that, considering the difficulty we are placed in by this most lamentable tragedy, you would kindly take command and navigate the schooner."

"I see," remarked I. "Well," I continued, "if such is the wish of you all, I have no objection to do as you wish. But—understand me—I will only consent to navigate the schooner back to the West Indies; I will not undertake the trouble and responsibility of carrying the ship to her destination and shipping a cargo. I disapprove, on principle, of slave-trading, which I consider an iniquitous traffic, and I will have nothing to do with it; but, if you are willing, I will navigate the ship back to Port Royal,—guaranteeing you immunity from capture upon our arrival, in consideration of the rescue and succour that you have afforded me,—and, when there, you will have no difficulty in procuring someone who will navigate the schooner from thence to Havana or any other port that you may choose to go to. Just talk it over among yourselves, and let me know what you decide on doing."

I could see that my proposal was not at all to Charpentier's liking, or, indeed, to the liking of any of the crew; but I cared not for that. I was quite determined to have nothing whatever to do with the kidnapping of any unfortunate blacks; and in the end they were obliged to give way, although Charpentier tried hard to dissuade me from my resolution; the result being, that immediately after I had ascertained our position at noon, we wore round and shaped a course for Martinique, that island being in a direct line with Jamaica. At first I was rather apprehensive that the disappointment of the men at so unprofitable a result of the voyage would cause them to be troublesome; but it did not. The question of turning back having once been settled, they all seemed to take the matter very philosophically, the fact that they were now relieved of the mate's tyranny perhaps reconciling them to such disappointment as they might otherwise have felt.

I need not dwell upon the return voyage, which was

singularly uneventful; suffice it to say that, favoured with fine weather and a fair wind all the way, we made an exceptionally smart run across the Atlantic, entering Port Royal harbour on the morning of the twenty-second day after bearing up, and eleven weeks to a day from the date of my abduction by Dominguez.

My sudden reappearance created quite a sensation among the dockyard people, my disappearance having been involved in so much mystery that all sorts of surmises had been indulged in to account for it. Some were of opinion that I had fallen overboard into the harbour, and had found a secure hiding-place in the maw of a shark; but there were others who, happening to have been present when I was summoned from Mammy Wilkinson's hotel upon my supposititious errand of help and rescue to young Lindsay, at once mentioned the circumstance, with the result that a very strong suspicion of foul play was aroused. My friend and patron, the admiral, was especially concerned upon my account, even going to the length of offering a reward of fifty pounds for such intelligence as should lead to my discovery; but it resulted in nothing, those worthies, Cæsar and Peter, perhaps being too much afraid to utter a word of what they knew. Then there occurred more frigate actions, resulting in so heavy a pressure of work, that nobody seemed to have any time to think about the mysterious disappearance of a somewhat obscure young lieutenant. But now that I had unexpectedly turned up again, safe and sound, I was overwhelmed with congratulations, while the admiral sent a party of police to the house to which I had been conveyed, with instructions that the two negroes were to be at once found and arrested. The house, however, proved to be empty when the police made their domiciliary visit; and, as for the negroes, their whereabouts was never discovered. Possibly the excitement of my reappearance, and the talk to which it gave rise, alarmed them and caused them to beat a hasty retreat to some other island.

To my great joy, I discovered that the *Diane* was not yet recommissioned, the repairs and alterations to her having been greatly delayed by the more pressing work of repairing the frigates, while the admiral—in the hope that I might still turn up, and with that extreme kindness that had marked all his treatment of me—had determined not to give the command of her to anyone else until she should be absolutely ready for sea. I therefore at once stepped into my former position, and lost no time in getting as many men to work upon her as could be spared. And there was the less difficulty in accomplishing this, that Morillo was believed to be more busy than ever, several outward-bound ships being overdue without the occurrence of any bad weather to account for their disappearance. Meanwhile, during the progress of the work aboard the brigantine, I gave myself up to the task of getting together a crew, of which my old friend Black Peter constituted himself the nucleus, while several former *Terns* volunteered, these again inducing other men of their acquaintance to come forward and join; so that by the time that the finishing touches were being put to the *Diane*, I had fifty-two first-rate men waiting to go aboard as soon as the ship should be ready to receive them. But I wanted five more to complete my complement, and these I picked up by making a raid one night upon the low boarding-houses in Kingston, where the crimps were in the habit of taking in sailors and keeping them in hiding until they had extracted from them every penny of their hard-earned wages.

At length, some five weeks from the date of my reappearance, the time arrived when the *Diane*, being ready for sea, with her guns mounted, provisions, water, and stores of every kind on board, and sails bent, hauled off alongside the powder hulk to ship her ammunition; and that delicate job having been successfully accomplished, under my personal supervision, I went up to Kingston to dine with the admiral prior to sailing, calling at the hotel on my way in order to change my clothes. As I entered the building, the head waiter—a negro—stepped forward and handed me a letter addressed in an unknown and foreign-looking handwriting to myself. I opened it at once, and found that it bore a date a full fortnight old, and read as follows, the language being English:—

"SEÑOR COURTENAY,—You have constituted yourself my especial enemy, and have apparently declared war to the knife against me. In return I now declare my determination to destroy you by whatever means may present themselves. Thrice have you injured me, either personally or through my agents; but rest assured that a day of reckoning will come, when you shall curse the hour that gave you birth. I will fight you wherever we may happen to meet, and let the strongest conquer. If you fear not to meet me, hoist a red swallow-tailed burgee to your fore royal masthead, that I may recognise your ship from others. . MORILLO."

"When did this letter arrive, and who brought it?" demanded I of the waiter, who stood by as I read the document.

"A black boy brought it, about half an hour ago, sah, an' said I was to be suah an' gib it you, sah, an' dat dar was no ansah, sah," replied the fellow.

"Did you know the boy?" demanded I.

"No, sah; nebber saw him befoah to my knowledge, sah," was the reply.

"Did you take enough notice of him to be able to recognise him should you happen to see him again?" asked I.

"I's afraid not, sah; those black boys are all exactly alike, you know, sah," replied the fellow, who was himself as black as the ace of spades.

"Well," said I, "if you *should* happen to see him again, and can manage to detain him until you can give him into custody, it will be worth five guineas to you. I should very much like to see that boy and ask him a question or two."

"All right, sah; if I see him I'll stop him, nebbah feah, sah," replied the waiter, with a grin; and therewith I hurried away to my room to dress.

# CHAPTER XIX

### THE END OF THE *GUERRILLA*

I ARRIVED at the Pen just in time for dinner, and found myself one of an unusually large party of guests, several men-o'-war being in port at the time, while a large contingent of civilians might always be met at the admiral's table. The old gentleman received me with all his wonted kindness and cordiality, introducing me to such of his guests as I had not met before, and relating over the dinner-table, with much gusto, the story of my abduction and escape. Then I produced Morillo's letter of defiance, which I took with me to show him, and which added a fillip to the conversation that lasted us until the cloth was drawn. We sat rather late over our wine, and when we rose to go the admiral invited me into his library for a moment, and said—

"Well, my lad, d'ye intend to accept that piratical rascal's challenge?"

"Most assuredly I do, sir, if I can but fall in with him," answered I.

# THE END OF THE *GUERRILLA*

"Very well," said the admiral, "you shall have every opportunity to give him the thrashing that he so richly deserves. There," handing me a packet, "are your orders, which you will find are that, while cruising against the enemy, and doing as much harm as you can to their commerce, you are to keep a bright lookout for Morillo, and either capture or destroy him at all costs. When do you sail?"

"The moment that I can get aboard, sir," answered I.

"That's right, that's right; you will then be able to make a good offing before the land breeze drops," returned the admiral. "Well," he continued, "good-bye, my boy, and a successful cruise to you. And if, when you return, you bring Morillo with you, or can assure me of his destruction, you shall have t'other swab; for I shall consider that you have well earned it."

And therewith I left him and drove into Kingston, where I routed out a boatman and made the best of my way aboard the *Diane*. An hour later the brigantine was under way, and threading her passage through the shoals to seaward under the influence of a roaring land breeze.

The question that now exercised my mind was, where was I to look for Morillo? In what direction should I be most likely to find him? It was a most difficult question to answer; but, after considering the matter in all its bearings, I came to the conclusion that his most likely haunt would probably be near one of the great entrances from the Atlantic to the Caribbean Sea, where he would be conveniently posted to intercept and plunder both outward and homeward-bound ships; although he would probably take care not to establish himself *too* near, lest he should run foul of any of our cruisers stationed in the same locality for the protection of British bottoms trading to and from West Indian ports. He would in all likelihood select a spot some two or three hundred miles away out in the Atlantic, from which he could command both the outward and the homeward routes of ships bound from and to Europe. I opened a chart of the North Atlantic and studied it carefully, trying to imagine myself in his place, and thinking what I should do under such circumstances; and reasoning in this way, I at length fixed upon a belt of ocean suitable for piratical purposes, and thither I determined to make my way, thoroughly searching every mile of intervening water as I did so. Then came the question whether I should select the Windward or the Mona Passage by which to make my way into the Atlantic; and after much anxious consideration I decided upon the Windward Passage, that being the channel most frequently used by our merchantmen. I accordingly set the course for Morant Point, and then went below and turned in.

When I went on deck next morning, shortly after daybreak, I found that the *Diane* had weathered the point and was now on the starboard tack, heading well up for Cape Mayzi, with the Blue Mountains already assuming the hue from which they are named, as the brigantine rapidly left them astern. It was a brilliant morning, with the trade wind piping up to the tune of half a gale; yet the little ship was showing her topgallantsail to it, and sheering through the rather short, choppy sea like a mad thing, with her yards braced hard in against the lee rigging, and the lower half of her foresail dark with spray, while the white foam hissed and seethed and raced past her to leeward at a pace that made one giddy to look at. That the *Diane* was a perfect marvel in the matter of speed—and a good sea-boat withal—was undeniable; and as I stood aft, to windward of the helmsman, and watched the little hooker thrashing along, I felt sanguine that, should we be fortunate enough to encounter Señor Morillo, he would have but small chance of escaping us by showing a clean pair of heels.

The following midnight found us handsomely weathering Cape Mayzi, the most easterly extremity of the island of Cuba, after which we held on until we had brought the southern extremity of Great Inagua broad abeam, when we again tacked, and so worked our way out to sea between the Handkerchief shoal and Grand Caicos, passing an inward-bound Indiaman on the way. I spoke this vessel, asking if they had sighted any suspicious craft of late; to which the skipper replied that four days previously he had been chased by a French brig, which he had contrived to elude in the darkness; and that he had on the following day sighted and spoken the British frigate

*Euterpe*, which had forthwith proceeded in quest of the brig. Thenceforth we sighted nothing until our fifth day out, when we fell in with the *Euterpe*, which had just returned to her station after an unsuccessful search. Two days later we sighted a British privateer, which made sail and tried to run away from us as soon as she made out our pennant, fearing—so the skipper said when we overhauled and compelled him to heave-to—that we should impress some of his men. But, as I had as many hands as I required, I let him go without compelling him to pay toll. His report was that the Atlantic was absolutely empty of shipping, he having sighted nothing but a British line-of-battle ship and three frigates during his passage across.

Finally, we reached the cruising ground that I had selected as being the most likely spot in which to meet Morillo; and there we cruised for a full fortnight, just reaching to and fro athwart the wind, under mainsail, topsail, and jib, and still there was no sign of the *Guerrilla* or of any other craft. At length I became so thoroughly discouraged that one night, soon after sundown, I went below, got out my chart, and proceeded to study it afresh, with a view to the selection of some other cruising ground; and at length, after long and anxious consideration, I fixed upon a new spot, for which I determined to bear up next day if by noon nothing had hove in sight.

It chanced, however, that at dawn next morning a craft was made out some ten miles to windward of us, and the officer of the watch at once came down below and called me. I went on deck immediately, to find that the day was just breaking, and the stranger even then only barely visible against the faint light that was spreading along the eastern horizon. As we stood looking, we made her out to be a square-rigged vessel, apparently of no great size, running down toward us under easy canvas; and the thought came to me that here was the *Guerrilla* at last, and that my patience was about to meet its reward. But a few minutes later—by which time, as I supposed, it had grown light enough to reveal our canvas to the approaching stranger—the craft suddenly hauled her wind; and I then saw that she was a brig. That she was not a merchantman was obvious from the fact that she was under such short canvas, all she showed being her two topsails, spanker, and jib—just such canvas as a privateer or gun-brig would show, in fact, on her cruising ground; and I at once set her down for one or the other. Of her nationality, however, it was impossible to correctly judge at that distance and in the still imperfect light; but there was a certain subtle something in her appearance that suggested France as the land of her birth. Meanwhile, as she had rounded-to on the same tack as ourselves, evidently with the intention of taking a good look at us before approaching too near, we held on as we were going, taking no notice whatever of her. In about a quarter of an hour, however, it became apparent that we were head-reaching upon her; whereupon she dropped her foresail, to keep pace with us, while we on our part took a small pull upon the lee braces, which enabled us to head up a point higher, and so gradually edge up toward her.

Such excessive caution as the stranger was now exhibiting convinced me that she could not be British; she must, consequently, be an enemy. And having once made up my mind upon this point, I very gradually braced our yards as flat in against the rigging as they would come, flattened in the main and jib sheets, and thus brought the *Diane* on a taut bowline, without, as I hoped, arousing the suspicion of the stranger, meanwhile keeping the telescope constantly levelled upon her in order that, should I see any hands in her rigging going aloft to make sail, we might follow suit without loss of time. But I did not wish to take the initiative, because by so doing I might possibly alarm them; while, so long as we both kept on as we were, we were gradually and almost imperceptibly closing her.

This state of affairs prevailed for about an hour, when suddenly — with the view, perhaps, of compelling us to disclose our intentions — the stranger tacked. Obliged thus to throw off the mask, we at once did the same, the hands—who had been standing by, waiting for orders—at the same time springing into the rigging to loose our additional canvas; and by the time that the little hooker was fairly round on the starboard tack, and the yards swung, our topgallant sail and gafftopsail were sheeted home and in the act of being hoisted, together with the flying jib, foretopmast staysail, and main and maintopmast staysails, while the fore tack was being boarded and the sheet hauled aft. This caused an immediate stir aboard the stranger, who, in her turn, at once set all plain sail to her topgallant sails, the wind being altogether too fresh for either of us to show a royal to it.

The manœuvres just described brought the brig about three points before our starboard beam and some eight miles to windward of us, both craft being now close-hauled on the starboard tack. There was a strong breeze blowing from the north-east, with a fair amount of sea on, and the day was brilliantly fine, with a rich, clear, crystalline blue sky, dappled here and there with puffs of white trade-cloud sailing solemnly athwart our mastheads; a splendid day for sailing, and we had the whole of it before us.

It soon became apparent that we were gaining upon the brig—weathering and forereaching upon her at the same time; and as it was now broad daylight, I sent the men to quarters, hoisted our colours, and fired a shotted gun to windward as an invitation to her to heave-to; but of this she took no notice whatever. By nine o'clock—at which hour I took an observation of the sun for my longitude—we had forereached upon the brig sufficiently to bring her a couple of points abaft our weather beam, and then, in accordance with the rule for chasing, we tacked again; whereupon she did the same, thus bringing us right astern and slightly to windward of her. It was now a stern chase, she being as nearly as possible seven miles ahead of us. The wind held steady, and hour after hour the two craft went plunging along at racing speed, the brigantine gaining steadily all the time, until by one o'clock the chase was within range, and we opened fire upon her with our long eighteen-pounder. Our shot flew close to her on either side,—as we could see by the jets of water thrown up,—but it was fully half an hour before we hit her, which we then did fair in the centre of her stern. She immediately shot into the wind, all aback, and it took them fully five minutes to box her off again, when— seeing, I suppose, that they could not now possibly escape us—her people clewed up her courses, hauled down topgallant sails and staysails, until they had reduced their canvas to what it had been when we first sighted her, hoisted French colours, and bore up for us.

It was at this time that we first made out the upper canvas of another vessel just appearing above the horizon in the northern board, and evidently steering in our direction ; and upon sending aloft one of the midshipmen who were acting as my lieutenants, he reported her as a craft of apparently about our own size. The fact that she was heading *toward* us led me to the conclusion that she must be either a privateer or a small cruiser like ourselves, —evidently attracted by the sound of our guns,—and as I did not wish for her assistance, if a friend, or the additional anxiety of having to fight her at the same time as the brig, if an enemy, I called the hands aft and made them a brief speech, impressing upon them the importance of settling the brig's business as promptly as possible, in order that we might be free to give the other stranger our undivided attention, if necessary. They answered with a hearty cheer, and went back to their guns; and a quarter of an hour later the brig rounded-to within biscuit-toss to windward of us, giving us her larboard broadside as she did so.

This was the beginning of a regular set-to, hammer and tongs, between us, the French fighting with the utmost courage and determination, and playing havoc with our rigging, which they cut up so severely that half a dozen of our people were kept busy aloft knotting and splicing. At length, however, when the fight had thus been raging for a full hour, with heavy loss on both sides, tacking suddenly under cover of the smoke of our starboard broadside, we shot across the brig's stern, raking her with a double-shotted broadside from our larboard guns, which had the effect of bringing both her masts down by the run, rendering her a wreck and unmanageable; and we now felt that she was ours.

But we were reckoning without our host—or rather, without the second stranger, whom we had been altogether too busy to give a thought to. As the smoke of our guns blew away to leeward, and we prepared to tack again preparatory to passing once more athwart the brig's stern, I got a full and clear view of the stranger, who—

approaching us from to windward—had hitherto been hidden from us by the brig and by the smoke of our combined cannonade. She was less than half a mile distant from us, and was at the moment in the very act of taking in her studding-sails. She was a brigantine, and a single glance at her sufficed to assure me that she was the *Guerrilla*, and that at last the feud between Morillo and myself was to be fought out to the bitter end. I had long ago prepared a red swallow-tailed burgee, such as the pirate had dared me to exhibit, and I immediately gave orders to hoist it at our fore royal masthead. The flag had scarcely reached the truck when I saw a *black* flag flutter out over the other brigantine's rail and go soaring aloft to her gaff-end. Morillo had evidently recognised my challenge, and was prompt to answer it.

Sweeping under the brig's stern again, at a distance of only a few fathoms, I hailed, asking whether they surrendered; but a pistol-shot, which flew close past my ear, was their only reply, so we gave them our starboard broadside, and then wore round to meet our new antagonist, leaving the brig meanwhile to her own devices.

I am of opinion that Morillo must have had a very shrewd suspicion as to our identity long before the exhibition of our burgee, because of the eager haste with which he bore down upon us. So eager, indeed, was he, that he carried his studding-sails just a minute or two too long; a mistake on his part, which enabled us to make a couple of short stretches to windward and secure the weather-gage before he was ready to round-to, although as soon as his people detected our purpose they worked with frantic haste to shorten sail.

The pirates opened the ball by giving us their whole larboard broadside while we were in stays, tacking toward them; but the guns were fired hurriedly, and did us no harm, the shot flying high over us and between our masts, without touching so much as a ropeyarn. Five minutes later we passed close across the *Guerrilla's* stern, making a half-board to clear her, and delivered our larboard broadside, with the eighteen-pounder thrown in, every shot taking effect and raking her from end to end. Morillo was standing aft by the taffrail, and as we passed near enough to hear the wash of the water about the pirate vessel's rudder, he suddenly snatched up a blunderbuss, and, singling me out, fired point-blank at me, one bullet knocking my cap off, while another lodged in my left shoulder, a third killing the man at our wheel, close behind me. The *Guerrilla* immediately ported her helm, while I, springing to our wheel, put it hard a-starboard, thus passing a second time athwart our antagonist's stern; and again we raked her mercilessly, this time with our starboard broadside. Keeping our wheel hard over, we swept round until we were once more in stays, the *Guerrilla* having tacked toward us a minute earlier, with the evident intention of raking us in her turn. We were just a little too quick for her, however, gathering way so smartly that, as we neared each other, it became evident that, unless one or the other of us tacked again, we must inevitably run foul of each other. I had no mind for this sort of thing, however, as we should probably hurt ourselves quite as much as our antagonist; so, holding on until we had only just room to clear the *Guerrilla*, and singing out for a second shot to be rammed home in the larboard guns, I eased our helm down just at the right moment, ranging up so close to the other brigantine that we almost grazed her side, when we exchanged broadsides at precisely the same instant, with terrible effect on both sides. At the same moment our topsail was thrown aback to deaden our way, and as the *Guerrilla* passed ahead our helm was put hard up and we paid square off across her stern, firing our starboard broadside into her as we did so. The result this time was absolutely disastrous to the pirates, for the guns were fired at the precise moment when the *Guerrilla's* stern was lifted up on the crest of a sea, while we were in the trough beyond; in consequence of which, our shot all struck her a trifle below her normal water-line, producing a very serious leak, which, even under the most favourable circumstances, it would have been exceedingly difficult to stop. But this was not the worst of it; the shot, by a lucky accident, so far as we were concerned, had somehow become concentrated, all of them taking effect upon the pirate's rudder and sternpost, with the result that the former was shot away, and the latter, as well as two or three hood-ends, so badly started that ere

## THE END OF THE *GUERRILLA*

ten minutes had elapsed it became apparent that the *Guerrilla* was rapidly filling.

Meanwhile, however, we held on across her stern, filling our topsail again, and tacking as soon as we had room; while the pirate brigantine, deprived of her rudder, shot into the wind and got in irons, obstinately refusing to pay off on either tack. This enabled us to sweep across her bows, pouring in our port broadside as we passed, raking her fore and aft, and bringing down her foremast by the run. Holding on for a few minutes, we next wore round —getting her starboard broadside as we passed—and then cut close across her stern again, raking her as before. By this time, however, it had become apparent that she was sinking, so, having once more tacked, we ranged up close athwart her stern, with our topsail aback, when, instead of firing, I hailed to ask if they surrendered.

"No, señor," replied Morillo himself, who was standing aft close to the now useless wheel, "we will *never* surrender! I wrote you a letter—which I hope you received —in which I said that I would fight you until my ship sinks under me; and I mean to do so. I also told you that my feud with you is to the death; so, take that!" and therewith the scoundrel quickly levelled a pistol and, for the second time that day, fired point-blank at me! And there is no doubt whatever that this time he would have slain me—for the pistol was pointed so truly that I actually looked for a moment right into the barrel of it —had it not been for the *Diane's* helmsman, who unceremoniously seized me by the arm in the very nick of time and quickly pulled me aside. As it was, the bullet whistled close past my ear. This dastardly act so exasperated our people that forthwith, without waiting for orders, they poured the whole of our port broadside into the devoted craft, completely demolishing her stern, so that for a few seconds, as we drew slowly athwart her wake, we got a full view of her decks, which were cumbered with killed and wounded, and literally streaming with blood. Still, by a miracle, Morillo himself survived this last destructive broadside of ours; for when the smoke blew away I saw him still standing erect and shaking his fist defiantly at us.

It was by this time evident to us all that the *Guerrilla* was a doomed ship; she was settling fast in the water, and to continue firing upon her would only be a waste of ammunition. We therefore filled our topsail and, a few minutes later, tacked, again getting a broadside from the sinking ship, when we stationed ourselves square athwart her bows—where we were pretty well out of the way of her fire—and, with topsail aback and mainsheet eased off, waited patiently for the final moment, which we saw was rapidly approaching. Yet, even now, Morillo persisted in firing at us with his two bow guns, compelling us to fire upon him in return; and so the useless fight went on, until the *Guerrilla* had settled so low in the water that the sea welled in over her bows at every plunge of her, rendering it impossible to any longer maintain their fire.

## THE END OF THE *GUERRILLA*

Then, with folded hands, we all stood by, watching for the end.

And a very melancholy picture it was upon which we looked. There was the illimitable expanse of ocean all round us, blue as sapphire, heaving in long, regular ridges of swell, and whipped into foam here and there by the scourging of the strong trade wind, with a rich blue sky above, dappled with whisps of trade-cloud, and the sun shining brilliantly down from the midst of them, causing the heaving waters to flash and glitter under his fiery beams, so that the sea that way was too dazzling to look at. And there, right in the centre of the glowing picture, lay the two brigantines—we with our bulwarks torn and splintered to pieces, our sails riddled with shot-holes, our rigging badly cut up, and our decks scored with shot-marks and littered with dead and wounded men; while the *Guerrilla* was an even more melancholy wreck than ourselves, as she lay heaving and rolling sluggishly, with her covering-boards awash and the sea sweeping her decks from stem to taffrail at every plunge, and the wreck of her foremast towing under her bows. There was not a soul visible on board her. When she first engaged us her decks had appeared to be crowded with men, but now most of them were either killed or wounded, and the few who had escaped seemed to have flung themselves down exhausted, for they had all disappeared. As for the craft herself, it was now only when she rose heavily upon the ridges of the swell that we could see her hull at all; and every plunge that she took into a hollow threatened to be her last. Yet she lingered, as though reluctant to leave the brilliant sunshine and the warm, strong breeze; lingered until I began to wonder whether she would not after all remain afloat, a water-logged wreck; and then, all in a moment, her stern rose high in the air, revealing her shattered rudder and sternpost, and with a long, slow, diving movement, she plunged forward, like a sounding whale, and silently vanished in a little swirl of water. We at once bore up for the spot where she had disappeared, —finding it easily by the torn and splintered fragments of wreckage that came floating up to the surface,—but her crew went down with her, to a man; for although we cruised about the spot for fully half an hour, we never saw even so much as a dead body come to the surface.

And so ended that terror of the seas, the *Guerrilla*, with her bloodthirsty pirate crew; and with her destruction ended the feud that had been thrust upon me by one of the most fiendish monsters in human form that ever sailed the ocean. It may perhaps seem to the reader a cold-blooded deed on our part to remain passively by and calmly watch the passing of those wretches to their account; but in reality it was an act of mercy, for their end was at least swift; whereas, had we saved any of them, it would only have been that they might terminate their career upon the gallows.

Meanwhile, the brig had dropped some six miles to leeward during the fight, and her crew had made the best of the opportunity by endeavouring to get some jury-spars aloft. The time, however, was too short for that, and when we ran down to them they were still in the thick of their work. But they had now had enough of fighting, for when I again hailed to ask if they surrendered, they at once replied in the affirmative; and in due course we took possession of the *Néréide* of Bordeaux, armed with twelve long nine-pounders, and with a crew originally of eighty-six men, of whom twenty-three were killed and fifty-seven wounded in her fight with us. We spent the remainder of that day in completing the rigging of the jury-masts that her people had begun, and made sail upon both craft just after sunset that same evening, arriving safely in Port Royal harbour some three weeks later.

And now, what remains to be said? The tale of my association with the fate of Morillo the Pirate is told; and all I need add is that when the account of my exploit was told, I received a great deal more credit and praise than I felt I really deserved; while, as for my friend the admiral—well, he was as good as his word, for within twenty-four hours of my arrival with my prize in Port Royal harbour, he handed me, with hearty congratulations and many kind words, the commission that entitled me to mount "t'other swab."

THE END

www.ingramcontent.com/pod-product-compliance
Lightning Source LLC
Chambersburg PA
CBHW030311240426
**43673CB00040B/1130**